"In *Value Creation Principles*, Madden introduces the pragmatic theory of the firm that positions the firm as a system fueled by human capital, innovation, and, at a deeper level, imagination. He challenges us to understand how we know what we think we know in order to better discover faulty assumptions that often are camouflaged by language. His knowledge building loop offers guideposts to design experiments and organize feedback to facilitate early adaptation to a changed environment and to avoid being mired in ways of thinking rooted in 'knowledge' of what worked well in the past—a context far different from the context of today. His book explains a way of being that enables those who work for, or invest in, business firms to see beyond accounting silos and short-term quarterly earnings and to focus on capabilities instrumental for creating long-term future and sustainable value for the firm's stakeholders. I can't recommend this astounding book enough especially given its deep and timely insights for our world today."

—John Seely Brown, former Chief Scientist for Xerox Corp and Director of its Palo Alto Research Center (PARC); co-author with Ann Pendleton-Jullian of *Design Unbound: Designing for Emergence in a White Water World*

"In contrast to existing abstract theories of the firm, Madden's pragmatic theory of the firm connects management's decisions in a practical way to a firm's life cycle and market valuation. The book promotes a firm's knowledge building proficiency, relative to competitors, as the fundamental driver of a firm's long-term performance, which leads to insights about organizational capabilities, intangible assets, and excess shareholder returns. *Value Creation Principles* is ideally suited to facilitate progress in the New Economy by opening up the process by which firms build knowledge and create value, which is a needed step in revising how neoclassical economics treats the firm."

—Tyler Cowen, Professor of Economics, George Mason University; co-author of the popular economics blog *Marginal Revolution*

"Bartley Madden rightfully points out that both textbook and more advanced economic theories of the firm fail to address the concerns of top management and boards of directors. He offers a tantalizing pragmatic alternative that directly connects to quantitative changes in the firm's market value. His framework gives recognition to the importance of intangible assets, and his pragmatic approach is quite complementary to the Dynamic Capabilities framework that strategic managers implicitly and sometimes explicitly employ."

—David J. Teece, Thomas W. Tusher Professor in Global Business, Faculty Director, Tusher Center for the Management of Intellectual Capital, Haas School of Business, University of California, Berkeley

"Drawing upon a long history of experience and research, Madden integrates management theory and firm valuation in *Value Creation Principles*. He hypothesizes the foundational importance of managerial processes to sustain knowledge building proficiency and demonstrates its relevance through case studies of important firms. Absent a culture of purpose, respect, experimentation, and learning, innovative processes degrade and hinder firm competitiveness. He convincingly deviates from traditional accounting standards and bedazzling quantitative methods in developing the pragmatic theory of the firm that is well suited to the New Economy's reliance on intangible assets and human capital. Underlying the entire exposition is Madden's clear understanding of market-oriented choice and the limitations of rigid hierarchies and bureaucracies, particularly in the complex systems that we call 'firms.'"

—Brian Singer, CFA, Partner, William Blair, Dynamic Allocation Strategies and former chairman of the CFA Institute

"In *Value Creation Principles,* Madden applies a holistic, systematic view of the firm to connect finance to the broader issues of managing firms through the creation of intangible assets. He provides a life-cycle lens that reveals the economic logic that drives levels and changes in stock prices over the long term. Management priorities need to be attuned to a firm's life-cycle position. He explains excess shareholder returns at a much deeper level compared to the popular factor studies in finance, while offering a blueprint for future research. The key to excess returns is shown to be intangible assets, and especially unique brands, that favorably contribute to a firm's long-term, competitive fade of profitability. The book should be read by anyone concerned with expanding the contribution of finance to business."

—Bobby J. Calder, Kelstadt Emeritus Professor of Marketing, Kellogg School of Management, Northwestern University

"Bart Madden has written an important book rooted in systems thinking. Understanding a systems approach to value creation by business firms is at the heart of his Pragmatic Theory of the Firm—a theory that is focused on the practical tasks of knowledge building and value creation. An important insight from this book is the ongoing and dynamic connection between a firm's knowledge building proficiency, long-term competitive fade of a firm's profitability, excess shareholder returns, and the concept of *firm risk* that differs from CAPM's *investor risk*. Firm risk, in Madden's words, is about obstacles that interfere with achieving the firm's purpose, which includes broad stakeholder advancement. *Value Creation Principles* provides insightful guideposts for managements, boards, and investors, as well as providing new thinking on academic research regarding the purpose of the firm."

—David R. Koenig, author of *Governance Reimagined: Organizational Design, Risk and Value Creation* and *The Board Member's Guide to Risk*

"*Value Creation Principles* takes a holistic approach to how firms create value and maintain a competitive advantage. Knowledge building, systems thinking, and a strong sense of purpose hold the key. Bartley Madden's wide-ranging command of the evolution of the theory of the firm leads to an inevitable conclusion: knowledge building proficiency rooted in sustainable capitalism leads to progress for the firm and for the economy."

—Michele Wucker, bestselling author of *The Grey Rhino: How to Recognize and Act on the Obvious Dangers We Ignore*

VALUE CREATION
PRINCIPLES

VALUE CREATION PRINCIPLES

The Pragmatic Theory of the Firm Begins with Purpose and Ends with Sustainable Capitalism

Bartley J. Madden

WILEY

Published by John Wiley & Sons, Inc., Hoboken, New Jersey.
Published simultaneously in Canada.

Limit of Liability/Disclaimer of Warranty: While the publisher and author have used their best efforts in preparing this book, they make no representations or warranties with respect to the accuracy or completeness of the contents of this book and specifically disclaim any implied warranties of merchantability or fitness for a particular purpose. No warranty may be created or extended by sales representatives or written sales materials. The advice and strategies contained herein may not be suitable for your situation. You should consult with a professional where appropriate. Neither the publisher nor author shall be liable for any loss of profit or any other commercial damages, including but not limited to special, incidental, consequential, or other damages.

For general information on our other products and services or for technical support, please contact our Customer Care Department within the United States at (800) 762-2974, outside the United States at (317) 572-3993 or fax (317) 572-4002.

Wiley publishes in a variety of print and electronic formats and by print-on-demand. Some material included with standard print versions of this book may not be included in e-books or in print-on-demand. If this book refers to media such as a CD or DVD that is not included in the version you purchased, you may download this material at http://booksupport.wiley.com. For more information about Wiley products, visit www.wiley.com.

Library of Congress Cataloging-in-Publication Data

Names: Madden, Bartley J., author.
Title: Value creation principles : the pragmatic theory of the firm begins
  with purpose and ends with sustainable capitalism / Bartley J. Madden.
Description: First Edition. | Hoboken : Wiley, 2020. | Includes
  bibliographical references and index.
Identifiers: LCCN 2020006300 (print) | LCCN 2020006301 (ebook) | ISBN
  9781119706625 (cloth) | ISBN 9781119706632 (adobe pdf) | ISBN
  9781119706649 (epub)
Subjects: LCSH: Organizational effectiveness. | Organizational learning. |
  Production management. | Value.
Classification: LCC HD58.9 .M343 2020 (print) | LCC HD58.9 (ebook) | DDC
  658.15/52—dc23
LC record available at https://lccn.loc.gov/2020006300
LC ebook record available at https://lccn.loc.gov/2020006301

Cover Design: Wiley
Cover Image: © sakkmesterke/Getty Images

Printed in the United States of America

V10018377_051120

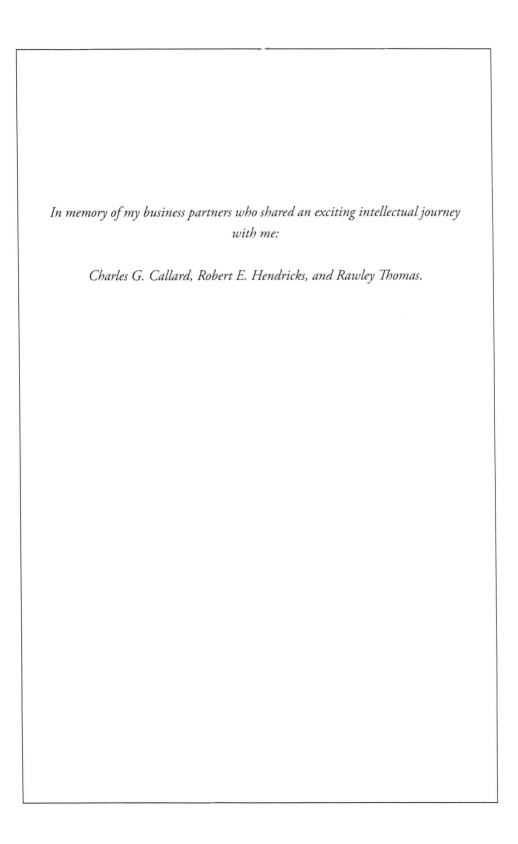

In memory of my business partners who shared an exciting intellectual journey with me:

Charles G. Callard, Robert E. Hendricks, and Rawley Thomas.

CONTENTS

Contents

Contents

PREFACE AND OVERVIEW

I strongly believe that a firm's long-term performance is a direct result of its knowledge-building proficiency. That belief is the result of my work in two research areas that normally are not connected—finance and knowledge building. First, by way of background, my career in finance began with the startup of the boutique research firm Callard Madden & Associates in 1969. Our primary mission was to understand levels and changes in stock prices worldwide and provide practical insights to enable portfolio managers to make better investment decisions. We devoted considerable effort analyzing management decision-making in the context of a firm's long-term financial performance quantified as life-cycle track records. Over many years I have been fortunate to work with talented colleagues at Callard Madden and later at HOLT Value Associates. Our research addressed a never-ending stream of problems in connecting a firm's accounting-based performance to its market valuation.

While this finance work was progressing, I got hooked on a second research area dealing with how we know what we think we know, which remains my ongoing intellectual passion.[1] The more I learned about the knowledge-building process, the clearer it became that knowledge building and value creation are opposite sides of the same coin. The

---

[1] Bartley J. Madden, 1991, "A Transactional Approach to Economic Research," *Journal of Socio-Economics* 20(1): 57–71; available at my website www.LearningWhatWorks.com. This article emphasizes how language affects our perceptions of the world. This important issue is reflected in the knowledge-building process used in many of the chapters in this book. See the 2017 TED talk by Lera Boroditsky, "How language shapes the way we think." See also Bartley J, Madden, 2012, "Management's Worldview: Four Critical Points about Reality, Language, and Knowledge Building," *Journal of Organizational Computing and Electronic Commerce* 22(4): 334–346, and Bartley J. Madden, 2014, *Reconstructing Your Worldview: The Four Core Beliefs You Need to Solve Complex Business Problems*, Naperville, IL: LearningWhatWorks.

more I analyzed management tasks such as strategy, innovation, employee engagement, development of new capabilities, etc., the more I realized that the root cause of a firm's long-term performance and returns to its shareholders is the firm's knowledge-building proficiency relative to competitors. This book makes what I believe is a strong case that a new holistic theory of the firm, built upon this foundational importance of a firm's knowledge-building proficiency, will improve thinking about the role of firms in society. Moreover, this new theory of the firm is labeled "pragmatic" because it facilitates systems thinking to analyze practical problems thereby leading to improved decision-making for managements, boards, and investors.

Theories of the firm tend to be narrow in scope and ignore how firm performance connects to market valuation. A notable advantage of the pragmatic theory is its explanation of what drives a firm's long-term financial performance and its returns to shareholders. The more one understands long-term stock prices, the better one appreciates the mutual interests of shareholders and other stakeholders.

As to understanding levels and changes in market valuations, my early research at Callard Madden was instrumental in developing the CFROI (cash flow return on investment) valuation model and related global database.[2] The CFROI research program is rooted in economically sound principles applied to the construction of long-term, life-cycle track records of a firm's financial performance; the forecasting of a firm's long-term net cash receipts; the calculation of warranted market valuations; and the decoding of investor expectations implied in stock prices. This unique research program was further advanced by HOLT Value Associates, which was acquired by Credit Suisse in 2002. A highly skilled team at Credit Suisse HOLT continues to advance the CFROI valuation framework as part of the Credit Suisse HOLT global database, which is used worldwide by many large money management organizations.

---

[2]CFROI is a trademark of CreditSuisse AG and its affiliates.

The seven chapters in the book can be distilled into the following fourteen key ideas:

1. **Purpose of the firm**—The pragmatic theory includes a statement of the firm's four-part purpose, as detailed in Chapter 1, which answers the questions: Why does a firm deserve the commitment and support of its stakeholders, and what unchanging principles will guide management's actions? Maximizing shareholder value is best viewed as the result of a firm successfully achieving its purpose.

2. **History of the theory of the firm**—The pragmatic theory is more comprehensive than other theories of the firm and treats the firm as a holistic system. As discussed in Chapter 1, this leads to insights that are otherwise unobtainable. The pragmatic theory integrates the firm as the critical unit of economic growth, thereby expanding upon the key ideas of Paul Romer, Robert Gordon, Joel Mokyr, and Edmund Phelps, as reviewed in Chapter 1.

3. **Knowledge building**—A firm's knowledge-building proficiency is the primary determinant of its long-term performance. Chapter 2 explains the knowledge-building process, including the subtle yet important impact of language.

4. **Performance improvement**—Chapter 3 uses knowledge building as a framework to explain the similarities and differences among three important approaches to improving the performance of firms: (1) Lean Thinking pioneered by Toyota; (2) the Theory of Constraints developed by Eli Goldratt; and (3) the recent work of Werner Erhard and Michael Jensen on an ontological/phenomenological model. By focusing on the knowledge-building components—purposes, worldview,

perceptions, actions and consequences, and feedback—any proposed performance-improvement program can be analyzed for its likely impact.

5. **Life-cycle framework**—Chapter 4 illustrates how the four stages of the life-cycle framework (high innovation, competitive fade, mature, and failing business model), which are typical of the long-term histories of firms, fit into the pragmatic theory. Instead of beginning with a model of risk and return and elegant mathematics tied to equilibrium, the life-cycle framework focuses on an individual firm delivering economic returns and reinvestment rates over its life cycle, thereby generating net cash receipts that drive market valuation.

6. **Excess shareholder returns**—Excess shareholder returns (positive/negative) result from life-cycle performance that deviates (better/worse) from initial expectations. The life-cycle valuation model helps to generate insights about a firm's historical performance and to improve forecasts of future financial performance, particularly when such forecasts are benchmarked against the firm's and its competitors' track records. In addition, the model helps gauge the implied expectations of investors embedded in a stock price at a specific time.

7. **Alternative view of risk**—The Capital Asset Pricing Model (CAPM) and related models define *investor risk* for an equilibrium setting in the context of the investor's portfolio. Research to advance these models is based on empirically tested factors (as proxies for risk) that seek to explain excess shareholder returns. CAPM equates higher average returns with higher risk. Managements can easily embrace the CAPM view of risk because it facilitates the calculation of a cost of capital. An alternative, although complementary, view of risk is presented in order to facilitate sharper thinking and improve decision making. *Firm risk* can differ from investor risk. Firm risk is about obstacles management faces that interfere with

achieving the firm's purpose. Firm risk increases (decreases) in lockstep with changes that degrade (improve) the likelihood of achieving the firm's purpose. An increase in firm risk, all else equal, means a greater likelihood for a firm to generate lower future financial performance. In the early stage of an increase in firm risk, management may choose to disregard the warning signs, but nevertheless those inside the firm have superior information compared to investors relying on public information. The key insight here is that there can be a substantial time lag between a significant change in firm risk and investor perception of this change. As such, an increase in firm risk will eventually be understood by investors and, all else equal, this adjustment process will cause a decline in the firm's market valuation. How does this adjustment process connect to models of investor risk like CAPM? The stock price declines in order to provide a high enough expected investor return to adequately compensate investors for the increased likelihood of future shortfalls in the firm's financial performance.

8. **Systems view**—A strong advantage of the pragmatic theory is its systems view of the firm which aids in dealing with complex problems like intangibles (e.g., brands), which dominate value creation and economic growth in the New Economy. The intangibles measurement problem impacts accounting-based performance measures, resource allocation, and market valuation. My blueprint, described in Chapter 5, for handling intangibles indicates that capitalization and amortization are warranted when the duration of expected benefits (economic lives) can be reasonably approximated. This improves the accuracy of economic returns and reinvestment rates, yielding more insightful track records. If economic lives are too speculative to estimate, the benefits from intangibles can be incorporated via more favorable long-term forecasts of competitive fade rates for economic returns and reinvestment rates.

9. **New research methodology**—A new way to conceptualize research about shareholder returns is presented in Chapter 5 with three levels of cause-and-effect logic: (1) correlation studies using financial variables as potential factors to better model risk and return; (2) targeted causes of excess returns such as intangibles, culture, and ESG (environmental, social, and governance) initiatives; and (3) utilization of a firm's knowledge-building proficiency as the preponderant cause of long-term value creation and ultimately shareholder returns.

10. **Crossover problem**—The knowledge-building process that is fundamental to the pragmatic theory sheds light on how accounting-based performance metrics, applied at lower levels in the firm, can be at cross-purposes with performance improvement actions keyed to process (nonaccounting) variables. The solution is to employ systems principles in the development of more effective language keyed to performance improvement.

11. **Management's priorities**—Chapter 6 explains, using well-known and prominent company examples, the underlying logic for management's priorities to change, dependent on the firm's life-cycle position, as follows: for the high innovation stage— test critical assumptions; for the competitive fade stage—build or acquire capabilities to expand; for the mature stage—adapt early to fundamental change; for the failing business model stage—purge a culture of business-as-usual.

12. **Organizational structure**—A critically important part of sustaining a knowledge-building culture that minimizes bureaucratic waste is a firm's organizational structure. In Chapter 6, the benefits and challenges from transitioning to flatter organizations are analyzed. The evolution of a large Chinese firm, the Haier Group, is reviewed focusing on its changes in organizational structure attuned to the company's size and competitive environment.

13. **Company histories**—Throughout this book, company histories are analyzed that spotlight a company's long-term life-cycle track record with its key comparison of economic returns (returns on capital) versus the cost of capital. These track records are essential for any long-term study of how firms create or dissipate value. Life-cycle track records applied to a firm's business units will improve resource allocation decisions, and are especially helpful for analyzing the risk and potential reward from owning a firm's shares.

14. **Progress Studies**—There is a growing demand for a new academic discipline, Progress Studies, that will advance our understanding of the complex system relationships involved with dynamism and economic growth. Integrating the pragmatic theory of the firm with Progress Studies will accelerate an understanding of the processes by which firms build knowledge, create value, and generate progress—a bottom-up, concrete body of knowledge using the individual firm as the unit of analysis, as it should be: the firm is the fundamental unit of capitalism.

In conclusion, I was fortunate to have two friends volunteer to extensively edit the entire manuscript. As to writing, both are perfectionists. Jack Reardon is the author of economics textbooks and the founding editor of the *International Journal of Pluralism and Economics Education*. Bryant Matthews is Global Director, Credit Suisse HOLT Research and the coauthor of *Beyond Earnings: Applying the HOLT CFROI and Economic Profit Framework*. Others at Credit Suisse have helped me on my journey: Jim Ostry, co-Head and Managing Director of Credit Suisse HOLT; Tom Hillman, Managing Director and head of HOLT's research team; and Rick Faery, Global Head of Corporate Insights Group, Credit Suisse Investment Banking. Especially useful comments were provided by Joe Cursio, Jerry Ellig, Maureen Ryan Healy, Keith Howe, Tom Malatesta, Jeff Ubois, and my sons, Greg Madden and Jeff Madden. I am grateful to Mark Frigo, who frequently invited me to present many of the ideas in this book to his MBA students at DePaul University. I appreciate the graphic design skills of Kimberly and Johnny Allgaeuer, who produced the book's many figures.

Finally, I am on the Executive Advisory Board of the Center for Advancing Corporate Performance (CACP) started at the Illinois Institute of Technology. I am working with Mark Ubelhart, David Koenig, and others to make CACP a world-class organization in providing practical insights about value creation for broad stakeholder groups using the business firm as the fundamental unit of analysis.

Part I

A Firm's Role in Society

1

OVERVIEW OF THE PRAGMATIC THEORY OF THE FIRM

In my experience, motivating employees with a sense of purpose is the only way to deliver innovative products, superior service, and unsurpassed quality over the long haul. ... An organization of highly motivated people is hard to duplicate. The motivation will last if it is deeply rooted in employees' commitment to the intrinsic purpose of their work.

—Bill George[1]

Business ethics, then, has to do with the authenticity and integrity of the enterprise. ... Those who cannot serve the corporate vision are not authentic businesspeople and, therefore, are not ethical in the business sense. ... In a company, a leader is a person who understands, interprets, and manages the corporate value system. Effective managers, therefore, are action-oriented people who resolve conflict, are tolerant of ambiguity, stress, and change, and have a strong sense of purpose for themselves and their organizations.

—Bowen H. McCoy[2]

---

[1] Bill George, 2003, *Authentic Leadership*. San Francisco: Jossey-Bass, p. 66.
[2] Bowen H. McCoy, 1997, "The Parable of the Sadhu," *Harvard Business Review* 75(3): 54–64.

Theories of the firm arise from the motivations of their developers. They initially define a firm in a way that is compatible with their objectives and their worldview. This chapter shows how theories of the firm evolved in the disciplines of economics, finance, and management. In addition, this review places the pragmatic theory of the firm in historical context, highlights the main differences separating the pragmatic theory from alternative theories, and provides an initial assessment of its usefulness.

THE NUCLEUS OF THE PRAGMATIC THEORY OF THE FIRM

Any theory of the firm involves an answer to this question: What is a firm? The pragmatic theory defines a firm as a dynamic system of coordinated activities that evolves as management and employees build knowledge in order to efficiently create value for customers, and that knowledge-building proficiency, relative to competitors, determines a firm's life cycle and the extent of rewards to its stakeholders over time.

How should the usefulness of the pragmatic theory of the firm be gauged versus other theories of the firm? Six metrics can help.

1. **Clarity about the firm's purpose.** Any theory about the functioning of a firm needs to be clear about how the purpose of the firm provides guidelines for creating value for all of the firm's stakeholders. As the above quote by Bill George, former CEO of Medtronic, emphasizes, a firm's purpose is its bedrock foundation.

2. **Source of competitive advantage.** The pragmatic theory specifies that the *source* of long-term competitive advantage (disadvantage) is a firm's knowledge-building proficiency being greater (less) than competitors. This stake in the ground can help management prioritize performance improvement projects. How often do we hear that capability X is the key to a firm's competitive advantage? But, shouldn't the question of interest

be: What is the source for improving capability X over time? And the answer circles back to a firm's knowledge-building proficiency.

3. **Understanding the firm's market valuation.** A strong suit of the pragmatic theory is how it connects a firm's core activities (e.g., work, innovation, and resource allocation) to its publicly traded market value (estimated for privately held firms). Currently, important issues tend to be analyzed without treating the firm as a dynamic, holistic system. For example, academic finance has a theory of asset pricing—the Capital Asset Pricing Model (CAPM) and its variations, which tie together risk and return. This equilibrium theory of asset pricing has been applied in accounting, management, and economic research because heretofore theories of the firm were incomplete due to ignoring key variables concerned with the market valuation of firms. However, the pragmatic theory of the firm provides new angles of thinking about important finance/management issues such as risk, cost of capital, intangible assets, competitive advantage, firm performance, resource allocation, and valuation. For many, this will be a transition that agrees with their business intuition by avoiding the constraint of firm risk being synonymous with the extent of co-movement (Beta) of a firm's stock price with the general market regardless of a firm's ability to be a viable competitor in an increasingly tough global business environment. The pragmatic theory leads to testable hypotheses about firm performance and shareholder returns (see Chapter 5).

4. **Source of improved operating performance.** The pragmatic theory predicts that performance of managerial tasks (e.g., strategy formulation, new product development, quality control, etc.) will improve as managers gain mastery in traversing the knowledge-building loop that is described in Chapter 2.

5. **Source of improved managerial decisions.** Management is well served by constructive skepticism as to what they think they know. The pragmatic theory views knowledge building as the foundation for value creation.

6. **Analysis of firms.** Not only managements, boards, and investors, but also academic researchers and business students can benefit from studying firms' long-term track records guided by the pragmatic theory of the firm. This promotes the study of value creation through deep understanding of the histories of firms, including a comprehension of what drives a firm's stock price over the long term—an especially important readout of long-term value creation. Moreover, economists tend to measure how value is created in a society via macroeconomic variables and industry analyses. The pragmatic theory of the firm equips economists (and their students) with a useful framework for evaluating the locus of value creation at the individual firm level, a highly beneficial microanalysis supplement.

The pragmatic theory of the firm addresses both the actual operations of a firm and a variety of practical needs for those relying on a theory of the firm—hence the label *pragmatic*. The next section presents a historical synopsis of how thinking about the theory of the firm has evolved. Keep in mind that theories have been tailor-made for certain academic disciplines and specific purposes and are not easily applied across disciplines. In contrast, the pragmatic theory of the firm should be useful across economics, finance, management, and other disciplines because it provides insights regarding each of the above six metrics.[3]

---

[3] For one view of the specific needs of finance researchers regarding a theory of the firm, see Luigi Zingales, 2000, "In Search of New Foundations," *Journal of Finance* 55(4) 1623–1653. Zingales focuses on capital structure, corporate governance, and valuation. For the needs of mathematically oriented economists concerned especially with why firms exist and how they are established, see Daniel F. Spulber, 2009, *The Theory of the Firm*. Cambridge: Cambridge University Press.

THE EVOLUTION OF THINKING ABOUT THE THEORY OF THE FIRM

If a theory of the firm is to be widely useful, it necessarily must deal with how a firm is managed. One of the earliest statements clearly acknowledging this need is found in an 1886 speech, "The Engineer as an Economist," presented to the American Society of Mechanical Engineers by Henry R. Towne, cofounder of the Yale Lock Manufacturing Company.

> There are many good mechanical engineers—there are also many good businessmen—but the two are rarely combined in one person. But this combination of qualities, together with at least some skill as an accountant, either in one person or more, is essential to the successful management of industrial works, and has its highest effectiveness if united in one person, who is thus qualified to supervise, either personally or through assistants, the operations of all departments of a business, and to subordinate each to the harmonious development of the whole [i.e., systems thinking].[4]

In 1911, Fredrick Taylor published *Principles of Scientific Management,* which focused in the extreme on quantitative measurement to develop "the one best way" to accomplish specific tasks. In short, management should develop the required knowledge and then command employees to follow the prescribed routines. Taylor's worldview did not embrace win-win partnerships that continually developed employees' problem-solving skills while simultaneously increasing job satisfaction.

Meanwhile, the economist Alfred Marshall's book, *Principles of Economics,* first published in 1890 and revised in eight subsequent editions, became the dominant economic textbook for decades. Marshall cemented the use of supply-and-demand curves, marginal cost, elasticity, and many other important concepts tied together as a system of partial equilibrium.

---

[4] Henry R. Towne, 1886, "Engineer as an Economist," *Transactions of the American Society of Mechanical Engineers* (7): 428–432.

His book became the foundation for neoclassical economics which is the guiding light for mainstream economics taught to students today.

Neoclassical economics exerts a heavy hand in how a theory of the firm is configured in economics textbooks. Market prices are a function of supply and demand, and given perfect competition, will generate an equilibrium in which resources are efficiently allocated. In this stylized world, a firm transforms labor and capital inputs by way of its production cost function to yield outputs. Equilibrium is attained and profit maximized when marginal cost equals marginal revenue. In a world of complete information and perfect competition, no excess profits are possible. Oftentimes, the neoclassical definition of the firm is referred to as a "black box" since the firm is a mechanism to maintain mathematical logic of an economic system in equilibrium. Peter Klein summarizes:

> In neoclassical economic theory, the firm as such does not exist at all. The "firm" is a production function or production possibilities set, a means of transforming inputs into outputs. Given the available technology, a vector of input prices, and a demand schedule, the firm maximizes money profits subject to the constraint that its production plans must be technologically feasible. That is all there is to it. ... In short: the firm is a set of cost curves, and the "theory of the firm" is a calculus problem.[5]

The Nobel economist Ronald Coase remarked: "Economists have tended to neglect the main activity of the firm, running a business."[6] In his celebrated 1937 journal article, "The Nature of the Firm," Coase asked a penetrating question: Why do firms exist? He explained that the alternative of individuals engaging in private transactions and employing contracts to duplicate a firm's activities can be excessively costly. Firms exist because they are more efficient at coordinating activities outside of the marketplace and within the boundaries of the firm.[7] This way of thinking led to the *transactions cost* theory of the firm with the objective of

[5] Peter G. Klein, 1996, "Economic Calculation and the Limits of Organization," *Review of Austrian Economics* 9(2): 3–28.
[6] Ronald Coase, 1988, "The Nature of the Firm: Origin, Meaning, Influence," *Journal of Law, Economics & Organization* 4(1): 3–47.
[7] Ronald Coase, 1937, "The Nature of the Firm," *Economica* 4(16): 386–405.

explaining the different organizational forms for a business.[8] The property rights approach extended the transaction cost perspective to address issues concerning the rights of control over assets.[9] The pragmatic theory of the firm is not concerned with deep explanations of why firms exist other than to have the opportunity to earn above-cost-of-capital returns. The pragmatic theory deals with practical issues concerned with managing firms.

In the first edition of *Capitalism, Socialism and Democracy* published in 1942, the economist Joseph Schumpeter argued that the neoclassical view of economic equilibrium minimizes the role of the entrepreneur. Furthermore, an evolutionary process of continuous innovation and creative destruction offers a more illuminating view of economic progress in a capitalistic society.

> As soon as quality competition and sales effort are admitted into the sacred precincts of theory, the price variable is ousted from its dominant position. ... But in capitalist reality as distinguished from its textbook picture, it is not that kind of competition which counts but the competition from the new commodity, the new technology ... competition which commands a decisive cost or quality advantage and which strikes not at the margins of the profits and the outputs of the existing firms but at their foundations and their very lives. This kind of competition is ... more effective than the other as a bombardment is in comparison with forcing a door.[10]

In 1959, Edith Penrose published *The Theory of the Growth of the Firm* in response to limitations of the neoclassical treatment of the firm. Her objective was to explain a firm's long-term growth. Penrose focused on the services obtainable from a firm's resources and laid the foundation for the resource-based view of the firm, which appeals to those dealing with a firm's strategy.

---

[8] Oliver E. Williamson, 1981, "The Economics of Organizations: The Transaction Cost Approach," *American Journal of Sociology* 87(3): 548–577.

[9] Sanford Grossman and Oliver Hart, 1986, "The Costs and the Benefits of Ownership: A Theory of Vertical and Lateral Integration," *Journal of Political Economy* 94(4): 691–719. Also, Oliver Hart, 1989, "An Economist's Perspective on the Theory of the Firm," *Columbia Law Review* 89(7): 1757–1774.

[10] Joseph Schumpeter, 1947, *Capitalism, Socialism and Democracy*. New York: Harper Perennial, p. 84.

Richard Cyert and James March coauthored *A Behavioral Theory of the Firm* in 1963, and they questioned the usefulness of profit maximization and perfect knowledge used in neoclassical economics. They stressed multiple goals (sales, market share, etc.) and *satisficing* as opposed to maximization, that is, a bounded rationality view of decision-making. Cyert and March were interested in process explanations—actual behavior and learning versus assumed rational behavior—missing from standard economic explanations of firm behavior. Their seminal work continued the development of evolutionary economics, which is reviewed below.

KINDRED SPIRITS FOR THE PRAGMATIC THEORY OF THE FIRM

The pragmatic theory of the firm combines value-creating components (discussed later in this chapter) to comprise a holistic system; focuses on relationships among these components (especially connections to a firm's market valuation); and utilizes a more detailed process for knowledge building by individuals versus other theories of the firm that stress organizational learning. Yet the theory certainly uses ideas that others have advanced in their work. Consider Peter Drucker, often referred to as the man who invented management. It is hard to overstate his impact on management thinking contained in 39 books and countless articles and op-eds. Based on his experience with fascism, and influenced by Schumpeter, Drucker argued that effective and responsible institutions were needed for a functioning society. He noted: "The fact is that in modern society there is no other leadership but managers. If the managers of our major institutions, and especially of business, do not take responsibility for the common good, no one else can or will."[11]

Drucker's insightful way of analyzing complex phenomena enabled him to predict emerging trends at an early stage (e.g., Japan's rise as an economic power, the transition to knowledge work, etc.). Drucker was a kindred

---

[11] Peter F. Drucker, 1973, *Management: Tasks, Responsibilities, Practices*. New York: Harper Business, p. 325.

spirit to the pragmatic theory in two significant ways. First, he believed that profit was not the firm's singular purpose but an essential requirement for a firm to survive and prosper. Second, he emphasized the importance of developing employees' knowledge-building proficiencies and adapting firms' organizational structures to productively utilize these knowledge workers.

Alfred Chandler published *Strategy and Structure: Chapters in the History of the American Industrial Enterprise* in 1962, which analyzed the long-term histories of large American firms and focused on the evolution of organizational structures to effectively manage expanding businesses. Chandler's 1977 book, *The Visible Hand: The Managerial Revolution in American Business,* is a historical analysis of the replacement of market mechanisms by firms in coordinating economic activity and allocating resources, in other words, the replacement of Adam Smith's invisible hand of the market with the visible hand of management. These two books showcased the role of managerial decision-making pertaining to strategy and organizational structure while significantly influencing future research.

Chandler's *Scale and Scope: The Dynamics of Industrial Capitalism* was published in 1990 and analyzed the growth and competitiveness of the major firms in the United States, Britain, and Germany after 1880. The book showed the unique importance in modern times of how firms and markets coevolve. To understand markets, one must understand firms. He made a strong case that managements' strategic and organizational choices over time coupled to proficiency in production and distribution plus overall managerial skill were the key determinants of the industrial development of these three countries. Chandler forcefully put firms on center stage as a dominant source of economic growth—for sure, a kindred spirit with the pragmatic theory of the firm. Chandler had a strong opinion about the firm as the fundamental unit of analysis.

> Just as I find the earlier growth of the industrial firm difficult to explain fully in terms of transactions, agency and other information costs, so I find it hard to explain the recent process of expansion and contraction with these same concepts. ... I am convinced that the unit of analysis must be the firm, rather than the transactions or contractual relations entered into by the firm. Only by focusing on the

firm can microeconomic theory explain why this legal, contracting, transacting entity has been the instrument in capitalist economies for carrying out the processes of production and distribution, for increasing productivity and for propelling economic growth and transformation.[12]

In 1982, Richard Nelson and Sidney Winter coauthored *An Evolutionary Theory of Economic Change*, which extends Schumpeter's view of continuous innovation and change as the path to progress in modern capitalistic economies. The intrinsic uncertainty of innovation, emphasized in their book, does not comport with the neoclassical assumption that firms "know" how best to maximize profits. Moreover, the wide range of observed performance of firms is consistent with an evolutionary perspective.

An evolutionary perspective on innovation and competition is closely aligned with a firm's competitive life-cycle framework, which is introduced in Chapter 4. Nelson summarizes:

> While a successful innovator is able to hold control over its new ways of doing things and reap the returns from the advantage they give it over its competitors for a certain period of time, almost always, aspects of new productive ways of doing things sooner or later become widely known, and the ability of the innovator to hold off its competitors from using that know-how generally is limited. As a result, the whole industry moves ahead over time. Market competition turns out to be an effective vehicle for evolutionary learning.
>
> This is a very different view of what markets do and how they work than articulated in today's standard economic texts. And yet, here too it would appear that many contemporary economists have a view of the advantages of market organization of economic activity, and competition, that is very much in line with the [evolutionary perspective]. *It is the theory they espouse when presenting formal economics that ignores this.* As we have argued, a major advantage of evolutionary economic theory is that it puts forth an abstract view of economic activity, and the role of markets and competition, that squares with what much of the profession actually believes.[13] (italics added)

---

[12] Alfred D. Chandler, 1992, "Organizational Capabilities and the Economic History of the Industrial Enterprise," *Journal of Economic Perspectives* 6(3): 79–100.

[13] Richard R. Nelson, "Economics from an Evolutionary Perspective." Chapter 1 in Richard Nelson et al. 2018, *Modern Evolutionary Economics: An Overview*. Cambridge: Cambridge University Press, p. 21.

Evolutionary economists view institutions (i.e., the rules of the game) as playing a central role in economic growth and how we got to where we are.[14] Nelson and Winter stress how a firm's effectiveness is tied to routines and organizational learning, which underpin a firm's capabilities. This line of thinking was further developed with the concept of dynamic capabilities (discussed below) that treats the firm as an evolving, dynamic system. The *Journal of Evolutionary Economics* began in 1991 to showcase interdisciplinary research attuned to disequilibrium and the dynamics of innovation and competition.

The importance of management's strategic decisions led to the resource-based view of the firm that emphasized difficult-to-copy resources presumed to be the source of competitive advantage. These resources include "all assets, capabilities, organizational processes, firm attributes, information, knowledge, etc., controlled by a firm that enable the firm to conceive of and implement strategies that improve its efficiency and effectiveness."[15]

A logical step from the resource-based view is to focus on a uniquely important resource—knowledge. Generating, sharing, and utilizing knowledge within the firm is a palpable means to improve the firm's effectiveness and potentially gain competitive advantage if the firm's knowledge process is difficult for others to reproduce. The knowledge-based view and a pragmatic theory of the firm concur that knowledge is the primary resource underlying value creation.[16] Researchers applying a knowledge-based view often select for analysis the group, the business unit, or most frequently the overall firm (similar to the evolutionary perspective); in contrast, a critical component of the pragmatic theory of the firm is the process

---

[14] Thorstein Veblen, 1898, "Why Is Economics Not an Evolutionary Science?" *Quarterly Journal of Economics* 12(3): 373–397.

[15] Jay Barney, 1991, "Firm Resources and Sustained Competitive Advantage," *Journal of Management* 17(1): 99–120. For an early description of the resource-based view, see B. Wernerfelt, 1984, "A Resource-Based View of the Firm," *Strategic Management Journal* 5(2): 171–180. For an insightful review of the challenges and opportunities for this way of thinking, see Jay B. Barney, 2001, "Is the Resource-Based 'View' a Useful Perspective for Strategic Management Research? Yes," *Academy of Management Review* 26(1): 41–56.

[16] Bart Nooteboom, 2009, *A Cognitive Theory of the Firm: Learning, Governance and Dynamic Capabilities*. Northhampton, MA: Edward Elgar Publishing.

whereby individuals improve their knowledge base.[17] Robert Grant, an early supporter of the knowledge-based view, agrees with the emphasis on individuals as the foundational unit of analysis for knowledge building.

> The emphasis upon the role of the individual as the primary actor in knowledge creation and the principle repository of knowledge, I believe, is essential to piercing the veil of organizational knowledge and clarifying the role of organizations in the creation and application of knowledge.[18]

Keep in mind that ways of thinking about the firm tend to focus on how value is *created*. However, important issues concern how value is *distributed*. There is a fundamental tension between the owners (principals) of the firm who have delegated decision-making to the managers (agents). Managers have superior information and may be motivated to serve their own personal interests instead, or as an integral part, of meeting the owners' objectives. On the one hand, principal–agent research is concerned with the design of optimal incentive contracts between principals and agents. On the other hand, researchers have been working on a better understanding of financial structure, governance, and shareholder activism. Consistent with these research objectives, the firm is defined as a legal entity serving as a nexus for contracts (formal and informal) between those working for, or interacting with, the firm.[19]

With his 1979 article, "How Competitive Forces Shape Strategy," Michael Porter began a highly influential body of work focused on formulating strategy.[20] He popularized the concept of five forces that

---

[17] For an insightful analysis of the level in the firm at which new value is created, see Teppo Felin and William S. Hesterly, 2007, "The Knowledge-Base View, Nested Heterogeneity, and New Value Creation: Philosophical Considerations on the Locus of Knowledge," *Academy of Management Review* 32(1): 195–218. For an argument about the importance of knowledge creating versus knowledge commercialization, see Ikujiro Nonaka, Ryoko Toyama and Toru Hirata, 2008, *Managing Flow: A Process Theory of the Knowledge-Based Firm*. New York: Palgrave Macmillan.

[18] Robert M. Grant, 1996, "Toward a Knowledge-Based Theory of the Firm," *Strategic Management Journal* 17 (Winter Special Issue): 109–122. See also, Robert M. Grant, "The Knowledge-Based View of the Firm." In David O. Faulkner and Andrew Campbell, 2003, *Oxford Handbook of Strategy*, Volume 1. Oxford: Oxford University Press.

[19] Michael C. Jensen and William H. Meckling, 1976, "Theory of the Firm: Managerial Behavior, Agency Costs, and Ownership Structure," *Journal of Financial Economics* 3(4): 305–360.

[20] For an updated version of this article, see Michel E. Porter, 2008, "The Five Competitive Forces That Shape Strategy," *Harvard Business Review*, 86(1): 79–93.

shape industry competition: rivalry among existing competitors, threat of new entrants, bargaining power of buyers, bargaining power of suppliers, and the threat of substitute products or services. The usefulness of the five forces was due to setting the firm in the context of a specified industry. Stable industries were a hallmark of the Old Economy with its reliance on tangible assets to create value. The New Economy changes the context so that the five forces perspective is less useful as a thinking template. The New Economy with access to global transportation and information flows brings both hypercompetition and expanded collaboration that blurs the boundaries of industries. Intangible assets keyed to knowledge building have come to dominate as a source of competitive advantage.

In our fast-paced New Economy, it is even more imperative to develop an intellectual structure that enables a fundamental understanding of how (and why) firms succeed and fail. To meet this need, the dynamic capabilities theory of the firm has evolved, principally through the work of David Teece. It integrates the work of Penrose, Chandler, and Schumpeter, each interested in the dynamic link between knowledge and innovation.[21] In a nutshell, this theory ties into the knowledge-building primacy promoted in this book as follows:

> Effective organizational learning—a continuous process in most industries—requires dynamic capabilities. These capabilities are activities that can usefully be thought of in three clusters: sensing opportunities (building new knowledge), seizing those opportunities to capture value, and transforming the organization as needed to adapt to the requirements of new business models and the competitive environment.[22]

Sensing, seizing, and transforming capture succinctly and comprehensively the critical responsibilities facing top management.

---

[21] The initial article, which has been extensively cited, articulating the core idea of dynamic capabilities is D. J. Teece, G. Pisano, and A. Shuen, 1997, "Dynamic Capabilities and Strategic Management," *Strategic Management* 18(7): 509–533. For a more comprehensive treatment, see David J. Teece, 2009. *Dynamic Capabilities and Strategic Management*. Oxford: Oxford University Press.

[22] David J. Teece, 2011, "Knowledge Assets, Capabilities, and the Theory of the Firm." Chapter 23 in Mark Easterly-Smith and Marjorie A. Lyles, eds. *Handbook of Organizational Learning and Knowledge Management*. Hoboken, NJ: John Wiley & Sons.

Whereas ordinary capabilities focus on doing things right, dynamic capabilities focus on doing the right things in an uncertain, rapidly changing environment. Dynamic capabilities are built (a learning process), not bought. Through the lens of dynamic capabilities, decision-makers see the firm as a system that poses continual challenges to realign the firm's tangible and intangible assets in hopes of achieving sustained superior performance. This sharply differs from competitive advantage being secured in the Old Economy by leveraging tangible assets which had a long productive life in a relatively stable environment. Both the dynamic capabilities theory of the firm and the pragmatic theory of the firm help explain the performance of firms and offer guideposts for practical decision-making.

In summary, most theories of the firm were constructed to fit specific disciplines and consequently are narrow in scope. In contrast, the pragmatic theory of the firm is broadly based and explicitly connects to firm valuation. It should be useful for those working in economics, finance, management, and accounting. The pragmatic theory treats the firm as a holistic system with a well-defined purpose. Its application should help management and all of the firm's stakeholders better achieve the firm's purpose.

INNOVATION AND ECONOMIC GROWTH

Economic growth is about being better off at the end of a time period compared to the beginning. Consider the early 1900s when transportation in cities was mainly via horse-drawn carriages. People continually inhaled pulverized manure courtesy of the many horses. Would city folks be materially better off with 3% growth in the "capital stock" of horse-drawn carriages? The innovation of the automobile made people decidedly better off versus merely incrementally expanding the existing means for providing transportation with its adverse effects and limitations. Henry Ford's ideas about manufacturing a low-cost automobile became reality through the Ford Motor Company. On one hand, consumer acceptance of the early electric/battery-powered automobiles would have benefited from an especially farsighted perspective of carbon emissions from the internal combustion engine. On the other hand, the cost of Ford's Model T was a fraction of the cost of the electric automobiles in production and enabled a mass market to develop. A multitude of ancillary businesses and large-scale employment gains were spawned from the birth of the automobile industry.

A strong case can be made that the critical role of firms in the innovation process has long been neglected by neoclassical (mainstream) economists primarily because it does not fit into their mathematical models. The issue is not just quibbling about the content of economic textbooks. Rather, one result is that the critical role of firms in economic growth is neglected in economic policy-making.

This section reviews how mainstream economics has dealt with innovation and highlights different perspectives for explaining economic growth. There is a ripe opportunity for a bottom-up, firm-based approach to economic growth. The pragmatic theory of the firm should contribute to that direction.

In the 1950s, Robert Solow noted the importance of technological change that spurs economic growth without adding more labor and capital. Solow's neoclassical growth model did not address the source of technological change. He labeled it as exogenous (i.e., outside of his model). Empirical studies identified the unexplained "residual" component of economic growth as remarkably big, implying that technological change has a genuinely big impact on economic growth.[23] As to technological change, think of the introduction of electricity versus the status quo of increased growth using more candles. In 1990, Paul Romer published a refined model that explained in mathematical terms (necessary in order to convince his peers) how technological change was endogenous, that is, an integral part of how his model generated economic growth.[24] In some

---

[23] Robert Solow, 1957, "Technical Change and the Aggregate Production Function," *Review of Economics and Statistics* (39)3: 312–320.
[24] Paul M. Romer, 1990, "Endogenous Technological Change," *Journal of Political Economy* 98(5): S71–S102.

ways, Romer's approach was a mathematical abstraction of the economic growth theme developed in the evolutionary economics approach.

For Romer, ideas are recipes to rearrange physical things in order to create value. Physical things are finite, but there is an infinite number of recipes to be discovered. Ideas do not suffer from diminishing returns that are characteristic of physical things; for example, over time it costs more to discover the next barrel of oil, to mine the next ton of copper, and so on. He is an optimist about the potential for significant future economic growth.

Romer's new growth theory involves three key principles. First, ideas are treated as goods which are "nonrival," meaning everyone can use them at the same time. Second, commercialization of ideas can lead to increasing returns, which contravenes the deeply entrenched economic concept of decreasing returns. For example, while initially expensive to produce, copies of Microsoft's operating system for personal computers are almost costless to reproduce. And third, incentives that make ideas partially excludable (e.g., patents) are needed in order for some ideas to be initially produced. In Romer's words:

> New growth theorists … start by dividing the world into two fundamentally different types of productive inputs that can be called "ideas" and "things." Ideas are nonrival goods that could be stored in a bit string. Things are rival goods with mass (or energy). With ideas and things, one can explain how economic growth works. Nonrival ideas can be used to rearrange things, for example, when one follows a recipe and transforms noxious olives into tasty and healthful olive oil. Economic growth arises from the discovery of new recipes and the transformation of things from low to high value configurations … a nonrival idea can be copied and communicated, so its value increases in proportion to the size of the market in which it can be used.[25]

Romer's insightful work improved the language of growth for economists, although still missing was the explicit role of firms. Consider Richard Nelson's critique of new growth theory.

---

[25]Paul M. Romer, 1996, "Why, Indeed, in America? Theory, History, and the Origins of Modern Economic Growth," *American Economic Review* 86(2): 202–206.

I would like to propose that the attempt to probe more deeply leads inevitably to three topics that continue to be repressed, or misspecified, in standard growth theory, including the new neoclassical growth models. These are, first, technology as a body of understanding and practice, and the processes involved in mastering and advancing technology. Second, the nature of the organizations, principally business firms, that employ technology and produce output. And, third, the nature and role of a wide variety of economic institutions that establish the environment within which firms operate.[26]

Many economists and historians have explained the historical sources of growth, providing reasons that ostensibly fit the data and were deemed plausible. Such explanations often undergird forecasts about future growth and policy proposals to boost economic growth. Three recent books summarize the core ideas of recognized leaders in this field.

In the 768 pages of *The Rise and Fall of American Growth: The U.S. Standard of Living Since the Civil War*, Robert Gordon, a professor at Northwestern University, takes issue with how various versions of neoclassical growth theory imply "steady state" growth consistent with their mathematical construction. Gordon documents in considerable detail how actual economic growth, measured as the standard of living, began to accelerate after 1870; was very rapid between 1920 and 1970; slowed thereafter although temporarily increasing from 1996 to 2004; and was followed by slower growth to this day. In addition to economic analysis, his book provides significant insights about technology developments and their impact on how people work and live.

Context matters. Gordon emphasizes that the information technology revolution of recent decades pales in comparison to the impact of inventions that powered economic growth from 1870 to 1970, which include electricity, urban sanitation, pharmaceuticals and chemicals, the internal combustion engine, and modern communications. And the magnitude of the improvement brought by these inventions, according to Gordon, will

[26]Richard R. Nelson, 2005, *Technology, Institutions, and Economic Growth*. Cambridge: Harvard University Press, p. 27.

not be repeated (e.g., "hoof and sail" to modern planes, polluting flames to electric lights, etc.).[27]

In Gordon's analysis, the 1970 to 1995 phase of the information technology revolution replaced mechanical calculators and typewriters with electronic calculators and memory typewriters, brought personal computers with word processing and spreadsheets, and in general enhanced the productivity of business firms. The 1995–2005 phase brought the Internet, search engines, electronic commerce, and broadband advancements. Gordon's point is that *these business-firm-oriented productivity gains are about done.* His view is that robots and artificial intelligence are evolutionary innovations, not revolutionary on the scale of the great inventions noted earlier. Consequently, he forecasts a continuation of low economic growth in the future.

Joel Mokyr, also a professor at Northwestern University, has a much more optimistic view of future economic growth. His latest book, *A Culture of Growth: The Origins of the Modern Economy,* explains what ignited the Industrial Revolution and rising living standards after nearly zero economic growth for thousands of years. Mokyr stresses the importance of cultural beliefs among the educated people in Europe between Columbus and the death of Isaac Newton in 1729. Contrary to the past, the new culture was about blending scientific research with practical know-how in order to better humankind. The notion that life should be about making progress was a radical departure from the past. This cultural transition involved breaking the chains of paralyzing reverence for "knowledge" developed in the past (e.g., Aristotle) and taking control of the knowledge-building process.

Although Europe transitioned, China did not with its imperial bureaucracy that maintained a strict allegiance to centuries-old "knowledge." Because Europe was fragmented, it spurred a competition for ideas between nations (not firms) to develop improved ships, navigation

---

[27]Nicholas Bloom, Charles I. Jones, John Van Reenen, and Michael Webb, 2017, "Are Ideas Getting Harder to Find?" National Bureau of Economic Research Working Paper 23782. The authors document that research effort is rising substantially while research productivity is declining. They note that the number of researchers needed today to achieve the doubling every two years (Moore's Law) of the density of computer chips is more than 18 times larger than the number required in the 1970s.

techniques, weaponry, and much more. In Europe, letters and books served as a network for exchanging ideas very quickly. The incentive to compete in knowledge building was the recognition (and opportunity for patronage jobs) accorded pioneers who solved important problems or made scientific discoveries. Mokyr believes that competition between nations, as long as it doesn't result in armed conflicts, is needed to maintain a pro-growth culture.[28] He looks at scientific knowledge building as the ultimate source of economic growth.[29]

Keep in mind that many support Gordon's analysis and also agree with Tyler Cowen's point that the low-hanging fruit of transformative innovation has been picked.[30] Mokyr's response is that the scientific process, which includes advancements in tools, continues at a strong pace today and will enable taller ladders to reach higher hanging fruit. Who forecasted that the development of the microscope would lead to the discovery of the germ theory of disease? Who can forecast the discoveries that will follow from today's expanding scientific toolbox (gene editing, nanotechnology, etc.) coupled to Internet-enabled locating and sharing of information?

Edmund Phelps is a Nobel economist who currently directs the Center on Capitalism and Society at Columbia University and is Dean of China's New Huadu business school, which makes sense given the remarkable success of the Chinese translation of his capstone book, *Mass Flourishing: How Grassroots Innovation Created Jobs, Challenge, and Change*. Phelps makes the case that the bedrock foundation that enables nations to prosper is society's

---

[28] For agreement that competition between nations that are in contact with one another drives technology advancements, see Jared Diamond, 1999, *Guns, Germs, and Steel: The Fates of Human Societies*. New York: W. W. Norton.

[29] Deidre McCloskey agrees with Mokyr's emphasis on the importance to economic growth of ideas and culture, although she may not fully share Mokyr's emphasis on the preeminence of scientific ideas. See Deidre Nansen McCloskey, 2016, *Bourgeois Equality: How Ideas, Not Capital or Institutions, Enriched the World*. Chicago: University of Chicago Press. For a comprehensive historical analysis of the importance of institutions to secure property rights and the rule of law, to minimize government-granted privilege, and to provide opportunities to innovate and invest emblematic of an inclusive market economy, see Daron Acemoglu and James A. Robinson, 2012, *Why Nations Fail: The Origins of Power, Prosperity, and Poverty*. New York: Crown Publishers.

[30] Tyler Cowen, *The Great Stagnation: How America Ate All the Low-Hanging Fruit of Modern History, Got Sick, and Will (Eventually) Feel Better*, 2011. New York: Dutton. Also see Patrick Collison and Michael Nielsen, November 16, 2018, "Science Is Getting Less Bang for Its Buck," *The Atlantic*.

embrace of what he terms modern values—desire to create, explore, and meet challenges.

> Flourishing is the heart of prospering—engagement, meeting chal-
> lenges, self-expression, and personal growth. … A person's flourish-
> ing comes from the experience of the new: new situations, new prob-
> lems, new insights, and new ideas to develop and share. Similarly,
> prosperity on a national scale—mass flourishing—comes from broad
> involvement of people in the processes of innovation: the conception,
> development, and spread of new methods and products—indigenous
> innovation down to the grassroots. This dynamism may be narrowed
> or weakened by institutions. … But institutions alone cannot create
> it. Broad dynamism must be fueled by the right values.[31]

Phelps does not deny the benefits of scientific advancements. However, he gives top priority to regaining the modern values that were the hallmark of high-economic-growth times enabling "intellectual growth that comes from actively engaging the world and moral growth that comes from creating and exploring in the face of great uncertainty." This flourishing goes beyond wages earned and is unfortunately absent from standard economic models.

These models miss indigenous innovation—a nation's home-grown, bottom-up innovating which can pervade the workplace and lead to well-earned satisfaction with the value of one's work. Earned success for employees of firms who may not be R&D superstars but who nonetheless creatively solve problems and seek out opportunities to create value is itself sufficient reward. While scientific discoveries are highly visible and newsworthy, business discoveries (knowledge building) are much less visible and rarely publicized even though they can be more important than scientific discoveries to the process of efficiently delivering high value to customers, says Phelps.[32] Indigenous innovation manifested in a nation's

---

[31] Edmund Phelps, 2013, *Mass Flourishing: How Grassroots Innovation Created Jobs, Challenge, and Change*. Princeton, NJ: Princeton University Press, p. vii.

[32] For a critique of Phelps's view about the relative importance of business versus scientific discoveries, see Joel Mokyr, 2014, "A Flourishing Economist: A Review Essay on Edmund Phelps's *Mass Flourishing: How Grassroots Innovation Created Jobs, Challenge, and Change*," *Journal of Economic Literature* 52(1): 189–196.

workforce directly ties into the overriding importance given to a firm's knowledge-building proficiency in the pragmatic theory of the firm.

In summary, the three books highlighted above show that Gordon, Mokyr, and Phelps take different approaches to better understand the causes of economic growth while not being constrained by the mathematical formalism of mainstream economics. How can we coalesce these insights into something more illuminating and useful for today's economy?

A deep understanding of the role of firms, however, takes a back seat in these books and other major works in economics. This is because the type of research needed differs from how economists typically work; in addition, the analysis of centuries of economic growth includes times when the modern firm did not exist. The economics literature has been concerned with why firms exist and how they are established, but little has been done on the contribution of firms to economic growth. Research about firms in the finance literature has focused on capital structure, governance, and especially, empirical studies about shareholder returns, risk, and market efficiency. Less work has been conducted that connects firm performance to overall economic growth. In the management literature, priority is given to different theories of the firm to serve as a thinking template to analyze the impact of strategy and other managerial levers on firm performance, but once again, little work has been done that connects firms to overall economic growth (i.e., a bottom-up approach to macroeconomics).

This state of affairs is one reason for this book. For example, in Chapter 3 I review three high-impact approaches to improving firm performance that illustrate the process of bottom-up economic growth. One approach, Lean Thinking, originated with Toyota's revolutionary Toyota Production System (a major business discovery) for producing high-quality cars at lower prices while engaging employees in improving their problem-solving skills. Is this not a significant example of the type of dynamism that Phelps says we need? Perhaps the ongoing worldwide adoption of Lean Thinking is an underappreciated boost to future economic growth.

What is needed is an improved language to analyze and discuss firm performance consistent with a bottom-up approach to economic growth. To this end, the pragmatic theory of the firm involves the firm's competitive life cycle and related life-cycle track records for individual firms, which are introduced in Chapter 4. These life-cycle track records facilitate the analysis of firm performance over long time periods, including insights as to how firm performance links to stock prices.

Let's now consider the purpose of the firm.

THE PURPOSE OF THE FIRM

The pragmatic theory of the firm necessarily is rooted in the purpose of the firm. At the present time, the firm's purpose, including its social role and responsibilities, is at the center of a worldwide debate about capitalism. There are no shortages of proposed ways to move forward. This includes the CSR (corporate social responsibility) movement; Michael Porter's shared value concept; conscious capitalism led by John Mackey of Whole Foods; ESG (environmental, social, and governance) scorecards; a corporate commitment to purge short-termism and focus on building long-term value, which is promoted by FCLT (Focusing Capitalism on the Long Term) among others; and the Center for Capitalism and Society at Columbia University, which focuses on fundamental analysis of what determines a country's dynamism.[33] Larry Fink, CEO of BlackRock, the largest worldwide investment management firm, emphasizes the foundational role of a firm's purpose.

---

[33] See Harwell Wells, 2002, "The Cycles of Corporate Social Responsibility: An Historical Retrospective for the Twenty-First Century," *University of Kansas Law Review* Vol. 51: 77–140. Available at SSRN: https://ssrn.com/abstract=1121899. Michael E. Porter and Mark R. Kramer, 2011, "Creating Shared Value," *Harvard Business Review,* January-February: 62–77. See John Mackey and Raj Sisodia, 2013, *Conscious Capitalism.* Boston: Harvard Business Review Press. Sakis Kotsantonis, Chris Pinney, and George Serafeim, 2016, "ESG Integration in Investment Management: Myths and Realities," *Journal of Applied Corporate Finance* 28(2) (Spring): 10–16. FCLT Global is dedicated to encouraging long-term behaviors in business and investment decision making, http://www.FCLTglobal.org. Robert G. Eccles and Michael P. Krzus, 2015, *The Integrated Reporting Movement: Meaning, Momentum, Motives, and Materiality.* Hoboken, NJ: John Wiley & Sons. The website for the Center for Capitalism and Society is https://capitalism.columbia.edu/.

Without a sense of purpose, no company, either public or private, can achieve its full potential. It will ultimately lose the license to operate from key stakeholders. It will succumb to short-term pressures to distribute earnings, and, in the process, sacrifice investments in employee development, innovation, and capital expenditures that are necessary for long-term growth. It will remain exposed to activist campaigns that articulate a clearer goal, even if that goal serves only the shortest and narrowest of objectives. And ultimately, that company will provide subpar returns to investors who depend on it to finance their retirement, home purchases, or higher education.[34]

For those engaged in the capitalism debate, and in order to improve how capitalism operates worldwide, it is first necessary to gain genuine clarity about the purpose of the firm. Many of those with a background in economics or finance assume that, whether privately held or publicly traded, the firm's purpose is simple and straightforward—maximize shareholder value (long-term profitability). As a pure, conceptual objective, this is sensible. The idea is to avoid investments that dissipate value while directing resources to investments that create value. But, stakeholder proponents contend that a singular purpose to maximize shareholder value will fail to generate commitment and support from the firm's stakeholders and will incentivize management to make decisions that most always shortchange nonshareholder stakeholders.[35] Stakeholder proponents say that, in practice, maximizing shareholder value results in an extreme focus by management on quarterly performance to the detriment of building long-term value. But there is a way out of this dilemma.

The four-part purpose detailed below resolves this dilemma and should be acceptable to both proponents of maximizing shareholder value and stakeholder proponents. A key insight is that *maximizing shareholder value is best positioned not as the purpose of the firm, but as the result of a firm*

---

[34] https://www.blackrock.com/corporate/investor-relations/larry-fink-ceo-letter, accessed on 19 December 2018.

[35] See R. Edward Freeman, 1984, *Strategic Management: A Stakeholder Approach.* London: Pitman Publishing. Also, R. Edward Freeman, Jeffrey S. Harrison, Andrew C. Wicks, Bidhan L. Parmar, and Simone de Colle, 2010, *Stakeholder Theory: The State of the Art.* Cambridge: Cambridge University Press.

successfully achieving its purpose.[36] The following four mutually reinforcing goals constitute a firm's purpose and should be supported by all the firm's stakeholders, including its most knowledgeable institutional owners.

1. Communicate a *vision* that can inspire and motivate employees to work for a firm committed to behaving ethically and making the world a better place. The large, diversified firm 3M has a vision of collaborative innovation "advancing every company," "enhancing every home," and "improving every life." Managements of firms that provide commodities and basic services can craft a vision based on the value received by their customers.

2. *Survive and prosper* through continual gains in efficiency and sustained innovation, which depend upon a firm's knowledge-building proficiency.[37] Managements and boards typically embrace a "grow the business" mindset which is suitable for firms in a stage of their life cycle wherein profitability exceeds the cost of capital consumed and genuine value is being created for customers. But this "business-as-usual" mindset causes problems as firms mature and what worked well in the past can easily become out-of-step with a changed environment. Orchestrating feedback about change is key to early adaptation. Otherwise, management eventually is faced with downsizing business units that are uncompetitive at their current size while helping employees who lose their jobs to transition to more viable job opportunities. To be sure, nothing works long term if a firm consistently fails to earn its cost of capital.

3. Work continuously to *sustain win-win relationships* with all of the firm's stakeholders. The brokerage and financial advisory firm Charles Schwab delivers products and services that "put clients

---

[36] Bartley J. Madden, 2017, "The Purpose of the Firm, Valuation, and the Management of Intangibles," *Journal of Applied Corporate Finance* 29(2): 76–86.
[37] Bartley J. Madden, 2018, "Management's Key Responsibility," *Journal of Applied Corporate Finance* 30(3): 27–35.

first." Some of its competitors, as a practical matter, put the generation of sales commissions first. The firm has a well-deserved reputation of management decision-making that gives priority to: "What's this going to look like through the eyes of the customers?" Over the long term, Schwab shareholders have been significantly rewarded.

4. Take care of *future generations*. What is needed is a genuine commitment by management and the board to ensure the sustainability of the environment. The early stage of the design of products and manufacturing processes should be focused on minimizing waste and pollution. We return full circle to the importance of a firm's knowledge-building proficiency. Smart design can reduce total product costs (and increase profits) while simultaneously reducing harm to the environment.[38] In addition, the application of a lean mindset across all of the firm's activities can reduce waste throughout the entire value stream of a product, including raw material procurement and end-of-life recycling. Knowledge-building proficiency tied to the four-part purpose is a viable route to taking care of future generations.

A firm that is successful in achieving its four-part purpose benefits society and the firm's stakeholders. For example, Intuitive Surgical has a vision that people needing medical intervention should recover as quickly and completely as possible. Intuitive Surgical is the global leader in robotic-assisted minimally invasive surgery. As illustrated in Chapter 6, its stock price has significantly appreciated as high profits were earned due to the exceptionally high value delivered to customers (surgeons and their patients). Surely, Intuitive Surgical's scientists, engineers, and other employees have been motivated, not by maximizing shareholder value, but

---

[38] See William McDonough and Michael Braungart, 2002, *Cradle to Cradle: Remaking the Way We Make Things*. New York: North Point Press. Also, William McDonough and Michael Braungart, 2013, *The Upcycle: Beyond Sustainability—Designing for Abundance*. New York: North Point Press.

by the opportunity to make the world a better (healthier) place through the products they design and manufacture.[39]

In summary, the four-part purpose addresses the foundational needs of all stakeholders. It answers the question of why employees should show up for work. It provides a solid base to deal with tough issues that involve not just capital expenditures on R&D or new manufacturing capabilities but decisions to fund new employee health benefits and expand local community programs. Management, in fact, needs a cost-of-capital guidepost to make logically sound decisions even though it can be exceedingly difficult at times to execute. In this manner, the firm and, by extension, society can get the most out of its limited resources.

The firm's purpose underscores that it is a complex system of interrelated components. With complex systems, analysis of a single component isolated from its relationships with other system components will yield insufficient understanding and, at times, lead to decisions that degrade rather than improve performance. Of utmost importance is how a firm's knowledge-building proficiency touches so many of the firm's activities and is intimately tied to the firm's purpose. Consider this summary by Brad Smith, CEO of Intuit, which has a stellar long-term track record of financial performance:

> The culture you create lays the foundation that enables every other part of the company to grow and succeed … job one in creating a culture is building a *purpose-driven culture*. … What is the bigger idea that we are all part of? … At Intuit, our mission is to improve our customers' financial lives so profoundly they can't imagine going back to the old way. … One way leaders can create an action-oriented environment is to match inspiration with rigor, adopting a rapid experimentation culture … [that] cuts through hierarchy (especially if leaders hold their own ideas to the same scrutiny of testing), creating an environment where everyone can innovate, and debate turns into doing.[40] (italics added)

---

[39] Andrew M. Carton, 2018, "I'm Not Mopping the Floors, I'm Putting a Man on the Moon: How NASA Leaders Enhanced the Meaningfulness of Work by Changing the Meaning of Work," *Administrative Science Quarterly* 63(2): 323–369.

[40] Brad Smith, 2016, "The Most Important Job of a CEO," Investors.intuit.com, accessed March 13, 2016.

FIGURE 1.1 **The purpose of the firm**

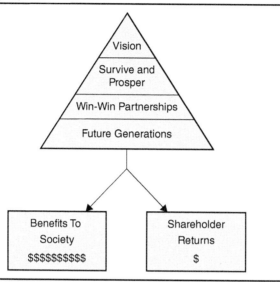

Source: Adapted from Madden (2016).[41]

The above quote captures the spirit of a high-performing firm. Figure 1.1 describes who really benefits from such high performance.

Figure 1.1 illustrates the core economic principle that society benefits from resources allocated to value-creating investments that at least earn the cost of capital. A firm's output, less the costs (including the cost of capital) of all resources used, provides a net benefit (surplus) to society. Meanwhile, a firm generates cash flows that drive its market valuation. So, a successful firm directly benefits both shareholders and society, but not equally.

The societal benefits from Henry Ford manufacturing an affordable automobile surely exceeded the investment returns achieved by the capital owners of Ford Motor Company. Also, consider the new HIV/AIDS drugs that entered the market after the late 1980s. The estimated benefit to the firms that developed these drugs was about 5% of the overall benefit to society from improved patient health.[42] This is why in Figure 1.1 there

[41] Bartley J. Madden, 2016, *Value Creation Thinking*. Naperville, IL: LearningWhatWorks, Figure 3.1.
[42] Tomas J. Philipson and Anupam B. Jena, 2006, "Surplus Appropriation from R&D and Health Care Technology Assessment Procedures." NBER Working Paper 12016.

are many more dollar signs in the box for societal benefits versus the box for shareholder returns.[43]

THE PRAGMATIC THEORY OF THE FIRM

As noted earlier, the pragmatic theory of the firm specifies that a firm's knowledge-building proficiency is the fundamental cause of a firm's survival and prosperity as well as a pathway to significant improvements across a firm's typically siloed activities. This theory is about *connectedness* among the firm's purpose, its major activities, and its long-term overall performance, with particular attention to long-term financial performance.

Employees improve their knowledge-building proficiency with experience in traversing the knowledge-building loop which is explained in Chapter 2. Success in understanding cause and effect reveals faulty or obsolete assumptions and leads to new assumptions whose reliability is then verified. Language matters and employees' knowledge-building proficiency improves with a habitual concern for questioning assumptions underpinning words describing the firm's activities. Attention to language can help guide experiments (similar to Intuit's experimentation culture) having the potential to negate "knowledge" which is now obsolete possibly due to a changed environment.

Figure 1.2 summarizes the key components of the pragmatic theory of the firm. The firm's purpose has been discussed. The remaining components of Figure 1.2 will be reviewed in the chapters to follow.

The pragmatic theory of the firm offers a more insightful template compared to existing theories of the firm. It reflects the following tenets about knowledge building and firm performance:

- The fundamental cause of a firm's long-term performance is its knowledge-building proficiency versus that of its competitors.

---

[43] For the period 1948 to 2001, Nordhaus estimates that innovators in the U.S. captured about 4% of the total social surplus from innovation. William D. Nordhaus, 2005, "Schumpeterian Profits and the Alchemist Fallacy Revised," http://ssrn.com/abstract=820309.

FIGURE 1.2 **Components of a pragmatic theory of the firm**

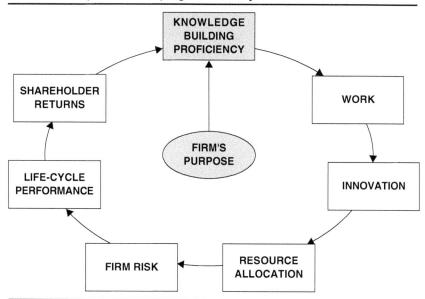

- Although competitive advantage is typically ascribed to a firm's capabilities, intangible assets, and the like, the *source* of these advantages is the firm's knowledge-building proficiency.
- A firm's performance—distilled into long-term, life-cycle track records of economic returns and reinvestment rates—offers insights about firm performance helpful to investors and other stakeholders and, in particular, can improve management's resource allocation decisions.
- Job satisfaction and retention of key employees improves as knowledge-building is made an integral part of employees' jobs.
- Innovation, whether in products, processes, or strategy, improves as more employees (including management) are engaged in knowledge-building experiences with the potential to discover faulty assumptions and generate insights.
- Firm risk (see Chapter 4) is best conceptualized as impediments to achieving a firm's purpose.

- Sustained shortfalls in profitability are typically assigned to changes in the external environment. But the real cause is a combination of management's inferior knowledge-building proficiency (lack of effective feedback and failure to question core business assumptions) and reliance on a business-as-usual culture of complacency.
- A comprehensive understanding of a firm's life-cycle performance (e.g., how a firm's economic returns fade over time) yields a conceptual roadmap for handling intangibles (see Chapter 5).
- A pragmatic theory promotes new thinking as to testable hypotheses. A section, "Excess Shareholder Returns and Three Levels of Cause-and-Effect Logic," in Chapter 5 highlights empirical tests for better linking a firm's performance to shareholder returns.

Since the pragmatic theory of the firm is rooted in a firm's knowledge-building proficiency, the next chapter includes practical insights about one's worldview, perceptions, and language that strongly influence how we build knowledge.

2

KNOWLEDGE BUILDING
AND FIRM PERFORMANCE

By detaching our self-image and self-worth from our beliefs, we should be more willing to stress test those beliefs instead of habitually defending them. This means that being who we are won't be tied up in maintaining a particular view, answer, opinion, or conclusion. Rather, we can define our "being" by how we think and converse. Defining everything we know as conditional—subject to change based on new evidence—can help decouple our egos from our beliefs.

—Edward D. Hess[1]

To be radically open-minded you must … sincerely believe that you might not know the best possible path and recognize that your ability to deal well with "not knowing" is more important than whatever it is you do know. … Radically open-minded people know that coming up with the right questions and asking other smart people what they think is as important as

[1] Edward D. Hess, 2014, *Learn or Die: Using Science to Build a Leading-Edge Learning Organization.* New York: Columbia University Press, p. 75.

having all the answers … what exists within the area of "not knowing" is so much greater and more exciting than anything any one of us knows.

—Ray Dalio[2]

THE KNOWLEDGE-BUILDING PATH TO IMPROVED PERFORMANCE

A major theme of this book is the paramount importance of a firm's knowledge-building proficiency in determining a firm's survival and prosperity over the long term. As such, a well-grounded understanding of what knowledge building entails is essential. The beginning point is four foundational ideas about building useful knowledge that can lead to improved performance.

First, to navigate through the world effectively in an energy efficient manner, our brains have evolved to use past experience to orchestrate perceptions and to guide actions. Our perceptions of what is "out there" are shaped by past experience. We see what our brains tell us to see.

Second, we experience the world as an objective, independent reality because this is such an efficient process for our daily lives. But perhaps it is not so efficient for dealing with highly complex problems. Experiencing the world as an independent reality is compounded by the fact that language itself promotes an independent reality, including a tendency to make conclusions about cause and effect based on initial perceptions.

Third, knowledge building is an integral part of living (and working) and the source of improved performance in achieving goals. As such, improving the process for improving firm performance—whether in product design, manufacturing, strategy, or culture—depends upon creative thinking attuned to effective knowledge building.

Fourth, a model of knowledge building should provide insights and reliable guideposts not only for the firm, but also for how business and science is conducted, and for decision-making in one's personal life.

---

[2] Ray Dalio, 2017, *Principles*. New York: Simon & Schuster, p. 188.

The remainder of this chapter establishes key points about building a useful and reliable knowledge base. Long-term successes and failures in business have their origin in management's skill, or lack thereof, in adapting a business model to change—skill in evaluating their *assumptions* about the external environment and how best to serve customers. Moreover, investors' assumptions about a firm's future financial performance guide their buy/hold/sell decisions. So, improving the process of how management and investors form assumptions that constitute what they "know" is not really a philosophical exercise, but rather a critically important prerequisite for making better decisions.

THE KNOWLEDGE-BUILDING LOOP

It is a difficult challenge to assemble quantitative data about how a firm's knowledge-building proficiency changes over time. Oftentimes, published empirical research about firm performance uses easily obtained financial data to facilitate high-powered econometric analysis favored by top academic journals in finance and accounting. This process can silently avoid important but hard-to-quantify problems that can otherwise lead to major insights. The importance of understanding hard-to-quantify phenomena, such as knowledge-building proficiency, is encapsulated in the following insight by Adelbert Ames, Jr. and his colleagues:

> Those who are wedded solely to a quantitative approach are all too frequently unwilling to tackle problems for which there are no available quantitative [data] … thus limiting themselves to research impressive only in the elaborate quantitative treatment of data. … But it is often forgotten that the value of an experiment is directly proportional to the degree to which it aids the investigator in formulating better problems.[3]

Ames pioneered work in visual perception illustrating how progress can be achieved by focusing on important variables whose measurement

---

[3] Hadley Cantril, Adelbert Ames, Jr., Albert H. Hastorf, and William H. Ittelson, 1949, "Psychology and Scientific Research," *Science* 110, Nos. 2862, 2863, 2864: 461–464, 491–497, 517–522.

requires significant creative thinking. He initiated a paradigm shift that focused on how observers participate in the perceiving process given their assumptions based on past experience. He defined perceptions as predictions that facilitate actions which can yield desired consequences. His work is central to the knowledge-building loop described below, which will be relied upon throughout this book.

Who was this man whom the great American philosopher John Dewey and the renowned British mathematician and philosopher Alfred North Whitehead referred to as a genius? Adelbert Ames, Jr. died in 1955 after creating some of the most memorable scientific demonstrations of the 20th century as part of his research on visual perception that anticipated major findings of modern neuroscience. John Dewey remarked: "It would not be possible to overstate my judgment as to the importance of your demonstrations with respect to visual perception … they bear upon the entire scope of psychological theory and upon all practical applications of psychological knowledge."[4]

The Ames Demonstrations in visual perception illustrate the importance of an observer's strongly held assumptions. His most famous demonstration, still reproduced in many contemporary psychology textbooks, is the Ames Distorted Room. When viewed through a peephole with one eye, an observer perceives a normal room. However, when a person in the room walks from one corner to the other, the observer's perception of that person's height radically changes. The room fails to meet the observer's firmly held assumptions, rooted in extensive past experience, about floors being level, windows rectangular, and that bigger is closer. The inability to purge these "faulty" (i.e., for the context of the Ames Distorted Room) assumptions—even when an observer learns about the room construction beforehand—dramatically demonstrates how one participates in the perceiving process. Interestingly, 21st-century neuroscience research supports the view that an observer's assumptions facilitate the process whereby the

---

[4]Hadley Cantril, ed., 1960, *The Morning Notes of Adelbert Ames, Jr.* New Brunswick, NJ: Rutgers University Press.

brain perceives the present as a means to predict the future.[5] Importantly, achieving outsized future performance gains may well begin with management's deep appreciation of how employees actually perceive their world at work.

In the academic literature on knowledge and the firm, there is debate about the locus of knowledge and the source of value creation. That is, should the foundational unit of analysis be the individual or a collective? Most research focuses on the social dynamics of collectives (teams, multidivisional collaborators, partnerships with universities, etc.), and the resulting knowledge is attributable to the entire organization. However, I side with the minority of researchers who emphasize the individual as the foundational unit of analysis.

Given my choice, the first task is to construct, from the perspective of the individual, a model for building knowledge. A useful model is depicted in Figure 2.1 illustrating how we go through life by traversing a knowledge-building loop while continually learning about what actions help achieve our purposes.

Since knowledge building continually occurs as an integral part of living, there is no particular starting point for Figure 2.1. The idea is that these components are intimately connected in an ongoing process that shapes one's knowledge base. Consider these components as guideposts that help audit how we know what we think we know.

The *knowledge base* shown in Figure 2.1 contains assumptions of varying degrees of reliability. Some are genetically hardwired due to being especially reliable and critically important to survival. That is why we fondly touch dogs but avoid touching snakes. Many of the assumptions we rely on as true tend to be based on easy to understand cause-and-effect experiences, such as touching a very hot object and the resulting effect of pain.

Knowledge is the result of a dynamic process often involving interactions with people who individually are traversing the knowledge-building

---

[5] Jakob Hohwy, 2013, *The Predictive Mind*. Oxford: Oxford University Press.

FIGURE 2.1 The knowledge-building loop

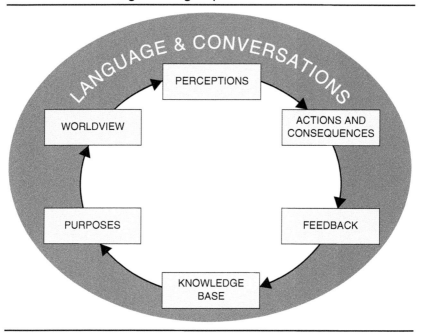

Source: Adapted from Madden (2012).[6]

loop and gaining different experiences.[7] The reliability of linear cause-and-effect analysis for nonliving things can lead to a false sense of confidence when the same logic is applied to complex systems, including human behavior.

An important component of the knowledge-building loop is one's *worldview* which is a part of, and a result of, traversing the knowledge-building loop in order to achieve one's *purposes*. It represents ideas and beliefs through which we interpret and interact with the world. In general, a worldview that favors a scientific approach for deeper understanding of causality and nonlinear system complexities improves

---

[6] Bartley J. Madden, 2012, "Management's Worldview: Four Critical Points about Reality, Language, and Knowledge Building to Improve Organization Performance," *Journal of Organizational Computing and Electronic Commerce* 22(4): 334–346.

[7] Even a scientist working alone on a problem still connects to the ideas of other scientists. See William Duggan, 2003, *The Art of What Works: How Success Really Happens*. New York: McGraw-Hill.

the knowing process and enables one to become more proficient in taking *actions* that produce desired *consequences*. A worldview that uses a systems lens to understand relationships among variables is more advantageous than a lens that treats variables as independent entities.

A critical component of the knowledge-building loop is *perceptions*. How we perceive our world is determined by how our brains function. In order to avoid sensory overload, we often operate on autopilot.[8] Our brains have evolved to enable us to quickly (subconsciously) act without having to consciously analyze multiple actions and likely consequences. This improves brain efficiency while minimizing energy consumption.[9] The brain stores past experiences to facilitate predictions via analogy to the past. The neuroscientist Chris Firth summarizes:

> By hiding from us all the unconscious inferences it makes, our brain creates the illusion that we have direct contact with objects in the physical world. … What I perceive are not the crude and ambiguous cues that impinge from the outside world onto my eyes and my ears and my fingers. I perceive something much richer—a picture that combines all these crude signals with a wealth of past experience. My perception is a prediction of what ought to be out there in the world. And this prediction is constantly tested by action.[10]

In other words, we actively participate in our perceptions of the world.[11] This tends to be ignored because it happens automatically. If you drive on the right side of the road and wait for an approaching car to pass before turning left, it is because you perceive the approaching car as too close. That perception is rooted in the assumption that bigger is closer. While

---

[8] Michael S. Gazzaniga, 2018, *The Consciousness Instinct: Unraveling the Mystery of How the Brain Makes the Mind*. New York: Farrar, Straus and Giroux.

[9] David Eagleman, 2011, *Incognito: The Secret Lives of the Brain*. New York: Pantheon Books.

[10] Chris Frith, 2007, *Making Up the Mind: How the Brain Creates Our Mental World*. Hoboken, NJ: John Wiley & Sons, pp. 17 and 132.

[11] John Dewey's later work in philosophy stressed how individuals participate in creating their realities; see Rollo Handy and E. C. Harwood, 1973, *Useful Procedures of Inquiry*. Great Barrington, MA: Behavioral Research Council and Franklin P. Kilpatrick, ed., 1961, *Explorations in Transactional Psychology*. New York: New York University Press. Ames noted that his visual demonstrations enabled people to experience his innovative concepts, which in his opinion could not be adequately communicated with words alone.

especially reliable in our past experience, it is not always true, as can be demonstrated with visual illusions.[12] Due to our participation in the perceiving process, we can unconsciously assign cause and effect to external variables even though our internal (unexamined) assumptions impact the analysis.[13] A similar line of thinking is reflected in the work of Teppo Felin, Jan Koenderink, and Joachim I. Krueger asserting that reality is constructed and expressed and that this is highly important to research in the social sciences.

We see both perception and rationality as a function of organisms' and agents' active engagement with their environments, through the probing, expectations, questions, conjectures, and theories that humans impose on the world. The shift here is radical: from an empiricism that focuses on the senses to a form of rationalism that focuses on the nature, capacities, and intentions of the organisms or actors involved.[14]

Another critical component of the knowledge-building loop is *feedback*. This signifies how one's knowledge base changes due to what is learned about the consequences of actions. An existing assumption may be supported or replaced due to improved understanding. Also, feedback serves a vital role in building confidence based on evaluation of alternative hypotheses.

Given our reliance on past experiences to shape our worldview and perceptions, a problem or an opportunity can be perceived so that it easily translates into a self-assured, favorite idea (hypothesis) as the obvious way to proceed. Who hasn't experienced an individual relentlessly promoting their favorite idea, safeguarded from hard-nosed feedback that could provide useful criticisms and possibly a superior idea?

What is needed is humility (as noted in the quotes from Edward Hess and Ray Dalio at the beginning of this chapter) as to what we don't know

---

[12] Richard L. Gregory, 2009, *Seeing through Illusions*. Oxford: Oxford University Press.

[13] For an insightful argument that our perceptions are shaped by natural selection to promote survival, not reveal truth, see Donald Hoffman, 2019, *The Case against Reality: Why Evolution Hid the Truth from Our Eyes*. New York: W. W. Norton & Company. In particular note the discussion in Chapter 3 of an exchange of letters between the author and Francis Crick.

[14] Teppo Felin, Jan Koenderink, and Joachim I. Krueger, 2016, "Rationality, Perception, and the All-Seeing Eye," *Psychonomic Bulletin and Review* published online December 7, 2016.

while traversing the knowledge-building loop, which will open the door wider to deeper understanding. Therefore, feedback about alternative hypotheses is hugely important in gaining confidence about a particular hypothesis because it withstands tests to refute it while convincing others of the soundness of one's analysis and conclusions. The new experiences gained from striving for eye-opening feedback may refute one or more strongly held beliefs, change your worldview, lift constraints, and provide access to a world of greater possibilities.

The role of language and conversations is prominently displayed in Figure 2.1 due to its significant influence throughout the knowledge-building process. Language has a pervasive influence in camouflaging assumptions while greatly simplifying the world. Our use of language is so automatic that we rarely consider that language implicitly assigns an independent existence to "facts" and "things." The English language uses noun-verb-noun construction that promotes linear cause-and-effect thinking based on variables being independent of one another. Improving the performance of complex systems, such as business firms, requires attention to systems thinking and relationships among variables. However, the words we use implicitly promote separation of subject versus object, organism versus environment, and so on.

That language is at work in how we perceive the world is important and verified, for example, by Lera Boroditsky's experiments.

> I thought that languages and cultures shape the ways we think, I suspected they shaped the ways we reason and interpret information, but I didn't think languages could shape the nuts and bolts of perception—the way we see the world. That part of cognition seemed too low-level, too hard-wired, too constrained by the constants of physics and physiology to be affected by language. ...
> I was so sure that language couldn't shape perception that I designed a set of experiments to demonstrate this. ... I had set out to show that language didn't affect perception, but I found exactly the opposite. It turns out that languages meddle in very low-level aspects of perception and without our knowledge or consent shape the very nuts and bolts of how we see the world.[15]

---

[15] Lera Boroditsky, 2009, "Operational Perceptual Freedom." In Ed. John Brockman, *What Have You Changed Your Mind About?* New York: Harper Perennial, pp. 342–343.

Because our use of language hides critical assumptions, this presents an opportunity to analyze what is behind the words in order to see new relationships and uncover different ways of handling problems (i.e., break the constraints imposed by language). The philosopher Ludwig Wittgenstein noted that "the limits of my language mean the limits of my world."[16]

The analysis of language in business has important practical applications. For example, consider how often the accounting word *cost* is encountered in business. System thinkers question proposals to increase the efficiency of a process just because of a targeted cost reduction in one part of the system. Is there a hidden assumption in the accounting cost approach? Yes. The assumption is that system components are independent of one another, and therefore the sum of local efficiency gains for individual components should translate directly into a cumulative gain for the entire system. But system components are invariably interdependent, and gains in local efficiencies do not directly accumulate into an overall system improvement. This connects directly to the Theory of Constraints (Chapter 3), which focuses improvement on the system's key constraint in order to quickly and efficiently improve overall system performance. Otherwise, opportunities to reduce costs can be found everywhere, and the biggest leverage point (the key constraint) is not prioritized.

The knowledge-building loop helps one develop a useful toolbox to deal with today's business challenges and to gain insights about a firm's past performance. For example, Lou Gerstner became CEO of IBM in 1993, when the firm's stellar, innovative successes were only dim memories and a serious cash shortfall was putting IBM on the road to bankruptcy. The following quote from Gerstner reflects his deep understanding that the root cause of the steep decline in IBM's profits was the fundamental deterioration of IBM's knowledge-building proficiency:

> When there's little competitive threat, when high profit margins and
> a commanding market position are assumed, then the economic and
> market forces that other companies have to live or die by simply don't

---

[16]Ludwig Wittgenstein, 1922, *Tractatus Logico-Philosophicus.* Trans. C. K. Ogden. New York: Harcourt, Brace & Co., www.gutenberg.org/files/5740/5740-pdf.pdf.

apply. In that environment, what would you expect to happen? The company and its people lose touch with external realities, because what's happening [*perceptions*] in the marketplace is essentially irrelevant to the success of the company.

This hermetically sealed quality—an institutional viewpoint [*worldview*] that anything important started inside the company— was, I believe, the root cause of many of our problems … leading to a general disinterest in customer needs [*lack of feedback*], accompanied by a preoccupation with internal politics. There was a general permission to stop projects dead in their tracks, a bureaucratic infrastructure that defended turf instead of promoting collaboration, and a management class that presided rather than acted [*lack of purpose*]. IBM even had a *language* all its own.[17] (italics added)

Gerstner made an important decision to revitalize the mainframe computer with CMOS technology, relentlessly communicated to employees how customer-focused teamwork was going to produce a better future, and successfully restructured IBM into a firm offering integrated solutions to customers. Throughout his tenure as CEO (1993 to 2002), he emphasized the need to "speak in plain, simple, compelling language that drives conviction and action throughout the organization."

In this book, historical analyses are presented for a diverse group of firms. These case studies emphasize the advantages of using the knowledge-building loop to better understand fundamental causes of long-term success and failure. Seeing beyond good/bad strategies, innovative/copycat products, and management's efficiency goals, a strong case is made for the overriding, bedrock importance of a firm's knowledge-building proficiency in determining the quality of a firm's strategy, innovation, and employee spirit—and ultimately determining a firm's long-term performance. Large-scale successes and failures often result from a management worldview being either adaptive or nonadaptive. The former promotes feedback to identify obsolete assumptions, either within the firm or the industry, and related new opportunities. The latter leads to a bureaucratic culture promoting a belief that what worked well in the past must surely work well in the future.

---

[17]Louis V. Gerstner, 2002, *Who Says Elephants Can't Dance?: Inside IBM's Historic Turnaround.* New York: Harper Business, pp. 117 and 189.

HUMAN BEHAVIOR, CULTURE, AND FIRM PERFORMANCE

Knowledge building (learning) is an integral part of living and occurs automatically as we strive to achieve our goals. One view of behavior considers actions fundamentally as a response to a stimulus. A different view, however, is slowly gaining support, that is, living organisms have purposes and control variables that are important to them. Perceptual control theory (PCT), developed by William T. Powers, treats living organisms as being wired with a hierarchical control system intent on making our perceptions of the current state of variables we want to control match our intended state for these variables (negative feedback control). Consequently, behavior is control of perception. Whether driving a car, hiking along a trail in rough terrain, or having a conversation at work, we as human control systems automatically take actions likely to control what is important to our purposes. To understand behavior, identify a person's purposes (goals) that are especially important to him or her. The "I get it" insight is that people do not respond to stimuli; they act to oppose disturbances to their controlled variables.

> The control-theory version of human nature—or the nature of organisms, for that matter—can be put succinctly. Organisms control. Whatever we see them doing, at whatever level of analysis we prefer, we see them controlling, not reacting. The old metatheory says that there is a one-way path through the organism, from cause to effect. The final effect is behavior. The new one says that there is a closed loop of action that has neither a beginning nor an end. The old concept says that behavior can be expressed as a function of independent variables in the environment. The new concept says that behavior is varied by the organism in order to control its own inputs. The old concept says that environments shape organisms. The new one says that organisms shape both themselves and their environments.[18]

Think of all the studies in the social sciences based on a stimulus-response mindset that are straightforward to design, to run, and to publish.

---

[18] William T. Powers, 1992, *Living Control Systems II: Selected Papers of William T. Powers.* Gravel Switch, KY: The Control Systems Group, pp. 256–257.

However, PCT's emphasis on control variables in order to understand behavior brings difficult challenges to identify and measure these variables. As such, the influence of PCT has been slowed in part due to the inertia from the huge past investment in stimulus/response journal articles and textbooks, plus the difficulty in transitioning to PCT-type studies. Nevertheless, an awareness of PCT equips one to be skeptical of much empirical research in management dealing with incentives, culture, new product design, and much more.[19]

The stimulus/response mindset often appears to be reliable, but inattention to control variables can lead to inaccurate predictions, especially when context changes. One revealing instance of control involved maintenance employees in a manufacturing facility.[20] Their performance was measured by the time needed to repair machines. The question for management was: How do we improve performance of the maintenance crews? Management could have used a stimulus/response mindset and perhaps offered bonuses (stimulus) for achieving especially fast repair times (response). However, management analyzed the situation more deeply and concluded that performance should be measured by the length of time between machine breakdowns. This led to improving employees' worldview and therefore *how they perceived problems*. Instead of doing a superficial quick fix, employees' new goal was to discover and fix the root cause of a machine's breakdown in order to *control* the time between machine breakdowns. This relates to the ontological/phenomenological model of performance developed by Werner Erhard and his colleagues

---

[19] See Chapter 5 in Bartley J. Madden, 2014, *Reconstructing Your Worldview: The Four Core Beliefs You Need to Solve Complex Business Problems*. Naperville, IL: LearningWhatWorks. Warren Mansell and Timothy Carey, 2009. "A Century of Psychology and Psychotherapy: Is an Understanding of 'Control' the Missing Link between Theory, Research, and Practice?" *Psychology and Psychotherapy: Theory, Research, and Practice* 82(3): 337–353. Richard S. Marken, 2009, "You Say You Had a Revolution: Methodological Foundations of Closed-Loop Psychology," *Review of General Psychology* 13(2): 137–145. If you thought the design of robots could benefit from a PCT perspective, you would be right. For example, Henry H. Yin, "Restoring Purpose in Behavior." In Gianlucs Baldassarre and Marco Mirolli, eds., 2013, *Computational and Robotic Models of the Hierarchical Organization of Behavior*. New York: Springer. The International Association for Perceptual Control Theory has a comprehensive website, www.IAPCT.org.

[20] Debra Smith, 2000, *The Measurement Nightmare: How the Theory of Constraints Can Resolve Conflicting Strategies, Policies, and Measures*. New York: St. Lucie Press, p. 4.

and discussed in Chapter 3. Their model focuses on language and conversations to change how the world occurs to people (perceptions) thereby opening up new possibilities for action.

Changing an adversarial relationship between management and employees is both a big problem and a big opportunity for improved performance. Steve Zaffron, CEO of the consulting firm Vanto Group, worked with a mining company in Peru that had a strong status system putting the direct descendants of the Spaniards at the top and the Indian workers at the bottom. Different color hats communicated an employee's status. The result was that the worldview of lower status employees impaired teamwork, promoted an "us versus them" culture, and constrained performance.

As part of fundamentally restructuring the firm's management system and changing how employees perceived the world, the different color hats were discarded. The same color hats for everyone became a powerful visual language that promoted teamwork.

> With that one change, the future shifted. The workers began to see their future and their role within the company completely differently—performance altered dramatically. The workers were able to see themselves as an integral, vital part of the mine's future. They were able to step outside their separate roles and experience themselves as part of a team. Few forces are as powerful in elevating a company's performance as a vision shared and owned at every level. When people take on their company's vision as their own, it becomes the generative force of the organization.[21]

The three steps to improve performance by changing how employees perceive the world are: (1) discover what constrains employees from fully utilizing their abilities; (2) create a way to remove that constraint in order to upgrade performance in achieving the goal of the system; and (3) effectively communicate how the change will enable employees to perform better in the future and, ideally, also improve their problem-solving skills.

Whenever the topic of human behavior and firm performance is discussed, attention is drawn to a firm's culture. This book makes the case for

---

[21] Steve Zaffron, 2012, "Breakthrough Leadership: From Ideas to Impact." https://stevezaffron.com/breakthrough-leadership-from-ideas-to-impact/.

the overwhelming importance of a firm's knowledge-building proficiency and therefore the need for a culture that nurtures and supports knowledge building. Typically, culture is defined as certain shared beliefs about how work should be done, and what is acceptable or unacceptable behavior. Referring to Figure 2.1, the following definition is more useful in general, and in particular, better fits with the pragmatic theory of the firm.

Culture is the language and conversations of management and employees that either strengthen or weaken: (1) beliefs about how work should be performed; (2) confidence in a win-win partnership between management and employees; (3) a commitment to mentoring of employees to continually improve their problem-solving skills; and (4) employee pride in what the firm stands for in the eyes of customers. A firm's culture is manifested in the worldview of those working in the firm and impacts their perceptions of both change in the external environment and opportunities to improve performance of internal operations.[22]

How should management orchestrate a major change in a firm's culture? The change should be grounded in knowledge building due to its obvious tie-in to improved performance. Moreover, by continuously improving their problem-solving skills and (simultaneously) their productivity, employees achieve intrinsic job satisfaction and a justified sense of earned success. However, it is reasonable to expect that an abstract conversation about a major change in how work is to be done will elicit resistance from employees.

For example, implementation of Lean Thinking, epitomized by the Toyota Production System, involves a strikingly big change in culture for employees accustomed to conventional manufacturing processes. Managers experienced in successfully transitioning to lean processes emphasize the need for initial demonstrations of productivity gains. This enables conversations focused on pragmatic feedback about how switching

---

[22] See Sameer B. Srivastava and Amir Goldberg, 2017, "Language as a Window into Culture," *California Management Review* 60(1): 56–69. Eccles and Nohria state: "The way people talk about the world has everything to do with the way the world is ultimately understood and acted in," Robert G. Eccles and Nitin Nohria, 1992, *Beyond the Hype: Rediscovering the Essence of Management*. Boston: Harvard Business School Press, p. 29.

to lean production methods in specific parts of a firm's manufacturing processes results in quantified performance gains, especially gains that are very substantial and not possible with the status quo manufacturing methodology. This is the type of language needed to gain commitment from employees.

ELEGANT, PARSIMONIOUS, AND RELIABLE THEORIES

Living brings continual experiences in traversing the knowledge-building loop as we expand our knowledge base and, over time, through our world-view we embrace theories about how the world works that we believe to be true. Theory construction begins with a worldview that shapes observations followed by descriptions of phenomena that lead to useful classifications. The next step is to focus on ideas about cause and effect that may change under different classifications of environmental conditions. A primary task is to identify which variables are critically important to the causal process. This is essential in order to develop a theory which can potentially be elegant, parsimonious, and reliable. For example, the pragmatic theory of the firm asserts that a firm's long-term performance is primarily the result of a firm's knowledge-building proficiency versus that of its competitors.

After a theory is crafted that may offer a superior handling of cause and effect, the next step is to systematically test the theory.[23] For a specified environment, when actual results significantly diverge from predictions, any outlier observations (anomalies) offer both opportunities to better understand the limits of a theory and clues for improving the

---

[23] In his famous essay, "The Methodology of Positive Economics," Milton Friedman asserted that a model or theory should be judged solely on the accuracy of its predictions and not on the realism of its assumptions. That this can easily facilitate elegant mathematical models that are of little practical value, or worse, uncritically accepted by policy-makers is an argument I made in Bartley J. Madden, 1991, "A Transactional Approach to Economic Research," *Journal of Socio-Economics* 20(1): 57–71. In personal correspondence, www.LearningWhatWorks.com/news.htm, Friedman replied, "I have no criticism of it [my argument] and it has no criticism of me." I interpret this to mean that in his own work he has addressed the issue of practical usefulness regardless of others who use the methodology of positive economics to produce elegant mathematical models built upon unrealistic assumptions that have little practical value. For a further critique of unrealistic assumptions, see Paul Pfleiderer, 2020, "Chameleon Models: The Misuse of Theoretical Research in Financial Economics." *Economica* 87(345): 81–107. Available at SSRN.com/abstract=2414731.

theory being tested.[24] In a famous article titled "Strong Inference," John Platt argued that focusing on excluding hypotheses (theories) is the key to efficient knowledge building in any area of inquiry. Here he comments about Pasteur shifting his research efforts to biology:

> Can anyone doubt that he [Pasteur] brought with him a completely different method of reasoning? Every two or three years he moved to one biological problem after another, from optical activity to the fermentation of beet sugar to the "diseases" of wine and beer, to the disease of silkworms, to the problem of "spontaneous generation," to the anthrax disease of sheep, to rabies. In each of these fields there were experts in Europe who knew a hundred times as much as Pasteur, yet each time he solved problems in a few months that they had not been able to solve. Obviously, it was not encyclopedic knowledge that produced this success, and obviously it was not simply luck, when it was repeated over and over again; it can only have been the systematic power of a special method of exploration. ... Week after week his crucial experiments build up the logical tree of exclusions.[25]

Of paramount importance is the specificity of a theory or hypothesis that can enable it to be falsified so that continual learning occurs. That is, theory construction is a continual journey of traversing the knowledge-building loop in order to test and improve a theory. We benefit from awareness that language often shields faulty assumptions from needed criticism. In addition, observations are not facts etched in stone but perceptions influenced by past experience that affect our assumptive worlds.

Researchers ought to be wary of prematurely fixating on a favorite theory or hypothesis that leads them (perhaps unconsciously) to produce data favoring their preference while shunning other explanations. Consider the question of why zebras have stripes.

---

[24] Christensen, Clayton M. and Michael E. Raynor. 2003., "Why Hard-nosed Executives Should Care about Management Theory," *Harvard Business Review* 81(9): 67–74.

[25] Platt, John R., "Strong Inference," *Science*, October 16, 1964, 146: 347–353. In this article, Platt emphasized the design of crucial experiments capable of excluding hypotheses (clear proof that an assumption is wrong) based on experimental results. Also see Douglas S. Fudge, 2014, "Fifty Years of J. R. Platt's Strong Inference," *Journal of Experimental Biology* 217: 1202–1204, in which the author writes that multiple hypotheses are needed "because of our tendency to become attached to our ideas, which can lead to science becoming an irrational argument among scientists, rather than a rational competition among ideas ... [Platt's vision] is one grounded in a firm belief in a knowable reality, and one in which good explanations rise out of the ashes of those shown to be false."

Tim Caro, professor of wildlife biology at the University of California at Davis, and his colleagues developed a now widely accepted explanation of why zebras have stripes.[26] Five hypotheses competed to explain their existence: (1) camouflage, (2) visual confusion for attacking predators, (3) temperature regulation, (4) social function, and (5) avoidance of biting flies. Support for the biting-flies hypothesis increased as empirical feedback from traversing the knowledge-building loop yielded confirming data while investigations of the other theories yielded essentially zero empirical support.

Would the biting-flies hypothesis hold beyond the African location where the original research focused on zebras? Additional research showed that in areas heavily infested with biting flies, animals evolved with bodily stripes. Checkmark for the biting-flies hypothesis. Also, it was discovered that biting flies have visual problems when confronted with stripes. Very big checkmark. Finally, why do zebras have such pronounced stripes? The researchers argued that unlike other hooved mammals living in the same environment, zebras have especially short hair making them highly susceptible to biting flies, adding another checkmark for the biting-flies hypothesis.

The knowledge-building process provides answers while simultaneously raising new questions. For example, why do biting flies encounter visual problems due to striped surfaces? And the cycle continues.[27]

Keep in mind that a useful theory improves behavior, that is, thoughts and actions that help achieve our purposes. A useful theory does not necessarily contain a revolutionary concept; it may simply spotlight what we have always seen but never meaningfully noticed. The theory may seem glaringly obvious once articulated. However, a powerful theory enables us to behave confidently because new actions are rooted in a more

---

[26] Caro, Tim, Amanda Izzo, Robert C. Reiner Jr., Hannah Walker, and Theodore Stankowich, "The Function of Zebra Stripes," *Nature Communications* 5 (April 2014), article number 3535, and Caro, Tim, 2016, *Zebra Stripes*. Chicago: University of Chicago Press.

[27] Further research showed that flies were not affected while approaching zebras, but the zebra stripes interfered with a controlled landing by the flies. Tim Caro et al., 2019, "Benefits of Zebra Stripes: Behaviour of Tabanid Flies around Zebras and Horses," February 20 PLOS ONE.

reliable understanding of cause and effect and therefore more likely to yield desired consequences.

Consider the Theory of Jobs to Be Done crafted by Professor Clayton Christensen and his colleagues at the Harvard Business School.[28] It facilitates a much deeper understanding of cause and effect for customer purchase decisions compared to a conventional analysis using customer satisfaction surveys. The theory's fundamental insight is rooted in language, specifically "buy" versus "hire." In contrast to simply using a product after you buy it, the new concept implies that you hire a product to make progress on a job that you want done. This is a new way of thinking that improves upon simply comparing a product to competing products. The theory motivates product developers to better align a product with the job customers are trying to accomplish.

So obvious you may say. But this big idea can forcefully impact the actions of innovators in order to achieve their desired consequences. For example, the design of new features of a product (or service) can lead to incremental advantages versus competitors' products and modest growth in sales. However, configuring a product to help customers make significant progress on needed jobs can lead to especially large growth in sales.

The popular QuickBooks accounting software, developed by the financial software firm Intuit, offers an insightful example of the usefulness of the Theory of Jobs to Be Done. QuickBooks initially generated remarkable sales growth even though it sold at a substantial premium. The competing software packages provided an ostensibly huge advantage in terms of comprehensive functionality versus the slimmed-down QuickBooks. Note that the Intuit product clearly enabled customers to excel in the job they wanted done, which did not involve more detailed accounting reports, or getting involved with accounting details. The customer's choice was to hire someone to handle the accounting chores or buy software that helped complete the needed business tasks while avoiding entanglements in accounting

---

[28] Christensen, Clayton M., Taddy Hall, Karen Dillon, and David S. Duncan, 2016, *Competing against Luck: The Story of Innovation and Customer Choice.* New York: Harper Business.

complexities. And, for them, QuickBooks was a compelling means to get the job done.

Rather than a narrow mindset focused on existing products, managers would benefit from a Jobs-to-Be-Done mindset that can lead to deep insights about the jobs customers hire their products to do. A significant benefit is new knowledge about jobs to be done that orchestrates redesigned product offerings for both existing and new customers.

There are two significant advantages for decision-making that follow from using the knowledge-building loop of Figure 2.1 with attention to the evaluation of alternative hypotheses. First, one can reach a recommendation that others find compelling due to the process used and the likelihood of a successful outcome if implemented. Second, the analysis can introduce an alternative hypothesis missing from the current majority view; even though this alternative is not accepted, it leads to more open-minded inquiry with the potential to discover genuine insights leading to a significantly improved decision.[29]

The next chapter analyzes the interrelationships among a firm's knowledge-building proficiency, work, innovation, and resource allocation.

---

[29] Charlan Nemeth, 2018, *In Defense of Troublemakers: The Power of Dissent in Life and Business.* New York: Basic Books.

3

WORK, INNOVATION, AND RESOURCE ALLOCATION

The biggest barriers to strategic renewal are almost always top management's unexamined beliefs.

—Gary Hamel[1]

A manager argued that he could either increase his business unit's margins or its sales, but not both. His chief executive reminded him of the time when people lived in mud huts and faced the stark choice between light and heat: punch a hole in the side of your hut and you let the daylight in but also the cold, or block up all the openings and you stay warm but sit in darkness. The invention of glass made it possible to overcome the dilemma—to let in the light but not the cold. How then, he asked his manager, will you resolve your dilemma between no sales or no margin improvement? Where is the glass?

—Dominic Dodd and Ken Favaro[2]

[1]Gary Hamel, 2012, *What Matters Now: How to Win in a World of Relentless Change, Ferocious Competition, and Unstoppable Innovation.* San Francisco: Jossey-Bass.
[2]Dominic Dodd and Ken Favaro, 2007, *The Three Tensions: Winning the Struggle to Perform without Compromise.* San Francisco: Jossey-Bass.

FIGURE 3.1 **Work, innovation, and resource allocation**

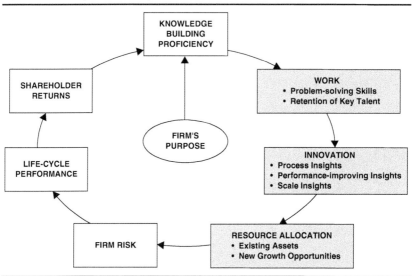

Figure 3.1 highlights three components of a pragmatic theory of the firm—work, innovation, and resource allocation—that will be analyzed in this chapter. Much of this chapter focuses on work because innovation and resource allocation are recurrent topics in other chapters. These three components are connected to one another and deeply rooted in a firm's knowledge-building proficiency.

In Figure 3.1, the firm's purpose is the beginning point because the other components are either managerial tasks to achieve the firm's purpose or related performance results.

Keep in mind that a theory is useful if it provides new angles of thinking about important issues that yield practical insights. In addition, a useful theory brings a deeper understanding of the phenomena of interest, makes important predictions, and reveals problems and opportunities that otherwise are unnoticed. Some examples, which are covered in detail in later chapters, include how the firm's competitive life-cycle connects to the life-cycle valuation model (Chapter 4). This model uses a forward-looking discount rate derived from current market prices (similar to a bond's yield-to-maturity) instead of a backward-looking discount rate based on a widely varying forecast equity risk premium coupled to a stock's Beta. The Beta approach is often taught to finance students even though the numerical answers should not be trusted, so say leading scholars in finance and accounting (more on this in Chapter 4). And the discussion of intangibles in Chapter 5 includes a method for investors to handle the qualitative nature of how intangibles impact competitive advantage by way of a long-term forecast of the "fade" rate of economic returns. In addition, Chapter 5 makes the case that the large-scale research program in mainstream finance focused on correlating factors with excess investor returns is of limited use to managements (for sure) and, with the exception of some quantitative factor investing styles, of limited use to investors. It's far better to focus on the root cause of excess returns for stocks, which is the difference between expected versus actual firm performance, which is easily expressed in life-cycle terms as economic returns and reinvestment rates.

In the following three sections, I will explain why Lean Thinking and the Theory of Constraints generate significant gains in the productivity of work in firms. Also, a new approach, the ontological/phenomenological model, orchestrates performance improvement based on how the world occurs to people. Extensive quotes from those especially knowledgeable about these three performance-enhancing initiatives are showcased.

LEAN THINKING—"NO PROBLEM IS A PROBLEM"

After World War II, Toyota had little financial resources when Tachi Ohno began the development of the Toyota Production System for manufacturing automobiles. Lean Thinking, as illustrated in Figure 3.2, is not a theory but a systematic way of thinking in order to rely less on investments in high-capacity machines and more on human capital to continually improve how work is done, and to minimize waste. Ohno's manufacturing insights originated with his study of how Henry Ford organized work in the 1920s so that iron ore mined on a Monday could be used to produce a car that rolled out of his assembly line on Thursday.

FIGURE 3.2 **Lean Thinking**

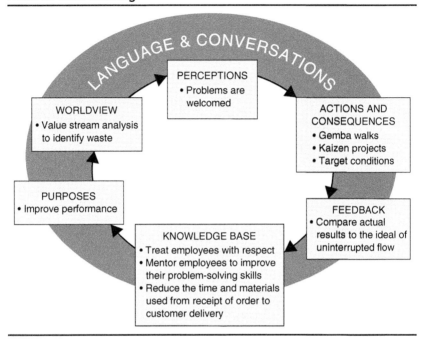

Ohno focused on pulling work through a factory, avoiding the conventional push system of mass production which uses high-capacity machines resulting in large work-in-process inventories that hide many sources of waste. He put it simply:

> All we are doing is looking at the time line from the moment the customer gives us an order to the point when we collect the cash. And we are reducing that time line by removing the non-value-added wastes.[3]

James Womack and Daniel Jones, two of the leading proponents of Lean Thinking, describe five fundamental lean principles as: "precisely specify *value* by specific product; identify the *value stream* for each product;

---

[3] Taiichi Ohno, 1998, *Toyota Production System: Beyond Large-Scale Production,* New York: Productivity Press, p. ix.

make value *flow* without interruptions; let the customer *pull* value from the producer; and pursue *perfection*."[4] When management nurtures and sustains a lean culture, expect high quality and less resources consumed, that is, less capital investment, less physical space, and less employee time to deliver value to customers. In a nutshell, Lean Thinking optimizes the flow of products or services through value streams which encompass the entire production process of a product, including suppliers and distributors. Skilled lean practitioners have a worldview distinctly different from one focused on using any means necessary to deliver accounting cost reductions. This worldview applies to service firms as well as manufacturing firms.[5]

What is the key mechanism for analyzing problems, evaluating proposed changes, overcoming implementation obstacles, and developing employees' problem-solving skills? Lean practitioners use the A3 report (named for the designation of a standard 11 x 17 piece of paper displaying the report).[6] The A3 report has been developed as a *specialized language* to describe the problem, focus on root causes, and outline a proposed solution, including implementation steps. A3 reports are an integral part of *kaizen* workshops that implement targeted improvements and *gemba*, that is, see for yourself in order to accurately perceive a problem in the workplace.

Lean Thinking, as practiced by preeminent firms like Toyota and Danaher, is best understood not as a set of tools (e.g., inventory reduction) but as a knowledge-building culture that continuously purges waste (including time) throughout a product's value stream. Such a culture does not rely on managers' "skill" in firefighting and workarounds to "fix" problems. Lean managers are skilled at asking the right questions. Lean employees learn by solving problems as part of a cognitive process that Toyota calls *kata*—a

---

[4] James P. Womack and Daniel T. Jones, 2003, *Lean Thinking: Banish Waste and Create Wealth in Your Corporation*, 2nd ed., New York: Free Press, p. 10.

[5] For an insightful description of the learning and leadership involved with transforming a medical practice into a lean organization, see Sami Bahri, 2009, *Follow the Learner: The Role of a Leader in Creating a Lean Culture*. Cambridge, MA: The Lean Enterprise Institute.

[6] John Shook, 2008, *Managing to Learn: Using the A3 Management Process to Solve Problems, Gain Agreement, and Lead*. Cambridge, MA: Lean Enterprise Institute.

pattern of thinking and behaving, which is described by Mike Rother, a leading expert on Toyota's culture:

> There is a human tendency to desire and even artificially create a sense of certainty [worldview]. It is conceivable that the point here is not that we do not see the problems in our processes, but rather that we do not *want* to see them because that would undermine the sense of certainty we have about how our factory is working. It would mean that some of our assumptions, some things we have worked for and are attached to, may not be true.
>
> Toyota's improvement kata involves teaching people a standardized conscious "means" for sensing the gist of situations and responding scientifically. This is a different way for humans to have a sense of security, comfort, and confidence. Instead of obtaining that from an unrealistic sense of certainty about conditions, they get it from the means by which they deal with uncertainty. This channels and taps our capabilities as humans much better than our current management approach, explains a good deal of Toyota's success, and gives us a model for managing almost any human enterprise.[7]

In the workplace the focus is on a target condition, that is, how a process operates to produce a specified outcome. By achieving the target condition, waste is eliminated—a highly disciplined, scientific approach. The essence of *kata* is rigorous experimentation and learning that becomes a way of life and supports a knowledge-building culture.

Win-win relationships between management and employees rooted in knowledge building are the foundation for a highly productive culture—the truth of that assertion is evidenced by the Fremont plant story.

In 1984, General Motors reopened an idle plant in Fremont, California, which had been well known for producing low-quality cars, coupled to low employee morale, high absenteeism, and frequent strikes. Not surprisingly, the Fremont plant was GM's worst-performing plant. This plant then became a joint venture with Toyota—New United Motor Manufacturing, Inc. (NUMMI). GM wanted to learn about Toyota's lean production system and also improve manufacturing to deliver high-quality small cars. One of the Japanese managers assigned to train American production

---

[7] Mike Rother, 2010, *Toyota Kata: Managing People for Improvement, Adaptiveness, and Superior Results.* New York: McGraw Hill, pp. 101 and 165.

supervisors in the NUMMI plant was Susumu Uchikawa. He explained that he did not want to hear "No problem" when asked about production. "No problem is a problem! Managers' job is to see problems!"[8]

Toyota hired 85% of the employees who previously produced GM's lowest-rated quality cars. These employees appreciated Toyota's noted respect for people and lean principles of standardized work, training, mentoring, and problem solving without blaming anyone.[9]

After a year, NUMMI was GM's best-performing plant with the highest-rated quality. A firm's long-term success in delivering quality products to customers depends upon management taking concrete actions that give employees a reason to participate in sustaining a win-win relationship. As part of the NUMMI contract with the United Auto Workers union, Toyota proposed eliminating the onerous job classifications that contravened the lean problem-solving approach of employees working in teams. The union agreed and Toyota willingly specified in the contract that during hard times, management salaries would be cut first, along with other actions taken to avoid layoffs. When demand for the plant's Chevy Novas sharply declined with sales plummeting 30% below expectations, Toyota changed the models produced in the plant and brought previously outsourced work into the plant. There were no layoffs and management further cemented a win-win relationship with employees. The pragmatic theory of the firm and Lean Thinking share a belief that a firm's success is tied to the people who build the knowledge that ultimately drives the value created for customers.

Regrettably, GM's top management and board failed to build upon NUMMI's success, which speaks volumes about the need to avoid a stifling bureaucratic culture that stymies adaptation to needed change. During the 2007–2009 recession, NUMMI was abandoned and the plant was later sold to Tesla Motors.

---

[8]John Shook, 2010, "How to Change a Culture: Lessons from NUMMI," *MIT Sloan Management Review* 51(2): 63–68.
[9]John P. Kotter and Dan S. Cohen, 2002, *The Heart of Change*. Cambridge, MA: Harvard Business Review Press, p. 2, notes: "Changing behavior is less a matter of giving people analysis to influence their thoughts than helping them to see a truth to influence their feelings."

NUMMI plainly shows the importance of respect for employees, which is an integral part of employees' continual learning, personal growth, and the satisfaction of experiencing a productive work life. Should we label this an HR (human resources) issue, a culture issue, a productivity issue, or perhaps even a moral issue? It's hard to settle on a single word. Perhaps a more useful approach is to rely on the pragmatic theory of the firm, which assumes the firm is a holistic system managed to sustain win-win relationships with all of the firm's stakeholders, especially employees.

THE THEORY OF CONSTRAINTS

Eli Goldratt's *The Goal: A Process of Ongoing Improvement* became a mega bestselling book. This was followed by a series of business books, videos, seminars, and a worldwide consulting organization to communicate the continual advancements of his work which was named the Theory of Constraints (TOC). It is rooted in comprehensive cause-and-effect thinking to solve problems (including overcoming obstacles to implementation) and generate substantial performance gains. TOC began as a production and scheduling management tool for manufacturing plants. This led to addressing ongoing improvements when constraints move outside of production and was applied to businesses other than manufacturing.

Due to a continual stream of notable insights that he generated over his lifetime, many labeled Goldratt a genius. He disagreed and maintained that his insights naturally flowed from a rigorous application of cause-and-effect analysis rooted in his training as a physicist. He would dissect seemingly complex business problems and avoid compromises in order to create breakthrough solutions that retrospectively seemed so simple. Goldratt typically described his approach as just commonsense. The hallmark of TOC is giving top priority to identify and fix a system's key constraint. The constraint is the roadblock, but also the maximum leverage point, to achieving big performance gains.

Figure 3.3 positions TOC in the context of the knowledge-building loop, as was done for Lean Thinking in Figure 3.2.

FIGURE 3.3 **The Theory of Constraints**

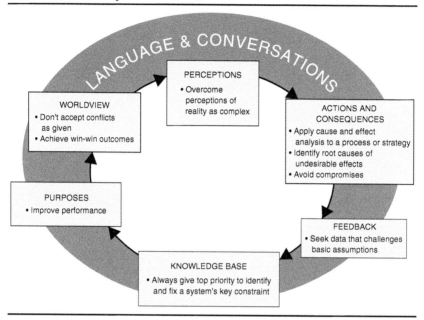

Early on, Goldratt criticized the spurious assumption that a resource standing idle is a "cost" reflective of waste and inefficiency. He argued that a system, such as a manufacturing plant, is optimized by a work pace that accommodates the processing speed of the key constraint. Avoiding work-in-process inventories due to overproduction resulting from keeping resources "working" at all times is not original to Goldratt. Henry Ford limited the space for work-in-process inventories in his automotive manufacturing lines. The Toyota Production System controls flow via a Kanban mechanism and skill in reducing setup times for different parts.

TOC involves systems thinking to avoid dealing with problems in isolation which frequently occur due to a firm being organized around separate activities. A system approach focuses on achieving the goal of the system and facilitates the discovery of root causes of undesirable effects. In Goldratt's words:

> The secret of being a good scientist, I believe, lies not in our brain power. We have enough. We simply need to look at reality and think

logically and precisely about what we see. The key ingredient is to have the courage to face inconsistencies between what we see and deduce and the way things are done. *This challenging of basic assumptions is essential to breakthroughs.* Almost everyone who has worked in a plant is at least uneasy about the use of cost accounting efficiencies to control our actions. Yet few have challenged this sacred cow directly. Progress in understanding requires that we challenge basic assumptions about how the world is and why it is that way. If we can better understand our world and the principles that govern it, I suspect all our lives will be better.[10] (italics added)

TOC's process of ongoing improvement consists of five steps.

- Identify the system constraint.
- Exploit the constraint through quick improvements using existing resources.
- Subordinate the nonconstraint activities to support further improvement of the key constraint.
- Elevate the constraint through actions that finally break the constraint.
- Repeat the process because after the original constraint is broken, the key constraint has moved elsewhere.

These steps represent cycles through the knowledge-building loop with preponderant focus on actions and consequences. TOC users are wary about sophisticated computer algorithms to optimize local efficiencies instead of optimizing the overall system. They focus on how the key constraint changes over time. For example, solving a major constraint in production can easily enable much higher output, thereby possibly moving the key constraint to marketing. Identifying such a shift is the purpose of the above Step 5.[11]

Goldratt devised the TOC Thinking Processes as a *language* of cause and effect (logical trees) that facilitated answers to three questions: (1)

---

[10] From the Introduction to the first edition of Eliyahu M. Goldratt, 1984, *The Goal: A Process of Ongoing Improvement.* Great Barrington, MA: North River Press.
[11] James F. Cox III and John Schleier, Jr., eds., 2010, *Theory of Constraints Handbook.* New York: McGraw Hill.

what to change, (2) what to change to, and (3) how to cause the change. The Thinking Processes helps analyze systems composed of myriad complex interactions. Importantly, the robust and comprehensive TOC logic enables hypothesis testing without the need for real-world experiments. Goldratt summarizes:

> This process of speculating a cause for a given effect and then predicting another effect stemming from the same cause is usually referred to as effect-cause-effect. … Every verified, predicted effect throws additional light on the cause. Oftentimes this process results in the cause itself being regarded as an effect thus triggering the question of what is its cause. In such a way, a logical tree that explains many vastly different effects can grow from a single (or very few) basic assumptions. This technique is extremely helpful in trying to find the root cause of a problematic situation. We should strive to reveal the fundamental causes, so that a root treatment can be applied, rather than just treating the leaves—the symptoms.
>
> Thus one of the most powerful ways of pinpointing the core problems is to start with an undesirable effect, then to speculate a plausible cause, which is then either verified or disproved by checking for the existence of another type of effect, which must stem from the same speculated cause.
>
> By explaining the entire process of constructing the Effect-Cause-Effect logical "tree" *we have a very powerful way to persuade others*.[12] (italics added)

TOC's extreme focus on the key constraint results in less attention (compared to Lean) to firm-wide employee learning and continuous interaction between managers at different levels. On one hand, an inefficient firm using a push production system with big buffers (e.g., inventories) is ripe for an immediate boost in performance via the introduction of TOC. On the other hand, an efficient firm with many years of experience using lean principles, and operating with a pull scheduling system, is not as susceptible to push-derived bottlenecks. Moreover, the efficient lean firm adds capacity in small, manageable increments as opposed to large capital expenditures typical of a batch manufacturing firm that can contribute to future bottlenecks.

---

[12]Eliyahu M. Goldratt, 1990, *What Is This Thing Called Theory of Constraints and How Should It Be Implemented?* Great Barrington, MA: North River Press, pp. 32–33.

TOC's Thinking Processes is a powerful language that enables fast and effective traversing of the knowledge-building loop. Goldratt was skilled in overcoming subtle constraints imposed by the use of common words.[13] The conventional view is that strategy exists at the highest level of a firm where management and the board agree on an overall direction that can distinguish the firm from its competitors. And tactics exist at lower levels where activities are shaped consistent with achieving success for the strategy. In contrast, Goldratt first defined strategy as the answer to the question: What for? and tactics as the answer to the question: How to? Second, Goldratt concluded that strategy and tactics should exist in pairs.

This arrangement is particularly useful for analyzing innovation—a new value proposition for better serving customers or a core strategy for a startup or ongoing firm. While some scholars of entrepreneurship make sweeping generalizations for an extreme focus on a process that accepts failures as long as one fails fast, TOC advocates argue for early and deep logical analysis to scrutinize the critical assumptions involved with delivering value.

Big ideas often exploit what has already been discovered but not fully exploited. The advantages of focusing on a system's key constraint to improve performance were known before Goldratt popularized the concept. Keep in mind that advancements invariably involve knowledge building. As for TOC, the Thinking Processes are the primary means to facilitate knowledge building. Once again, we see that knowledge building and value creation are opposite sides of the same coin.

ONTOLOGICAL/PHENOMENOLOGICAL MODEL

Werner Erhard is uniquely skilled in connecting ideas in new ways that provide insights about human behavior attuned to practical needs. His work has been applied to individual, organizational, and social transformations (www.wernererhard.com) and is the foundation for a distinctly different

---

[13] For examples in business of the role of language in masking obsolete assumptions, see Bartley J. Madden, 2014, *Reconstructing Your Worldview: The Four Core Beliefs You Need to Solve Complex Business Problems*. Naperville, IL: LearningWhatWorks.

FIGURE 3.4 OPM framework

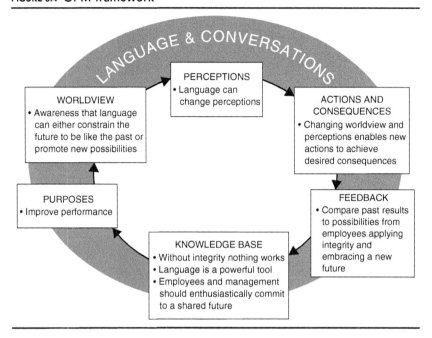

approach to leadership keyed to performance improvement via an onto-
logical/phenomenological model (OPM), which he and his colleagues have
developed in recent years. This model is gaining worldwide attention and
is packaged as course material for classroom use.[14]

The name of this model seems to suggest that it is abstract, steeped
in philosophy, and a tough challenge to comprehend. Not so. The
knowledge-building loop (Figure 3.4) neatly packages the key OPM
components which are summarized as follows:

> Integrity, authenticity, and being committed to something bigger
> than oneself form the base of "the context for leadership," a context
> that once mastered, leaves one actually being [ontology] a leader. It is
> not enough to know about or simply understand these foundational
> factors, but rather by following a rigorous, phenomenologically

---

[14]Werner Erhard, Michael C. Jensen, Steve Zaffron, and Jeri Echeverria, 2017, "Course Materials for:
Being a Leader and the Effective Exercise of Leadership: An Ontological/Phenomenological Model,"
SSRN abstract=1263835.

[direct experience] based methodology, students have the opportunity to create for themselves a context that leaves them actually being a leader and exercising leadership effectively as their natural self-expression.[15]

As shown in Figure 3.4, OPM includes the following strongly held beliefs: without integrity nothing works; language is a uniquely powerful tool; and a person's worldview about the future is not etched in stone, rather a person can see the future as a repeat of the past or a future with potential for new and rewarding experiences. OPM logic begins with performance being driven by action. And action is closely connected with how a situation occurs for an individual. This connection is viewed as the source for performance improvement. Moreover, language (including what is said and unsaid) can be used to affect how situations occur, thereby impacting performance. OPM clearly has a sharp focus on changing how individuals perceive the world, which typically is missing from management's "to do" list for achieving performance gains.

A key distinguishing feature is OPM's lack of concern for searching for cause-and-effect relationships in the work environment as typically seen in approaches to improve performance. Instead, the focus is on how employees' performance correlates with their perceptions.

> Action is a correlate of the way the circumstances on which and in which a performer is performing *occur* (show up) for the performer. ... "Occur" does not require the performer to pay any attention to, think about, understand, analyze, or interpret that which is registered.
>
> The world we *interact* with (act on and by which we are acted on) is the so-called objective world. However, while most of us don't give any thought to it, in a fundamentally important sense the world we actually *respond to* and *react to* is the world as we perceive it, what we have termed the *occurring* world.
>
> If we are dealing with life *as lived,* or performance *as lived* (the perspective of this new paradigm of performance), seeing and treating the objective and occurring worlds from the perspective of them

[15]Scott Snook, Nitin Nohria, and Rakesh Khurana, 2012, *The Handbook for Teaching Leadership: Knowing, Doing, and Being.* Los Angeles: Sage Publications, p. xxiv.

being two distinct *and* separate worlds obscures the way we actually live life and live performance. ... The *as-lived* perspective allows access to the *source* of performance.[16] (italics in original)

OPM lays a path for management to deliver effective leadership and achieve significant performance improvement. The key is to gain employee commitment to a future distinctly better than the past. Consequently, the envisioned future becomes the context for the present so that employee perceptions change, enabling new possibilities to emerge. However, a necessary ingredient for sustained superior performance is integrity (i.e., keeping one's word). The importance of integrity is summarized by Michael Jensen:

> Integrity is important to individuals, groups, organizations, and society because it creates workability. Without integrity, the workability of any object, system, person, group or organization declines; and as workability declines, the opportunity for performance declines. Therefore, integrity is a necessary condition for maximum performance. As an added benefit, honoring one's word is also an actionable pathway to being trusted by others.[17]

In their book, *The Three Laws of Performance,* Steve Zaffron and Dave Logan emphasize that individuals function with an implicit view of the future that shapes how the world occurs to them and thereby impacts their performance. So, to rewrite their default future requires the use of language involving promises and commitments from and to the individual. As previously noted, this necessitates leadership attuned to how employees perceive the firm in general, and their work environment in particular, which highlights the need for a purpose of the firm that employees feel is a win-win partnership.

Using the knowledge-building loop as a general-purpose analytical template facilitates comparison of OPM to other improvement approaches, such as TOC. For example, TOC's Thinking Processes, with their

---

[16] This quote is from pages 49 and 52 of a comprehensive presentation of the OPM framework, Werner Erhard and Michael C. Jensen, 2010, "A New Paradigm of Individual, Group, and Organizational Performance." SSRN Working Paper, abstract=1437027.

[17] Michael C. Jensen, 2009, "Integrity: Without It Nothing Works," *Rotman: The Magazine of the Rotman School of Management,* Fall: 16–20.

extensive logical diagrams, focuses on cause and effect, enabling users to discover root causes of problems. This clarity as to what needs to be done (and why) can change how the world is perceived. This directly ties into a critical takeaway of OPM, that is, language is the means for employees to reset their worldviews by purging the tendency to see the future as an extrapolation of the status-quo past. TOC's persuasive logic—the language of logical trees—can replace skepticism about living a new reality with a logically sound belief that a new environment of substantial performance gains is realistically achievable.

Lean Thinking, TOC, and OPM rely on managers who fully understand the payoffs from continual knowledge building. Such a knowledge-building culture depends upon having the right people on board for key leadership positions. Ram Charan, Dominic Barton, and Dennis Carey recommend elevating human resources (HR) to the same level as finance with high-level decision-making guided by the CEO, the CFO, and the CHRO (chief human resources officer). They emphasize the importance of talent, especially for what they call the 2 percenters who create disproportionate value:

> Most executives today recognize the competitive advantage of talent, yet the talent practices their organizations use are vestiges of another era. They were designed for predictable environments where lines and boxes defined how people were managed. As work and organizations become more fluid—and business strategy comes to mean sensing and seizing new opportunities in a constantly changing environment, rather than planning for several years into a predictable future—companies must deploy talent in new ways. In fact, talent must lead strategy.[18]

The way that key employees are compensated should ideally be linked to the creation of long-term value. Relevant to this point is a study of managers responsible for corporate R&D. No relationship was found between short-term incentives and measures of innovation. However, among firms

---

[18]Ram Charon, Dominic Barton, and Dennis Carey, 2018, *Talent Wins: The New Playbook for Putting People First*. Boston, MA: Harvard Business Review Press.

with centralized R&D organizations, "more long-term incentives are associated with more heavily cited patents, more frequent awards, and patents
of greater originality."[19]

INNOVATION

Ideas about innovation range from proposals that lack empirical support
but have gained shelf space in bookstores with catchy titles describing
"the keys to creativity" to empirically grounded, helpful proposals such
as design thinking. Businesspeople who embrace design thinking tend to
mimic the practices of top-rated design firms like IDEO. Highly skilled
designers are extraordinarily skeptical of initial *perceptions* as to what
constitutes the "design problem" and apply multiple ways of observing
the situation while questioning the validity of existing assumptions. A
hallmark of design thinking is building prototypes of proposed design
solutions. Prototypes are crude but function well to quickly generate
feedback that either supports or negates a design idea. This is similar to
startup firms that focus intently on quickly proving or disproving the core
assumptions about their business model and learning more about their
target customers.

Invariably when discussing innovation, the question arises as to how
to achieve the "Aha!" moment—that novel solution or big idea that can
eliminate a problem or even invent a new future. Is this basically analysis
and brainstorming? Not really, as William Duggan writes:

> Neuroscience has overturned that old [split brain] model of the brain.
> We now know that analysis and creativity are not two different func-
> tions on two different sides of the brain. In the new model—called
> *learning and memory*—analysis and creativity work together in all
> modes of thought. You cannot have an idea without both.

The new science of learning-and-memory reveals at last how creative
ideas form in the mind. When you do something yourself or learn what

---

[19] Josh Lerner and Julie Wulf, 2007, "Innovation and Incentives: Evidence from Corporate R&D,"
Review of Economic and Statistics 89(4): 634–644.

someone else did, those details go into your memory. When you face a new situation, your brain breaks down the problem into pieces and then searches through your brain for memories that fit each piece. It then makes a new combination from those pieces of memory. The combination is new, but the elements are not. These three steps—break it down, search, combine—are very different from the two conventional steps of analyze and brainstorm.[20]

Innovation in the firm can be categorized as *process insights, performance-improving insights,* and *scale insights.*[21] The previous descriptions of TOC and Lean Thinking highlight how process insights are developed and implemented. Although one specific process improvement may provide a minuscule gain to the overall productivity of a system, the continual generation of process insights can aggregate to substantial performance gains. Arranging tools on an assembly line to minimize the steps taken by employees is one example. Absent such continual improvement, a process degrades and eventually becomes a drag on the firm's competitive position.

Performance-improving insights add functionality to products, making products easier to use, and ideally distinguish them versus competitors' products. These insights typically dominate management's priority lists and sustain cash flows from the firm's existing assets.

Investing in new business ideas may lead to scale insights. These insights are breakthrough ideas that create revolutionary products and services and also new business models of exceptional effectiveness such as Amazon's Internet platform. Scale insights not only bring unique value to customers but also spawn ancillary business opportunities and large-scale growth in

---

[20] William Duggan, 2013, *Creative Strategy: A Guide for Innovation.* NY: Columbia University Press; see pp. 98–100 for a useful critique of design thinking. Also, see Eric R. Kandel, 2007, *In Search of Memory: The Emergence of a New Science of Mind.* New York: W. W. Norton and Company. In 2000, Eric Kandel was awarded the Nobel Prize for his research on the physiological basis of memory storage in neurons. The insightful neuroscience research done by Jeff Hawkins provides theoretical support for the learning and memory model; see Michael S. Gazzaniga, 2008, *Human: The Science behind What Makes Us Unique.* New York: HarperCollins, pp. 362–371.
[21] Clayton M. Christenson, "A Capitalist's Dilemma, Whoever Wins on Tuesday," op-ed., November 3, 2012, *New York Times.*

new, meaningful jobs. Consider job creation that evolved from the introduction of railroads, automobiles, and intermodal freight containers, each resulting from especially important scale insights involving transportation.

Management and the board should continually invest for the future even if such investments are incompatible with, or at times even compete with, the firm's existing assets. Therefore, innovation involves an organizational structure consistent with knowledge building and insightful feedback. This is not a new concept but merely a commonsense conclusion consistent with the long-term track records of highly successful firms.

As the Old Economy, focused on physical assets and local manufacturing, is replaced by the New Economy with globalization, intangible assets, and Internet-based businesses, many people are left behind, looking for new jobs. So, how does innovation impact jobs created and lost? One answer is that entrepreneurs start firms and create jobs in parallel with the commercial success of their ideas. Meanwhile, mismanaged firms lacking a viable innovation culture continually focus on cutting costs as a means to improve profitability, and failing/bankrupt firms fire their employees. It follows that economic policy should eliminate regulations that constrain entrepreneurs from starting new businesses since startups are such a fertile ground for breakthrough ideas.

RESOURCE ALLOCATION

As firms grow larger and more mature (earning approximately cost-of-capital economic returns or perhaps lower), management tends to focus exclusively on near-term cash flows and maintaining or improving their competitive position and market share. This translates into improving the performance of existing products. In this environment, opportunities for new products or services can be analyzed and easily rejected if they require capabilities not currently available. Worse, management with a worldview focused in the extreme on improving existing products can become so insulated that they are unable to perceive emerging opportunities, which never even get to the analysis stage. For example, on the road to bankruptcy, East-man Kodak produced a significant inventory of patents emblematic of their R&D proficiency. However, alongside this technical skill for innovation, management created a bureaucratic culture that assumed business-as-usual would produce success in the future. For example, management repeatedly forecasted that its cameras and film would maintain a wide leadership over digital photography. One forecast for the year 2020 was that the photography market would be 30% digital and 70% traditional film where Kodak was dominant.[22] Management with a worldview rooted in never-questioned assumptions will surely fail to get useful feedback about a changing environment and will lose the opportunity to adapt early to a new world.

Innovation is about adapting to, and sometimes leading, change which involves the smart allocation of resources. Some existing business units of a firm may have degrading prospects due to competitors with significant comparative advantage or declining long-term customer demand. Business-as-usual investments in these business units should be avoided. Easy to say. Yet the history of large firms that have failed illustrates a sustained business-as-usual mindset toward investments similar to Eastman Kodak.

At times, concern with market valuation is mislabeled as short-termism that lacks concern for nonshareholder stakeholders. But this can miss the fundamental point that long-term value creation benefits from management's use of the following economic criterion for making decisions: cash outlays need to earn a return-on-investment (ROI) that at least equals the cost of capital consumed. A more refined version of this criterion used in financial analysis is that outlays must have an expected positive net present value (NPV). Application of this criterion is often difficult, but in principle it is the right path to make best use of society's scarce resources.

Put differently, what should be management's decision process for the following types of proposed outlays: (1) decrease product prices;

---

[22] Paul Snyder, 2016, *Is This Something George Eastman Would Have Done? The Decline and Fall of Eastman Kodak Company*. Self-published, CreateSpace Independent Publishing Platform.

(2) increase all employees' salaries; and (3) hire the unemployed who live in the vicinity of a firm's production facility? Each proposed outlay benefits a stakeholder of the firm—customers, employees, and the local community. A stand-alone criterion of stakeholder benefit clearly does not work because the answer is always yes. Management needs the NPV criterion as a guidepost in order to deliver sustainable, long-term, economically sound benefits to the firm's stakeholders.[23]

A holistic system (Figure 3.1) promotes analysis of interrelationships of a firm's key components. How work is organized, for example, can impact resource allocation via acquisitions, which in turn impacts firm valuation. Art Byrne, former CEO of the Wiremold Company, a classic lean success story, noted that inventory is "sleeping money" that can be used to "free up a lot of cash that is currently being wasted … that can be reinvested in new products, new equipment, or acquisitions that will help expand our market share." He emphasized that the typical reason for big inventories in a manufacturing plant is due to lengthy setup times for switching a workstation to manufacturing a different part. That lengthy setup times are an unfortunate reality is a spurious assumption according to skilled lean practitioners. For example, Wiremold employees reduced setup times for injection molding machines from 2.5 hours to 2 minutes and a rolling mill from 14 hours to 6 minutes. These extraordinary improvements in setup times mirror Toyota-style manufacturing efficiency.

Order-of-magnitude reductions in setup times was a necessary step in achieving and sustaining large inventory reductions that funded Wiremold's acquisitions. Note that expertise in lean manufacturing, which is rooted in knowledge building, was the critical ingredient in doing more with less and improving the economic returns in Wiremold's core business. Moreover, this skill in manufacturing was then extended to inefficiently managed firms which were acquired. The result was a value-creation acquisition strategy grounded in Wiremold's knowledge-building proficiency. This ties into a prediction of the pragmatic theory of the firm: in today's

---

[23] Michael Jensen, 2002, "Value Maximization, Stakeholder Theory, and the Corporate Objective Function," *Business Ethics Quarterly* 12(2): 235–256.

economy, acquisitions that exploit or extend a firm's knowledge-building proficiency tend to create greater long-term shareholder value versus acquisitions based on a cost reduction/synergy rationale.

> Our lead times went from 4–6 weeks to 1–2 days. We were growing and gaining market share. We freed up over half our floor space and used the cash from the inventory reduction to purchase 21 companies over the course of about 9 years. ... We increased operating income by 13.4x and enterprise value by just under 2,500% over these same 9 years.
>
> For acquisitions this focus on increasing inventory turns was a home run. Not only did we free up the cash to do the acquisitions in the first place but most of them were only turning inventory about 3x. ... We knew we would be able to get those turns up to 6x by the end of the first year and to about 10x by the end of the third year. Combined with the rest of our lean implementation we were able, for the most part, to get all of our purchase price back in cash by the end of the third year and then those companies were contributing cash towards the next new product or the next acquisition.[24]

Because their workplace is organized by value streams and oftentimes a cellular layout so that products (or services) flow in response to the pull of customer orders, lean employees are better able to see the entirety of a product or service, to identify waste, and to receive more useful feedback about the actions and consequences of their work activities (learning). Lean employees have an opportunistic worldview—problems are welcomed as illustrated in Figure 3.2. This performance-enhancing worldview was transferred to employees of firms that Wiremold acquired.

The long-term performance of Wiremold illustrates how a firm can be managed as a holistic system of interrelated activities. The firm's expertise in Lean Thinking led to value-creating acquisitions as a critical component of its resource allocation strategy. This way of thinking sharply differs from short-termism that views financial performance as something to be engineered by cutting costs and doing whatever it takes to hit short-term accounting targets—absent any meaningful mindset about building

---

[24]Art Bryne, "Ask Art: Why Does Boosting Inventory Turns Matter So Much?" September 13, 2018, *The Lean Post*.

long-term value and respect for employees who ultimately determine performance.

The above example shows how substantial performance gains for a firm are mutually beneficial to customers, shareholders, employees who are continuously increasing their human capital (problem-solving skills), and society in general. Understanding the histories of firms like Wiremold illustrates how analysis of the microeconomics of a firm provides a bottom-up understanding of macroeconomics as discussed in Chapter 1.

THE KEY CONSTRAINT IN SUSTAINING A KNOWLEDGE-BUILDING CULTURE

Let us focus on one of society's most important aims: large-scale economic benefits. As previously noted, the three complementary managerial approaches reviewed in this chapter are fundamentally concerned with improving performance via fast and effective traversing of the knowledge-building loop. This suggests that a scale insight—consistent with boosting dynamism as recommended by Edmund Phelps—would be to figure out how to remove the key constraint that blocks firms from effectively implementing a knowledge-building culture in the spirit of top-performing lean firms. Recall the previous quote from Mike Rother about how the Toyota Production System enhances employee ability to deal with uncertainty "channels and taps our capabilities as humans much better than our current management approach." The key constraint is that too many firms use a management approach that does not embrace purpose, respect for people, and continuous experimentation and learning at all levels of the firm to the extent needed to sustain a knowledge-building culture and a highly productive and fulfilling way of life for the firm's employees.

What are the essential tasks involved in breaking this key constraint? Some possibilities can be gleaned from the history of the Danaher Corporation, generally acknowledged as America's preeminent lean firm. The Danaher story is another concrete example of how microeconomics focused on firm performance connects to macroeconomics.

The fundamental value-creation driver for Danaher is its knowledge-building proficiency with emphasis on experimentation and learning. The label "Lean" can be misleading when it is used to represent lean tools (e.g., *kaizen*) giving the impression that implementation of lean tools is enough to achieve sustained high performance. Danaher labels its managerial approach the Danaher Business System (DBS) whose purpose is to improve innovation, quality, delivery, and cost to the firm's customers (i.e., value creation). DBS is Danaher's version of the Toyota Production System.

Steven and Mitchell Rales were experienced financial dealmakers when they began in the early 1980s to build Danaher into a preeminent high-performance firm. One of their early acquisitions was Jake Brake, which was the first American firm to implement Lean Thinking. Based on the performance gains at Jake Brake, the Rales brothers insisted that everyone commit to DBS as a way of life at Danaher extending from top management to the factory floor, including all of the firm's activities, not just manufacturing.

All of Danaher's top managers are exceptionally skilled in lean know-how and regularly teach classes to employees. This contrasts with the many situations where lean is not sustained in firms due to a lack of involvement with top management. Furthermore, Danaher's operating companies use extensive real-time data metrics for both process variables and financial variables in order to provide continuous hard-nosed, factual feedback to improve performance.

As to hiring outside managers, care is taken to avoid people with "bad habits," that is, those "skilled" in achieving results in ways inconsistent with DBS and sustainable business processes but typical of many current management cultures. Danaher acquires firms that have solid long-term prospects but typically lack operational efficiency in ways that the implementation of DBS can greatly improve. Danaher takes pride in being a learning machine, and that extends to insights gained from acquired firms that are then transferred to other Danaher operating companies. In 2016, Danaher reorganized into two separate businesses—Fortive

Corporation for industrial businesses and Danaher Corporation for science and technology businesses.

What prevents CEOs from following Danaher's lead for delivering sustained high performance? Let's begin with the notion that context matters. Typically, CEOs are in their leadership positions because of their past success in working in firms with hierarchical, command-and-control organizational structures. They demonstrated skill by taking charge and producing results that fit the command-and-control structure. Instead of systematic experimentation for dealing with the future, the typical environment was to lay out a plan and then do whatever is needed to meet or exceed the planned accounting targets for that part of the system for which they had responsibility. Moreover, if their educational background includes an MBA, their business school experiences have likely further emphasized specialized, quantitative planning and control.

These experiences differ markedly from work experiences within an organizational structure rooted in a knowledge-building culture that relies less on authoritative control and more on lower-level employees taking responsibility to solve problems and continually improve processes. Such a culture encourages experimentation and feedback that can reveal root causes of problems and obsolete assumptions at all levels of the organization while encouraging system thinking to cut across activities and optimize overall system efficiency.

The hierarchical command-and-control organizational structure has deep roots and is difficult to change. Of the firms that attempt to transition and sustain Lean Thinking across all their key activities, a reasonable estimate is that 4% to 7% have succeeded in the past.[25] However, the ongoing debate about capitalism discussed in Chapter 7 will draw attention to key elements of the firm's purpose: vision, survive and prosper, win-win partnerships, and taking care of future generations. This reexamination of the role of the firm in society will likely accelerate a transition to a holistic purpose-based view of the firm which also involves a

---

[25]Art Bryne, 2007, *The Lean Turnaround Action Guide: How to Implement Lean, Create Value, and Grow Your People*. New York: McGraw Hill Education, p. 3.

transition away from the conventional hierarchical command-and-control structure. A holistic purpose-based view of the firm improves upon the maximizing-shareholder-value purpose so prevalent in mainstream finance. The next chapter focuses on a key component of the pragmatic theory of the firm—the life-cycle framework for connecting a firm's long-term financial performance to its market valuation.

Part II

The Pragmatic Theory of the Firm Connects Innovation and Valuation

4

LIFE-CYCLE PERFORMANCE AND FIRM RISK

Because inflection points undermine the very assumptions on which a business is based and which have come to be taken as "facts" by most decision-makers, it is often difficult for leaders to imagine a different world. It is this failure of imagination that so often leads to strategic surprise.

It is crucial ... that data that challenge embedded orthodoxies be presented along with information that supports the common view. Otherwise ... people will continue to do business in the echo chamber of their existing assumptions.

—Rita McGrath[1]

The proof that a firm has succeeded is the fact that people are willing to pay for offerings in ways that result in a greatly profitable business. That

---

[1]Rita McGrath, 2019, *Seeing Around Corners: How to Spot Inflection Points in Business Before They Happen.* Boston: Houghton Mifflin Harcourt, pp 51–52 and 56.

financial state is merely society's reward to the business for fulfilling its unmet needs.

—Mark L. Frigo and Joel Litman[2]

Figure 4.1 highlights life-cycle performance and firm risk—the primary topics in this chapter and two components of the pragmatic theory of the firm. The objective is to gain insights about the connection between a firm's financial performance and its market valuation, including the troublesome issue of risk and cost of capital.

The order of topics in this chapter follows the timeline for research done at Callard Madden & Associates beginning in 1969. This was a time when I wrote Fortran programs using punched cards. I remember late nights trying to get the attention of computer operators because the drum-and-pen printer was running out of ink and degrading the

FIGURE 4.1 Life-cycle performance and firm risk

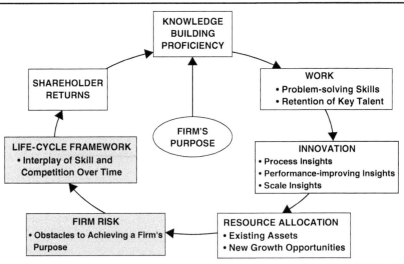

---

[2] Mark L. Frigo and Joel Litman, 2007, *Driven: Business Strategy, Human Actions, and the Creation of Wealth.* Chicago: Strategy & Execution LLC, p. 53.

production of my primitive life-cycle company charts. The commonsense idea then was to initially study the long-term histories of business firms by plotting time series of relevant corporate performance variables. A firm's economic returns and its reinvestment rates were obvious choices because they determined the cash flows that drive a firm's market valuation. I developed the inflation-adjusted CFROI (cash-flow-return-on-investment) as an estimate of a firm's economic returns.[3] A life-cycle framework was used based on the empirically validated assumption that a firm's economic returns regress (fade) toward the cost of capital over the life of the firm.[4] No matter how successful a company may have been in the past, competition eventually results in most companies eventually becoming average or worse.

The next logical step was a life-cycle valuation model enabling a firm's warranted valuation to be calculated at any point in time. With this valuation model, expectations implied in stock prices at a point in time could be expressed as future life-cycle performance. Keep in mind that this research program began with a focus on individual firms and how different levels of life-cycle performance would likely lead to shareholder returns sharply different than the general market, that is, a disequilibrium viewpoint attuned to the needs of active money managers who were Callard Madden clients.

The early research at Callard Madden set the foundation for a commercial research program later continued by HOLT Value Associates, which was acquired by Credit Suisse in 2002. Today, many of the world's largest money management firms are clients of Credit Suisse HOLT and receive a global database covering more than 20,000 companies and a life-cycle valuation model. The purpose of this research program is to develop a deep understanding of, and practical tools for, linking a firm's financial performance to levels and changes in stock prices on a worldwide basis.

---

[3] Bartley J. Madden, 1999, *CFROI Valuation: A Total System Approach to Valuing the Firm*. Oxford: Butterworth-Heinemann.

[4] George Stigler, 1963, *Capital and Rates of Return in Manufacturing Industries*. Princeton, NJ: Princeton University Press.

THE FIRM'S COMPETITIVE LIFE CYCLE

In a market-based economy, not only is competition ubiquitous, but it provides a reliable guidepost for assessing a firm's long-term future. This is not a new idea. The allocation of resources as part of a competitive process was discussed by Adam Smith. In the mid-1800s John Stuart Mill noted:

> On an average (whatever may be the occasional fluctuations) the var-
> ious employments of capital are on such a footing as to hold out,
> not equal profits, but equal expectations of profits. ... If the chances
> of profit (in a business) are thought to be inferior to those in other
> employments, capital gradually leaves it, or at least new capital is
> not attracted to it; and by this change in the distribution of capi-
> tal between the less profitable and more profitable employments, a
> sort of balance is restored.[5]

In 1887, the economist Francis A. Walker emphasized the role of managerial skill in determining winners and losers in the competitive battle:

> The excess of produce which we are contemplating comes from
> directing force to its proper object by the simplest and shortest
> ways; from saving all unnecessary waste of materials and machinery;
> from boldly incurring the expense—the often large expense—of
> improved processes and appliances, while closely scrutinizing outgo
> and practicing a thousand petty economies in unessential matters;
> from meeting the demands of the market most aptly and instantly;
> and, lastly from exercising a sound judgment as to the time of sale
> and the terms of payment. It is on account of the wide range among
> the employers of labor, in the matter of ability to meet these exacting
> conditions of business success, that we have the phenomenon in
> every community and in every trade, in whatever state of the market,
> of some employers realizing no profits at all, while others are making
> fair profits; others, again, large profits; others, still, colossal profits.[6]

Just before the stock market crash of 1929, the well-known economist Irving Fisher famously commented that stocks had reached a permanently higher plateau. In contrast, the investment analyst Dwight C. Rose applied

---

[5] John Stuart Mill, 2004, *Principles of Political Economy*. Amherst, NY: Prometheus Books, p. 393.
[6] Francis A. Walker, 1887, "The Source of Business Profits," *Quarterly Journal of Economics* 1(3): 265–288.

the life-cycle principles discussed in this chapter in an insightful analysis of the stock market, "Common Stocks at the Current Price Level," given at the December 27, 1928, joint annual meeting of the American Statistical Association and the American Economic Association:

> Do these changed conditions necessarily mean that the *average* corporation is going to show larger earnings on its capital? ... Is it not more likely that the principal beneficiary from all these influences will be the consumer rather than the producer or the investor? The average efficiency of business has increased. Those that do not keep up with the times must fall by the wayside in competition; those that are ahead of the times will show a correspondingly greater progress; but the *average* company will do little better than the average company has done in the past. In the last analysis we have a competition of capital seeking investment in any enterprise offering more than the average return, and more capital will continue to pour into such enterprises until the return of the average concern is on a basis commensurate with that in other fields. ... But the fact that industry is growing and earnings increasing does not necessarily mean large profits to the common stock investor if all of these favorable factors have been discounted in an inflated market price.

Figure 4.2 comports with how firms typically perform over the long term. It illustrates transitional stages over a life cycle that captures the dynamics of a firm's profitability and growth. Management at the beginning (startup) of the *high-innovation* stage needs to quickly confirm or refute the key assumptions about how their firm can efficiently provide value to customers beyond what established firms can do. Successful commercialization of an innovative business model results in economic returns accelerating beyond the cost-of-capital. If the innovation can be scaled, then big reinvestment rates are made which further boost the firm's market valuation.

High economic returns, especially if accompanied by high reinvestment rates that signal a substantial market opportunity, are a magnet for competitors. At the *competitive fade* stage, other firms attempt to duplicate the originator's innovation. The subsequent fade rates depend upon a firm's competitive advantage, in particular, its adaptability driven by the firm's

FIGURE 4.2 **The life-cycle framework**

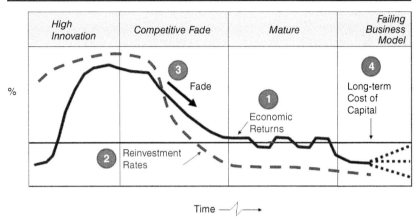

knowledge-building proficiency. Over the long term, the firm's economic returns fade toward the cost of capital and its reinvestment rates regress (fade) toward an economy-type growth rate.

In the New Economy, which puts a premium on intangible assets (see Chapter 5), network-based platforms can become more valuable as more users join (e.g., Facebook, Amazon). A bigger user base (hence, a larger firm) can actually slow the fade of economic returns and reinvestment rates. This is distinctly different from the Old Economy, which was dominated by tangible assets (e.g., plant and equipment) with large firms competing for share of a product market that typically grew at close to an economy rate.

Eventually, the firm matures and earns close to cost-of-capital economic returns, and its reinvestment rates slow considerably. At the *mature* stage, the challenge facing management is how best to improve the efficiency of existing assets and sustain its core competencies while also investing in new opportunities, some of which may have the potential to obsolete existing products or services.

A firm's competitive advantage may dissipate so completely (rapid fade of economic returns) that it now operates at a competitive disadvantage. The hallmark of the *failing business model* stage is business-as-usual complacency and a bureaucratic culture in which management sees the future as a mirror image of past business success.[7] Lacking in knowledge-building proficiency, timely and insightful feedback is missing about important changes in the external environment. Meanwhile, competitors typically become more efficient at providing value to the firm's customers. At this stage, restructuring is needed—more than likely led by new management. The firm will either successfully restructure or eventually close shop with individual business units sold, often at bankruptcy prices.

In summary, the life-cycle framework illuminates the typical path of a firm over the different life-cycle stages of Figure 4.2. At times, a firm surprises investors and delivers economic returns and reinvestment rates that sharply diverge from the typical fade patterns. After Steve Jobs returned to Apple, he rejuvenated Apple's innovation DNA and the firm's subsequent economic returns and reinvestment rates dramatically improved to the benefit of Apple's shareholders.

Implementation of the life-cycle framework requires adjustments to accounting data in order to calculate economic returns and reinvestment rates. Additional measurement challenges are encountered in calculating the investor discount rate and forecast fade rates needed for the life-cycle valuation model (described below). Briefly, four key decisions were made in the early 1970s at Callard Madden that laid the foundation for the research progress ongoing at Credit Suisse HOLT.

First, economic returns, reinvestment rates, and the investor discount rate need to be inflation adjusted (i.e., "real") This is the only sensible way to display long-term time series of these variables and accurately reflect levels and trends. In addition, forecasted real variables are then directly comparable to their historical counterparts and across countries which have experienced quite different inflation environments.

Second, the life-cycle valuation system is comprised of interrelated parts. As such, a CAPM/Beta cost of capital or any other discount rate calculated independently of how net cash receipts are forecast is avoided.

---

[7] See the discussion of Kmart and Walmart in Bartley J. Madden, 2014, *Reconstructing Your Worldview: The Four Core Beliefs You Need to Solve Complex Business Problems*. Naperville, IL: LearningWhatWorks pages 10–13. Also see Chapter 4 in Bartley J. Madden, 2010, *Wealth Creation: A Systems Mindset for Building and Investing in Businesses for the Long Term*. Hoboken, NJ: John Wiley & Sons.

Instead, a forward-looking (market-implied) investor discount rate is calculated consistent with the forecasting procedures used for net cash receipts and attuned to current stock prices.

Third, CFROI (cash-flow-return-on-investment) is a real internal rate-of-return metric that improves upon conventional RONA (return-on-net assets) by adjusting accounting data to reflect the economics of cash-in and cash-out projects. Keep in mind that CFROIs are comparable across companies on a global basis and comparable to real (inflation-adjusted) discount rates.

Fourth, the valuation system comprised of the life-cycle track records and valuation model is designed to be continuously improved. For example, improvement in the CFROI calculation for a particular class of companies typically enables better forecasts of future CFROIs and improved historical tracking of warranted values versus actual stock prices. This involves considerable work but leads to more accurate and insightful life-cycle track records. While critically important for understanding the past and making forecasts for the future, track records have heretofore not been given much attention by mainstream finance researchers. This is regrettable since the construction of life-cycle track records on a global basis is a source of continual new measurement problems—a highly useful situation because this promotes continual learning—and a gateway to a deeper understanding of how firms create or dissipate value.

The improved calibration of economic returns via CFROI facilitates measurement of the long-term average economic returns earned by industrial firms as displayed in Figure 4.3. In recent years, aggregate CFROIs in the U.S. have exceeded global aggregate CFROIs.

For Figure 4.3, the bars represent asset-weighted CFROIs. From 1950 to 1985, the data is primarily U.S. firms and thereafter the universe of firms is global. The data indicate that the *long-term economic return* on total assets (not just equity) for industrial firms is approximately 6% (adjusted for inflation), which is displayed as a horizontal line in Figure 4.3. A plausible conclusion is that a benchmark *long-term cost of capital* (weighted average

FIGURE 4.3 Aggregate CFROIs for global industrial firms, 1950–2017

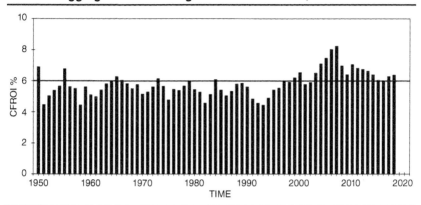

Source: Based on data from Credit Suisse HOLT global database.

of debt and equity) for the typical (not highly levered with debt) industrial firm is 6%, once again adjusted for inflation.[8]

In the next two sections, life-cycle track records are displayed for Nokia and Amazon, including brief company descriptions in order to better understand management behavior and the resulting long-term financial performance. The life-cycle charts are comprised of three panels. The top panel displays a firm's economic returns calculated as CFROIs, which are inflation-adjusted (real). A horizontal dark line is drawn at 6% as a benchmark real cost of capital. *When analyzing long-term time series of CFROIs, adjustments for inflation are critically important in order to more accurately measure levels and trends.* The middle panel contains annual real asset growth rates. The bottom panel displays a relative wealth index, which is a stock's total shareholder return (dividends plus price appreciation) relative to the total return of the appropriate index for the general market (e.g., the S&P 500 for U.S. firms). Outperformance is seen as a rising trend for the relative wealth line; market-matching performance is recorded as a flat trend; and underperformance of the index shows as a declining trend.

---

[8] The real cost of capital was estimated at 5.95% in Eugene F. Fama and Kenneth R. French, 1999, "The Corporate Cost of Capital and the Return on Corporate Investment," *Journal of Finance* 54(6): 1939–1967.

A PARANOID OPTIMIST RESTRUCTURES NOKIA

Nokia is a Finnish multinational company that began in 1865 as a pulp mill, later produced rubber and cable products, then evolved into telecommunications and consumer electronics. Nokia management made an astute decision to focus on mobile phones. This led to the steep rise in CFROIs from 1992 to 2001 as shown in the top panel of Figure 4.4, which displays Nokia's life-cycle track record. These high CFROIs were accompanied by high asset growth (middle panel) and the combination led to Nokia's stock price outperforming the STOXX Europe 600 stock index (bottom panel). By 1998 Nokia had become the best-selling mobile phone brand with close to a 50% share of the global market.

Due to innovation by Apple and Google, Nokia's fall was swift and by 2012 the firm had entered the failing business model stage. Risto Siilasmaa then became CEO and later transitioned from CEO to chairman of Nokia. He understood that Nokia's culture had become dysfunctional and innovation was stalled, partly because of Nokia's deep involvement with carriers that did not like fast-paced change. Siilasmaa described the competitive landscape as follows:

> Apple and Google were starting from scratch in the smartphone universe. They could use the latest technology and forge new alliances. We were weighed down by a load of bad legacy: old code, out-of-date architectures, compromising contracts, and development teams spread around the world using different tools and speaking different languages, all held together by rubber bands and chewing gum.[9]

Apple's strategy was to develop an ecosystem with a self-reinforcing cycle for its platform—enhance the user experience leading to more developers producing apps for Apple phones, which in turn leads to a better user experience and more consumers becoming Apple users. Nokia could not catch up and reached out to Microsoft to form a partnership that included using Microsoft's operating system for smartphones. Financial

---

[9]Risto Siilasmaa, 2019, *Transforming Nokia: The Power of Paranoid Optimism to Lead through Colossal Change*. New York: McGraw-Hill Education, p. 36.

FIGURE 4.4 Nokia 1988–2018

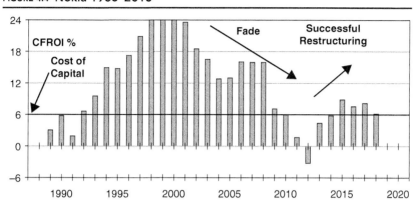

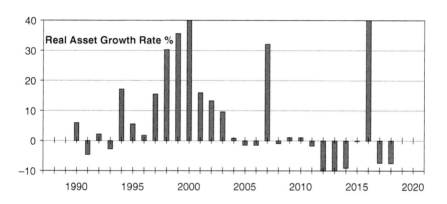

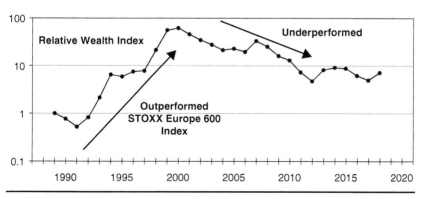

Source: Based on data from Credit Suisse HOLT global database.

performance continued to deteriorate. One cannot overstate the difficulty of revitalizing a firm with over 100,000 dispirited employees and on the brink of bankruptcy.

An important point emphasized throughout this book is that the root cause of value creation or dissipation resides in the degree of a firm's knowledge-building proficiency. Siilasmaa was well-positioned to orchestrate a needed knowledge-building culture. He labels such a culture "paranoid optimism"—hard-nosed reality checks coupled with a positive outlook for the future rooted in scenario-based thinking. This is an application of the knowledge-building loop of Figure 2.1. He assessed Nokia's dysfunctional management system and the way forward as follows:

> The subconscious assumption was that our past success guaranteed our future success. The unspoken message I heard was: We are Nokia. We invented this industry. ... Nobody does it better.
>
> ... learning to recognize four toxic symptoms of success: Bad news doesn't reach you or your team. ... Your team doesn't dig for negative news or hard facts. ... Decisions are constantly postponed and watered down. ... There is often just a single plan with no alternatives.
>
> ... by instilling a culture that is characterized by data-driven analysis, regular deep dives to understand root causes, and constant paranoia regarding competitors and markets, a culture that encourages communicating bad news quickly and an imperative for always being presented with alternatives, you can combat the toxicity of success and better prepare to withstand the storm.[10]

Siilasmaa led Nokia's board of directors to rapidly reinvent the firm's business model. Finances were improved by the sale of its mobile and device business to Microsoft. A previously neglected business was NSN (Nokia Siemens Networks), a joint venture with Siemens focused on telecommunications infrastructure. Nokia bought out Siemens. Finally, Alcatel-Lucent, a global telecommunications equipment company, which owned Bell Laboratories, was acquired, elevating Nokia as a major supplier for global wireless infrastructure. These bold initiatives fit a vision of a programmable world with massive connectivity and a large-scale business opportunity to

---

[10] Risto Siilasmaa, 2019, *Transforming Nokia: The Power of Paranoid Optimism to Lead through Colossal Change*. New York: McGraw-Hill Education, pp. 54–57.

enable software-driven networks to operate seamlessly. For Nokia to earn and sustain CFROIs in excess of the cost of capital, the firm needs to be a leader in the transition to 5G wireless technology (Ericsson and Huawei are especially strong competitors).

A CASE STUDY OF INNOVATION—AMAZON

That knowledge building and value creation are two sides of the same coin is evident in Jeff Bezos, Amazon's founder and CEO, explaining the firm's ability to innovate at a fast pace even as the firm continues to rapidly grow:

> The key is starting with customers, and working backwards—that's the kind of thing that has become a habit at Amazon. We also have an eagerness to invent that is a deep part of our culture, as is a willingness to think long-term. We can work on things that don't need to work perfectly for five, six or seven years; there aren't many companies willing to take on that kind of time horizon. And then finally, we have a culture of operational excellence—and I mean that in the sense that Toyota might mean it: we're constantly looking for and finding defects, doing root-cause analysis and working to fix and improve things—that's a big part of who we are.
>
> When you apply those four things—customer focus, invention, investment, and operational excellence—they work together synergistically in all the different parts of our business.[11]

Figure 4.5 displays Amazon's life-cycle track record beginning in 1995.

In the early years, Amazon's stock price was volatile as investors struggled to understand and forecast Amazon's future. By the mid-2000s Amazon was established, and investors understood that the firm's exceptionally high asset growth rates (see middle panel of Figure 4.5), which depressed CFROIs, were creating substantial long-term value. That is why a "weak" quarterly earnings report could result in a rising stock price as investors learned more about the new investments undertaken. From 1997 to 2018, Amazon outperformed the S&P 500 about 100-fold (bottom panel).

---

[11] James Quinn, 2016, "One Eye on the Consumer, the Other on the Future," *Rotman Magazine* Spring: 80–84.

FIGURE 4.5 Amazon 1995–2018

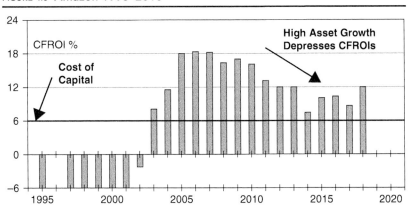

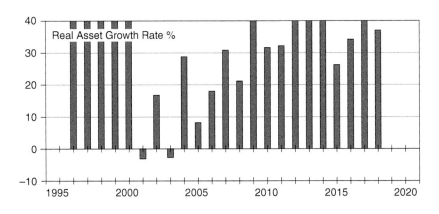

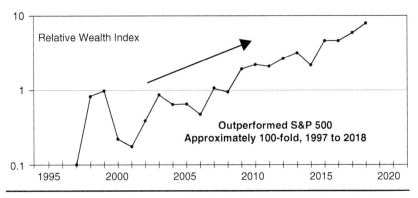

Source: Based on data from Credit Suisse HOLT global database.

An insightful perspective on Amazon's business model is that of a virtuous cycle. Low prices, wide selection, and online convenience improve the customer experience, building more traffic on Amazon's platform that in turn attracts more sellers and customers. Amazon Prime delivers expedited shipping at no charge for those customers who subscribe to the equivalent of a warehouse club membership. This enhances the customer experience and the virtuous cycle continues. Note that Amazon's low margins not only benefit customers but are a disincentive for potential competitors who typically are attracted to high-margin businesses. Also, Amazon's scale is a further disincentive for new competitors to attempt to duplicate Amazon's business model.

Recall in Chapter 2 the discussion of the subtle yet important impact of language in revealing assumptions that block alternative ways to better serve customers. During a meeting about Amazon's fundamental purpose, Bezos quickly composed and distributed a single paragraph that began: "We are the Unstore."[12] He emphasized that the traditional retail rules (assumptions) simply are not applicable to Amazon. For example, contrary to traditional retailers, Amazon provides both superb personalized service and low prices; publishes both negative and positive product reviews; and provides used products to compete with new products.

In his 1997 letter to shareholders, Bezos noted in his description of Amazon's decision-making approach: "We will continue to make investment decisions in light of long-term market leadership considerations rather than short-term profitability considerations or short-term Wall Street reactions." Since that first letter to shareholders Amazon has been true to this long-term value creation discipline, and experiments with innovative ideas that could result in a leadership role in a business with sizable revenues. The firm accepts failures, such as its Fire mobile phone, as a necessary part of a bold innovation process. Capabilities developed from failed projects can be utilized in other projects such as the Kindle

---

[12] Brad Stone, 2013, *The Everything Store: Jeff Bezos and the Age of Amazon.* New York: Little Brown and Company, p. 183.

e-book reader and the Alexa virtual assistant (part of Echo speakers and other devices) which are game changers.

AWS (Amazon Web Services) is an example of how Amazon's innovative culture combined with in-house capabilities spawned a new industry of substantial size. By year-end 2019 the annualized revenue rate for AWS will likely exceed $30 billion. AWS frees people from the traditional high-cost and time-wasting process of storing data and developing software code on computers and servers owned by others, or even in-house facilities. With on-demand AWS cloud computing platforms, customers pay for what they use and can instantly scale up their projects. Customers no longer worry about where to store data or security or availability. Instead, customers focus on developing innovative ways to use their data. AWS is a major game changer.

THE LIFE-CYCLE VALUATION MODEL

Contrary to other theories of the firm, the pragmatic theory explicitly addresses the issue of a firm's market valuation. Over the long term, stock prices represent an especially knowledgeable vote on a firm's ability to achieve its purpose. The pragmatic theory incorporates life-cycle track records coupled to the life-cycle valuation model to provide a lens not only to understand a firm's past performance and shareholder returns, but also to identify the most important current issues impacting future shareholder returns.

Let us begin understanding the life-cycle valuation model by noting the language choices. I prefer to avoid the use of "intrinsic value," which might imply a fixed "true" point on the valuation scale. Instead, I use "warranted value" whereby a value is warranted by a specific forecast of long-term net cash receipts and the assignment of a specific investor discount rate. In addition, I favor the use of "net cash receipts," calculated as the firm's after-tax cash inflows less reinvestment.

FIGURE 4.6 **Life-cycle valuation model**

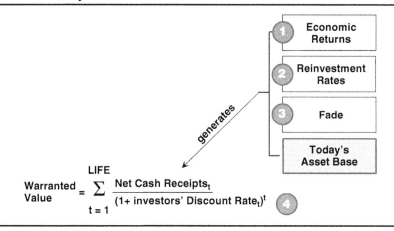

$$\text{Warranted Value} = \sum_{t=1}^{\text{LIFE}} \frac{\text{Net Cash Receipts}_t}{(1+ \text{investors' Discount Rate}_t)^t}$$

The life-cycle valuation model of Figure 4.6 displays a discounted-cash-flow calculation of a firm's warranted value.[13] The forecasted stream of net cash receipts is generated by applying a forecast fade rate to economic returns and a fade rate to reinvestment rates. I use "reinvestment rate" and "asset growth" interchangeably although the sums reinvested each year coupled to ROIs on these specific outlays actually drive the net cash receipt stream. All variables are inflation-adjusted.

In actual practice, the life-cycle valuation model is a window to experience how, on average, stock prices reflect forecasts that are astute and difficult to bet against. For those of us who have been in the trenches for decades doing life-cycle research that links firm performance to valuation, it is not at all newsworthy that the stock market is "efficient," on average, in making long-term forecasts (setting prices). In fact, many times after working through the economic effects of complicated accounting issues,

---

[13] A comprehensive description of the life-cycle valuation model and the CFROI as a proxy for economic returns first appeared in Bartley J. Madden, 1999, *CFROI Valuation: A Total System Approach to Valuing the Firm*. Oxford: Butterworth-Heinemann. For updated calculation details for CFROI and related valuation variables, see David A. Holland and Bryant A. Matthews, 2018, *Beyond Earnings: Applying the HOLT CFROI and Economic Profit Framework*. Hoboken, NJ: John Wiley & Sons.

one learns that the market typically has already incorporated the economic impact in prices.[14] In a similar vein, decoding investor expectations implied in current stock prices reveals forecasts that oftentimes a knowledgeable investor agrees with, that is, there are no easy ways to place a bet on the table, especially so for larger firms.

The most important skill an investor can possess is superior forecasting ability for fade rates of economic returns and reinvestment rates. Analysis of how firms have faded historically provides forecasting guidelines. Note that in studying a firm's life-cycle track record and related fade rates one is actually analyzing competitive advantage. Instead of merely a qualitative discussion of the magnitude of a firm's competitive advantage, life-cycle track records enable a visual and quantitative assessment of competitive advantage. This is one reason for including life-cycle performance as a component of the pragmatic theory of the firm.

For established firms, sustained failure to earn the cost of capital reflects below-average managerial skill and potential trouble adjusting to major changes in the environment. In addition, these firms typically have a culture of complacency and a business-as-usual mindset. Traditional retailers such as Kmart, Sears, and J. C. Penney operated in relatively stable retail environments until Walmart upended their business model, followed by Amazon's Internet platform efficiency in serving retail customers. As these firms headed toward bankruptcy, their stock price volatility increased, but this was coincidental to increased firm risk, not a leading indicator.

What large retail firm was not hurt by Walmart's growth or, recently, by the growing dominance of Amazon? The answer: Costco. Its highly skilled management consistently achieves economic returns well in excess of the cost of capital. A detailed discussion of Costco's business model and its ability to exploit change is presented in Chapter 5. The key point here is that the life-cycle framework is helpful for gauging managerial skill and raising early questions about a firm's ability to survive and prosper.

---

[14] For an illustrative example, see the description of how unreasonably high discount rates for Taiwanese companies were traced to a missing cash expense in calculating CFROIs in Bartley J. Madden, 2010, *Wealth Creation: A Systems Mindset for Building and Investing in Businesses for the Long Term*. Hoboken, NJ: John Wiley & Sons, pp. 90–91.

WHAT DOES A STOCK PRICE SAY ABOUT A FIRM'S FUTURE INVESTMENTS?

Managements, boards of directors, and investors should pay attention to the stock market's assessment of their firms' future profitability in order to judge the economic soundness of management's planned future investments. "Business as usual" is typically not strategically sound for firms priced with significant *negative values* for future investments, which means that current stock prices imply expected ROIs on future investments that are less than the firm's cost of capital.

A popular mathematical treatment for the value of a firm's existing assets is to calculate a normalized level of earnings. This is then treated as a perpetuity by assuming depreciation charges are automatically reinvested every year in the future to maintain today's asset base. Hence, dividing these earnings by the cost of capital provides a present value for existing assets as if depreciation charges represented future mandatory outlays to exactly duplicate today's asset base. Actually, this is a mathematical fiction that assumes a world of zero change. Investments in the future will actually be made in projects that offer the most economically promising opportunities as management adapts to a changing world. The perpetuity method incorrectly boosts the value of existing assets and therefore implies a much lower value of future investments. Why? Since the value of future investments is the total value of the firm less the estimated value of existing assets, too high an estimated value for existing assets necessarily lowers the estimated value of future investments.

A more useful estimate of the value of existing assets is the present value of future cash flows from the wind-down (zero new investment) of existing assets, including the value of released nondepreciating assets such as net working capital. For example, an oil and gas exploration company has reserves which will dissipate (wind down) over time as future cash flows are generated. The present value of those cash flows represents the value of existing assets. Deducting this estimated value of existing assets (principally reserves) from the firm's total market value leaves the implied value of future investments.

FIGURE 4.7 % Future and the firm's life cycle

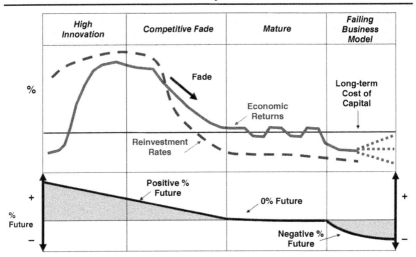

The % Future metric expresses the implied value of future investments as a percent of the firm's total market value. The lower portion of Figure 4.7 plots % Future for a firm as it transitions over the four life-cycle stages. In the high innovation stage, a high % Future reflects expectations for future investments to earn ROIs well in excess of the cost of capital and vice versa for the failing business model stage.

Figure 4.8 shows selected industrial firms that are ranked highest on % Future and lowest as of January 15, 2020.[15] For example, the highest ranked firm Adobe has debt and market value of equity totaling $174 billion and deducting an estimated value of $27 billion for existing assets yields an implied value of $147 billion for future investments. Expressing this as a percent of the firm's total market value yields 85 % Future. In a similar fashion, the lowest ranked % Future is Ford, which has an implied value for future investments of a negative $39 billion yielding −55 % Future.

---

[15] The % Future metric was developed in Bartley J. Madden, 1999, *CFROI Valuation: A Total System Approach to Valuing the Firm*. Oxford: Butterworth-Heinemann. The metric is occasionally used in performance scorecards in *Forbes* magazine. Also, the advantages of the % Future metric are discussed in Chapter 7 in Jeff Dyer, Hal Gregersen, and Clayton M. Christensen, 2011, *The Innovator's DNA: Mastering the Five Skills of Disruptive Innovators*. Boston: Harvard Business Review Press.

FIGURE 4.8 % Future for selected industrial firms, January 15, 2020

COMPANY	TOTAL FIRM SBIL	EXISTING ASSETS SBIL	FUTURE INVEST SBIL	% FUTURE
ADOBE	174	27	147	85
INTUIT	72	14	58	81
MASTERCARD	329	65	264	80
PAYPAL	140	32	108	77
INTUITIVE SURGICAL	72	18	54	75
MONSTER BEVERAGE	37	9	27	75
ILLUMINA	49	13	36	74
NETFLIX	173	47	126	73
NIKE	174	53	121	70
DANAHER	141	44	97	69
MICROSOFT	1,363	437	926	68
AMAZON	999	334	665	67
AT&T	539	521	18	3
WALGREENS	91	90	1	1
VERIZON	410	419	−9	−2
NORFOLK SOUTHERN	68	73	−5	−7
CONOCOPHILIPS	97	106	−10	−10
SPRINT	62	74	−11	−18
ARCHER DANIELS MIDLAND	38	47	−9	−25
CARNIVAL	48	62	−14	−30
CHEVRON	284	387	−103	−36
EXXON MOBIL	403	550	−146	−36
GENERAL MOTORS	95	130	−35	−37
FORD	70	109	−39	−55

Source: Based on data from Credit Suisse HOLT global database.

The next section addresses the assignment of the investor discount rate for use in the life-cycle valuation model.

FORWARD-LOOKING, MARKET-IMPLIED DISCOUNT RATE

The mainstream finance approach to the assignment of a valuation model's discount rate is to use an accepted theory such as CAPM or Arbitrage Pricing Theory. An empirically more useful approach that continues to gain broader academic support is to measure the market-implied discount rates from current stock prices, which advantageously provides a forward-looking discount rate similar to the yield-to-maturity for a bond.[16]

A forward-looking discount for a bond takes an expected stream of net cash receipts (interest and principal payments) and a known market price for the bond, and then derives the market-implied discount rate—the familiar yield-to-maturity. A regression equation could then connect variables likely to affect the demanded return for a bond. For example, credit quality and trading liquidity could be independent variables, and the demanded return for the bond would be the dependent variable. With this regression equation, for example, the estimated yield-to-maturity for a bond not yet traded could be estimated based on its estimated credit quality and trading liquidity.

While conceptually straightforward for bonds, this methodology is challenging for equities. The challenge is that future net cash receipts are not promised like they are for bonds, so plausible forecasts consistent with investor expectations need to be estimated. The Credit Suisse HOLT global database maintains such forecasts and therefore is able to correlate key variables in a regression equation to estimate market-implied discount rates for firms based on market prices at a particular time. While the methodology is not proprietary, remember that the closer the monitored forecasts match actual investor forecasts, the more accurate the market-implied discount rates.

Figure 4.9 displays the Credit Suisse HOLT market-implied discount rate (weighted average of debt and equity) for a firm of standard size and leverage.[17]

---

[16] The first use of a market-implied discount rate that identified the impact of size and financial leverage is in Bartley J. Madden, 1998, "The CFROI Valuation Model," *Journal of Investing* 7(1): 31–43. The key empirical finding was summarized in Exhibit 9 of that article which was reproduced and discussed in S. David Young and Stephen F. O'Byrne, 2001, *EVA and Value-Based Management: A Practical Guide to Implementation.* New York: McGraw-Hill, pp. 423–425. See also Kevin K. Li and Partha Mohanram, 2014, "Evaluating Cross-sectional Forecasting Models for Implied Cost of Capital," *Review of Accounting Studies* 19(3): 1152–1185.

[17] Technical details, including standard size and leverage, are explained in Chapter 7 of David A. Holland and Bryant A. Matthews, 2018, *Beyond Earnings: Applying the HOLT CFROI and Economic Profit Framework.* Hoboken, NJ: John Wiley & Sons.

FIGURE 4.9 U.S. aggregate market-implied investor discount rates, 1976–2019

Source: Based on data from Credit Suisse HOLT global database.

From the early 1980s to the height of the dot-com bubble in 2000, the discount rate declined as inflation and personal tax rates declined. Note that taxable investors will raise their demanded pre-personal-tax returns to offset higher taxes on capital gains and dividends. Inflation causes investors to pay capital gains taxes on nominal "gains," which when deflated are not real gains. So, the decline in both inflation and personal tax rates was a sound economic reason for taxable investors to lower their demanded returns.[18] Since 2000, the discount rate (weighted average of debt and equity) has trended around 4.5% real until an upward spike that coincided with the financial crisis of 2007–2009. Thereafter a monetary policy of quantitative easing resulted in a declining discount rate.

THE ROOTS OF MODERN FINANCE

Language matters. Two seminal articles coauthored by Franco Modigliani and Merton Miller (M&M) on capital structure and dividends in 1958 and 1961, respectively, were useful to many in finance given their

[18] See the data displays and discussion in Chapter 4 and Appendix A of Bartley J. Madden, 1999, *CFROI Valuation: A Total System Approach to Valuing the Firm*. Oxford: Butterworth-Heinemann. Market-implied (real) discount rates in the 1960s and 1970s approximated 6%.

straightforward mathematical language that effectively communicated cause-and-effect relationships.[19] This was a sharp turn from the vague and nonmathematical language previously used in the finance literature.

The Capital Asset Pricing Model (CAPM) and the efficient market hypothesis are rooted in the notion of risk and expected investor return in an equilibrium setting. Securities are assumed to be efficiently priced with all relevant valuation information about firms embedded in stock prices. Unfortunately, the stronger one's commitment to market efficiency (weak, semi, and strong-form), the less relevant are valuation models and the construction of a firm's financial track record. In contrast, historical track records and valuation sensitivities to forecast firm performance are critical to the life-cycle framework. A valuable learning opportunity is missed by many, or at least, relegated to a lesser status: namely the evaluation of a firm's financial performance in a manner that connects to its stock price over time.

With CAPM as a foundation, modern finance evolved via elegant mathematical logic, tied to restrictive assumptions about investor behavior and market structure, that described the investment world. The resulting logic, given the assumptions made, is tight, and finance textbooks are well-oiled machines for analyzing risk in an equilibrium environment. The worldview promoted is based on efficient markets and a theoretical CAPM view of risk and expected return linked via Beta, which reflects the degree of sensitivity of a stock with the general market. As a practical matter, the more volatile the stock price, the higher the Beta. Alternatives to CAPM, such as the Arbitrage Pricing Theory, still retain the core concept of higher returns demanded by higher variability (Beta).[20]

Finance students' worldview is shaped by the notion that systematic risk reflected in Beta is paramount because it cannot be diversified away in

---

[19] Franco Modigliani and Merton H. Miller, 1958, "The Cost of Capital, Corporation Finance and the Theory of Investment," *American Economic Review* 48(3): 261–297; Merton H. Miller and Franco Modigliani, 1961, "Dividend Policy, Growth, and the Valuation of Shares," *Journal of Business* 34(4): 411–433.

[20] Stephen A. Ross, 1976, "The Arbitrage Theory of Capital Asset Pricing," *Journal of Economic Theory* (13): 341–360.

a portfolio, whereas unsystematic (idiosyncratic) risk can. The argument is that for investors to achieve higher returns they need to accept higher systematic risk. Importantly, especially high and low Beta stocks have not consistently yielded the returns predicted by CAPM.[21] Nevertheless, that higher relative stock price variability (volatility) implies higher risk and expected investor return is a widespread belief.

CAPM provides a formula for a firm's cost of equity capital, a key component to a firm's weighted average cost of capital. The equity cost of capital based on CAPM equals the risk-free rate plus Beta times the equity risk premium, which is the expected return for the equity market in excess of the risk free rate. Based on the range of answers this formula produces in practice, it is truly dysfunctional. However, finance students and many valuation practitioners often apply this formula for use with their valuation models. Stephen Penman, who has authored multiple textbooks on financial accounting and valuation, is not a fan of CAPM/Beta:

> Under the CAPM, one estimates a beta (with considerable error) then multiples it by the "market risk premium." The latter is anyone's guess; estimates of this number in textbooks run from 3 percent to 10 percent! (Fancier asset pricing models compound the problem.) The fundamental investor must be honest in investing and, honestly, we don't know the cost of capital. Guessing at it builds speculation into a valuation.
>
> We can understand the risk in a business but thinking we can compress this understanding into one number called the cost of capital is a fiction. I see our failure to get hold of the cost of capital as the most disappointing aspect of modern finance, not that we haven't tried.[22]

Ask students who have completed their MBA finance courses what word comes to mind after one hears "risk" and they will likely say "covariance,"

---

[21] Eugene Fama and Kenneth French, 1992, "The Cross-Section of Expected Stock Returns," *Journal of Finance* 47(2): 427–465. This early article on the lack of predictability of Beta shows that after holding firm size constant, investors achieve the same, if not lower, returns from high-beta stock portfolios compared to low-beta stock portfolios. For an especially comprehensive discussion of the pitfalls of CAPM/Beta see Eric Falkenstein, 2009, *Finding Alpha: The Search for Alpha When Risk and Return Break Down*. Hoboken, NJ: John Wiley & Sons.

[22] Jacob Wolinsky, August 10, 2011, "My Interview with Stephen Penman: Professor of Accounting at the Columbia Business School," ValueWalk.com.

or "volatility," or "Beta." That is the result of CAPM's long-lived popularity, which is due in no small part to it being an elegant way for finance professors to present a logically beautiful sequence of teaching steps involving clever statistical/mathematical manipulations.

Keep in mind that investors should be wary of firms that have consistently failed to sustain economic returns at least equal to the real cost of capital of approximately 6%. Often such firms, if operating in a relatively stable industry, will exhibit a Beta of less than 1.0, implying lower risk than the market. But that stability can radically change in the future.

FIRM RISK OFFERS A DIFFERENT MINDSET

The CAPM/variability mindset about risk evolved from assumptions about investors' knowledge and behavior. As described above, this led to the CAPM equity cost of capital calculation that gained widespread use for investors' valuation models and for managements' resource allocation decisions. In contrast, the market-implied approach makes no assumptions about investor behavior or preferences, it merely conveys how investors are pricing assets at any given time. This approach facilitates empirical work about the impacts of personal tax rates, inflation, and economic conditions on the investors' demanded real return.

Although this book is not designed to present a new theory for quantitively deriving a firm-specific cost of capital, it does offer a fresh perspective to improve management's thinking about risk, thereby leading to improved decision-making. The beginning point is the purpose of the firm.

In Chapter 1, the firm's purpose was described as having four components:

- Communicate a vision that can inspire and motivate employees to work for a firm committed to behaving ethically and making the world a better place.
- Survive and prosper through continual gains in efficiency and sustained innovation.

- Work continuously to sustain win-win relationships with all of the firm's stakeholders.
- Take care of future generations.

Firm risk can differ from investor risk. Firm risk is about obstacles management faces that interfere with achieving the firm's purpose. Firm risk increases (decreases) in lockstep with changes that degrade (improve) the likelihood of achieving the firm's purpose. An *increase* in firm risk, all else equal, means a greater likelihood for a firm to generate *lower* future financial performance. In the early stage of an increase in firm risk, management may choose to disregard the warning signs, but nevertheless those inside the firm have superior information compared to investors relying on public information. For example, reviewed below are Enron's unethical behavior (not nurturing win-win relationships) and Union Carbide's disregard for maintenance and safety (not taking care of future generations) leading to an explosion at a toxic chemical plant in India. The key insight here is that there can be a substantial time lag between a significant change in firm risk and investor perception of this change. As such, an increase in firm risk will eventually be understood by investors and, all else equal, this adjustment process will cause a decline in the firm's market valuation. How does this adjustment process connect to models of investor risk, like CAPM? The stock price declines in order to provide a high enough expected investor return to adequately compensate investors for the increased likelihood of future shortfalls in the firm's financial performance.

Conceptually, firm risk includes business risk (i.e., myriad factors impacting sales, margins, etc.), plus activities of competitors and potential technological obsolescence—all of which impact a firm's ability to earn the cost of capital. However, I use *firm risk* in a broader way than *business risk* since firm risk varies based on top management's leadership skill to deliver on all four components of the firm's purpose. Included are the design of processes and a management that "walks the talk" to provide a safe working environment that delivers high quality to customers in an ethical manner, protection of its databases from cyberattacks, avoidance of creative accounting practices, and oversight by a board of knowledgeable directors committed to achieving the firm's purpose. When processes are poorly managed and/or employees incentivized to hit performance targets that require them cutting corners, the cost to the firm's reputation can be high.

Samsung Electronics unveiled its Galaxy Note7 smartphone beating the launch of Apple's iPhone7. However, shoddy quality control processes resulted in the phones overheating and catching fire. A massive recall followed. Worse, the replacement units were faulty and also recalled. The total cost of this quality control problem exceeded 5 billion dollars. This example emphasizes that firm risk is attuned to ways that increase or decrease the chances for incurring serious economic costs, including a firm's reputation and the value of its brands.

Consider management behavior that results in a culture in which employees believe they can behave unethically (not punished, perhaps rewarded) as long as they achieve or exceed short-term performance targets. This causes a *rise in firm risk* because it condones unethical behavior, which is eventually manifested in a declining stock price as investors learn about the consequences of this way of operating. Unethical behavior can hide management's inability to create value for a time but eventually business reality arrives. Enron was named "America's Most Innovative Company" by the business magazine *Fortune* every year from 1996 to 2001. However, *Fortune* magazine should have replaced "most innovative company" with "most deceptive company." Enron's top management employed whatever deceptive practices it could get away with in order to generate rising profits (off-balance-sheet hiding of debt, etc.) and pay huge bonuses. They built a culture that stamped out dissent, hid information so employees were unable to understand the overall business (including the unethical practices), and cooked the books while continually lying and hyping the stock to investors, including their employees.[23] Enron's bankruptcy wiped out shareholders' investments

---

[23] Bethany McLean and Peter Elkind, 2003, *The Smartest Guys in the Room: The Amazing Rise and Fall of Enron*. New York: Penguin.

and employees' savings. Top management's behavior was diametrically opposite the four components of the firm's purpose. Enron is a classic case of exceedingly high firm risk that eventually led to bankruptcy.[24]

Firm risk entails a long-term time horizon. Taking care of future generations by designing products and services to reduce waste and pollution and concern for operational safety is easy to shortcut when management has a singular focus on near-term financial results. When large-scale disregard for environmental impacts becomes an accepted way of doing business, *firm risk increases*. As investors see evidence of the negative consequences involved, the firm's stock price will suffer. The Bhopal disaster—the world's worst industrial disaster—occurred at a Union Carbide plant in India. The plant produced a pesticide using particularly toxic ingredients and had a history of serious safety problems and employee deaths. As the profitability of the plant declined, large cost-cutting measures were initiated, already low maintenance expenditures were cut further, and skilled employees were replaced with much less skilled and less expensive workers.[25] The precise cause of the disaster has been debated, but that is not the main issue. Management was the *cause* of a culture of disregard for workers and the people living in the surrounding community that was so plainly evident that a local reporter published an article with the prescient warning "Wake up people of Bhopal, you are on the edge of a volcano."[26] The volcano erupted in late 1984 with a massive leak of toxic gas. The subsequent deaths and long-term health problems were mind-numbing.

The above examples of Enron and Union Carbide illustrate that firm risk covers important issues (e.g., unethical behavior) that are difficult to quantify and may be hidden from accounting-driven performance metrics for an extended period of time. Nevertheless, firm risk, as defined and illustrated above, is a practical guidepost for managers and boards of directors.

---

[24] For an insightful analysis of Enron's culture, see Clinton Free and Norman Macintosh, 2006, "Management Control Practice and Culture at Enron: The Untold Story," SSRN working paper https://ssrn.com/abstract=873636.

[25] Stuart Diamond, January 28, 1985, "The Bhopal Disaster: How It Happened," *New York Times*, Section A, p. 1.

[26] The Week, 2012, *How to Be Really Well Informed in Minutes*. London: Ebury Press, pp. 222–225.

SUMMARY OF KEY IDEAS

Finance discussions about risk, the investor discount rate, the cost of capital, and valuation calculations can become mired in abstract mathematical arguments. The following key ideas may provide practical insights.

- The investor discount rate is best handled as a forward-looking, market-implied rate.
- Firm risk is fundamentally driven by obstacles to achieving the firm's purpose, and increases with a short-term-oriented culture focused on meeting accounting targets and earning bonuses with little concern for how results are achieved.
- As a practical matter, a useful long-term benchmark for a firm's cost of capital is 6% (inflation adjusted); see Figures 4.3 and 4.9.
- Management can control (but not eliminate) firm risk. Control varies as to the type of risk. For example, there is higher control in minimizing unethical behavior and designing products to reduce waste and pollution, but lower control in minimizing sensitivity of operations to overall economic activity. However, feedback about changes in the external environment (knowledge-building proficiency) can help early adaptation and circumvent business-as-usual complacency that can lead to a failing business model.
- A valuation model is best viewed as a system in which the discount rate is contingent upon the process for estimating future net cash receipts. To insert a discount rate that is not connected to the forecasting process for net cash receipts is a recipe for error.
- Conceptually, a more optimistic (pessimistic) forecast adjustment to a firm's warranted value calculation could be handled via a higher (lower) net cash receipt forecast or a lower (higher) investor's discount rate. The more one gains experience with life-cycle track records, the more comfortable one becomes in relying on adjustments to the net cash receipt forecast, that is, more

(less) favorable fade forecast of economic returns or reinvestment rates, which can be judged for plausibility by comparison to the life-cycle track records of the firm and its competitors.

- The usefulness of a track record for a firm (or a business unit of a firm) depends on the accuracy of economic returns derived from historical accounting data. With the growing importance of intangibles, the economic return calculation becomes more challenging, but also more important, as we will see in the next chapter.

A RESEARCH METHODOLOGY FOR ADVANCING THE LIFE-CYCLE FRAMEWORK

This section describes technical details involved with empirical research that advances the life-cycle framework. In the early 1970s at Callard Madden & Associates, my work in developing the life-cycle valuation model started with the concept of a completed project for a firm with known after-tax cash expenditures and receipts. A real ROI for the project can be computed as the internal rate of return after adjusting expenditures and receipts so that they are in units of constant purchasing power, that is, adjusted for inflation or deflation via the GDP Deflator. The "economic return" referred to throughout this book is conceptually an average of the real ROIs achieved on a firm's portfolio of projects. To compute more accurate track records, the CFROI metric is adjusted for inflation and many accounting biases to better estimate the economic return.[27]

My original model of a firm's capability to generate cash receipts was based on a firm configured as a portfolio of ongoing projects (see Figure 4.10) with the following inputs: time series of project ROIs, asset configuration (percent nondepreciating and specified life for depreciating assets), reinvestment rates, financial leverage, and dividend payout. For a

---

[27] For those interested in the conceptual thinking involved with technical details see Bartley J. Madden, 1999, *CFROI Valuation: A Total System Approach to Valuing the Firm*. Oxford: Butterworth-Heinemann. An up-to-date description of CFROI and the life-cycle valuation model is presented in David A. Holland and Bryant A. Matthews, 2018, *Beyond Earnings: Applying the HOLT CFROI and Economic Profit Framework*. Hoboken, NJ: John Wiley & Sons.

FIGURE 4.10 **The firm as a portfolio of projects**

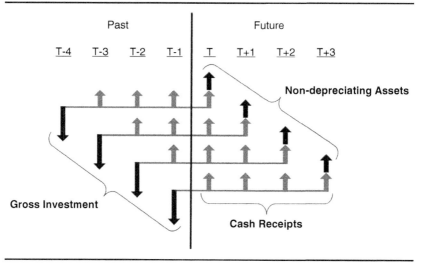

specified time series of interest rates and the GDP Deflator, accounting balance sheets and income statements were generated, thereby enabling a time series of net cash receipts to be calculated for valuation purposes. The resulting period-by-period warranted equity valuations plus dividend payments produced a total shareholder return which was then verified to match the assigned equity cost of capital.

The perspective of the firm as an ongoing portfolio of projects as specified in Figure 4.10 clearly contains simplifications such as equal cash receipts over the project life. However, it is a useful model to generate accounting statements and a time series of net cash receipts. It is also useful as a learning laboratory to investigate accounting biases that distort the measurement of economic returns. Such a learning laboratory can address the magnitude of measurement problems ignored by valuation-model builders who rely solely on mathematical models independent of real-world accounting complexities. For example, valuation textbooks contain models that often use Earnings/Book where book is common equity. The models presented in these textbooks often ignore the many problems with Earnings/Book, including the impact of inflation.

How important is it to ignore the impact of inflation on Earnings/Book calculated from accounting statements?

Figure 4.11 displays a simulated firm with financial leverage, asset life and percent nondepreciating assets, plus dividend payout similar to a typical industrial firm.[28] Every year the firm invested in 6% real ROI projects—known information, which is a key advantage of the simulation. Time series data for the U.S. GDP Deflator and nominal interest rates were incorporated in order to produce simulated accounting statements for the firm from 1890 to 1994.[29] The calculated CFROIs each year matched the 6% real project ROIs. However, the time series of calculated Earnings/Book oscillated widely due to varying historical inflation rates. The important lesson here is that we should be wary of using ostensibly elegant mathematics divorced from the complexities of real-world accounting data.

FIGURE 4.11 Simulated Earnings/Book

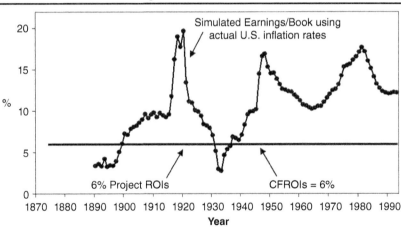

Source: A version of the above figure first appeared in Bartley J. Madden, 1996, "The CFROI Life Cycle," *Journal of Investing* 5(2): 10–20.

---

[28] Simulations have had limited use in finance and accounting. An exception is Paul M. Healy, Stewart C. Myers, and Christopher D. Howe, 2002, "R&D Accounting and the Tradeoff between Relevance and Objectivity," *Journal of Accounting Research* 40(3): 677–710.
[29] The actual inflation (and deflation) rates and corporate bond yields used to produce Figure 4.11 are displayed in Figure 2.3, Bartley J. Madden, 1999, *CFROI Valuation: A Total System Approach to Valuing the Firm.* Oxford: Butterworth-Heinemann.

Simulations can enable learning about complex systems in ways superior to purely mathematical approaches. For example, the economic life of tangible assets is straightforward, although quite complicated for intangible assets. Simulations may help develop quantitative metrics that tie outlays for intangibles to accounting data, to forecasts of net cash receipts, and ultimately to market valuations. Keep in mind that the conventional RONA used to approximate ROI is heavily influenced by the accounting life of tangible assets and even the choice of depreciation method. For example, RONA, which is net income plus after-tax interest divided by net assets, is impacted by the effect of depreciation charges (life of plant and equipment) on net income. Asset life also affects net plant via depreciation reserves and consequently impacts net assets. RONA masks the ROI impact of intangibles whose economic lives typically do not match the average life for tangible assets that is working behind the scenes in the RONA calculation. This measurement problem could be analyzed productively beginning with a creative description of a firm's typical project, similar to Figure 4.10, and incorporating outlays for both tangible and intangible assets, with particular attention to the lack of precision for the economic lives of intangibles.

Throughout this book CFROIs are displayed as a proxy for a firm's economic returns. Figure 4.12 shows the state-of-the-art inputs to the calculation of Amazon's 2013 CFROI, which was displayed as part of Amazon's track record earlier in this chapter.[30]

The CFROI of 12.0% is based on accounting data from Amazon's 2013 10-K report that provided the following variables as inputs to the ROI calculation: $38.581 billion of gross operating assets, which includes capitalized R&D of $14.910 billion; $4.539 billion of nondepreciating assets; life of depreciable assets of 5.4 years; and after-tax cash flow of $9.480 billion.

Free cash flow is popular for valuation models yet multiple definitions are used. An alternative is net cash receipts, which has a precise definition.

---

[30] Extensive, detailed explanations of the calculations involved with Amazon's 2013 CFROI are contained in David A. Holland and Bryant A. Matthews, 2018, *Beyond Earnings: Applying the HOLT CFROI and Economic Profit Framework*. Hoboken, NJ: John Wiley & Sons, pp. 63–103.

FIGURE 4.12 **Amazon's 2013 CFROI**

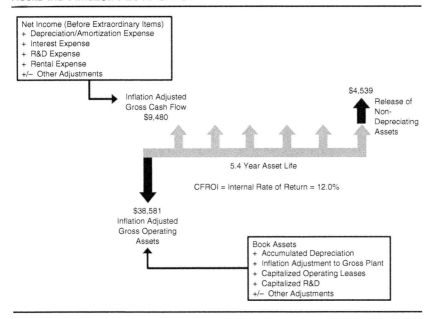

Source: Based on data from Credit Suisse HOLT global database.

Figure 4.13 displays how to calculate net cash receipts from the firm's perspective, and equivalently, from the capital suppliers' perspective.

As noted earlier, net cash receipts represent the numerator of the life-cycle valuation model (Figure 4.6). The denominator contains the investor discount rate. Substantial changes in a firm's stock price are almost always driven by changes in expectations for long-term net cash receipts. However, substantial changes in the overall stock market tend to be driven by discount rate changes.

During the 1970s, my partner at Callard Madden & Associates, Charles G. Callard, worked on connecting macroeconomic variables to forecasts of the stock market. In particular, Callard developed the concept of a demanded return (cost of equity capital) that compensated investors for the effects of inflation, nominal tax rate on capital gains, and dividend tax rates. The demanded return for maximum-tax-bracket investors was especially important since they owned a large portion of the U.S.

FIGURE 4.13 Two equivalent calculations of net cash receipts

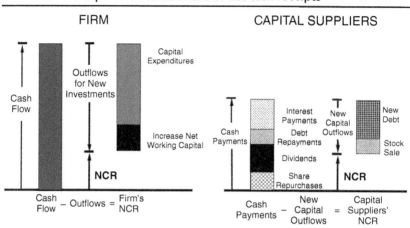

equity market at that time. My 1999 book, *CFROI Valuation: A Total System Approach to Valuing the Firm*, includes a description of Callard's discount rate insights.[31] Forecasting changes in the demanded return by maximum-tax-bracket investors, keyed to legislated changes in tax rates for dividends and especially capital gains, has proven useful for forecasting stock market reactions to tax law changes. One might think that the decline in percentage ownership of U.S. equities by maximum-tax-bracket investors due to ownership gains by tax-free institutions would have eroded the usefulness of this approach. The counterpoint is that changes in personal tax rates on investment income (especially capital gains) significantly impact venture capital and dynamism (as described in Chapter 1)—both of which are critically important to economic growth.

BETTER ESTIMATES OF THE INVESTOR DISCOUNT RATE

Callard and I chose not to use the CAPM/Beta cost of capital. Instead, we developed a database that contained monitored net cash receipt forecasts

---

[31] See Chapter 4 of Bartley J. Madden, 1999, *CFROI Valuation: A Total System Approach to Valuing the Firm*. Oxford: Butterworth-Heinemann.

for a large number of publicly traded firms. At a point in time each firm has a known total market value via its stock price and an estimated market value of its debt. Each firm had security analysts' forecasts of near-term earnings and forecasted, long-term net cash receipts driven by fade rates for both CFROIs and reinvestment rates. A key element is *standardized fade forecasts based on firm characteristics.* The investor discount rate is the market-implied discount rate, which equates a present value of forecast net cash receipts to the known total market value for the firm. Importantly, in contrast to a CAPM/Beta or similar calculations, *this discount rate is attuned to the life-cycle valuation model's forecasting process for net cash receipts.*

Empirical analyses of a firm's fade patterns led to standardized fade forecasts.[32] For example, consider two firms earning the same above-cost-of-capital economic returns. All else equal, the firm with a higher reinvestment rate tends to fade faster; and, all else equal, if one firm has much less variation in its annual economic returns, it tends to fade at a slower rate. The former with its high growth quickly attracts competitors due to the size of the market opportunity and the latter with its reduced variation reflects high managerial skill. Firms currently earning approximately the cost of capital exhibit zero fade on average.

Fade rates, CFROIs, reinvestment rates, and the investor discount rate coupled with a firm's asset base constitute a *valuation system* continuously improving beginning with the Callard Madden days. This improvement process has been accelerated by Credit Suisse HOLT with its global database covering over 20,000 publicly traded firms worldwide. For example, more accurate CFROI calculations lead to improved life-cycle track records and sharpened calibration of historical fade rates that in

---

[32] For early empirical work on fade rates see Bartley J. Madden, 1996, "The CFROI Life Cycle," *Journal of Investing* 5(2): 10–20. This early work was later reproduced by Credit Suisse HOLT using more rigorous econometric techniques. Other empirical studies include: E. F. Fama and K. R. French, 2000, "Forecasting Profitability and Earnings," *Journal of Business* 73(2): 161–175; Robert R. Wiggins and Timothy W. Ruefli, 2002, "Sustained Competitive Advantage: Temporal Dynamics and the Incidence and Persistence of Superior Economic Performance," *Organization Science* 13(1): 82–105; Robert R. Wiggins and Timothy W. Ruefli, 2005, "Schumpeter's Ghost: Is Hyper-competition Making the Best of Times Shorter," *Strategic Management Journal* 26(10): 887–911; Jens Kengelbach, Hans le Grand, and Alexander Roos, 2007, "Performance of Abnormal Returns and Possible Applications for Company Valuation," SSRN working paper ssrn.com/abstract=1002041.

turn improve both the assignment of forecast fade rates, and ultimately, better estimates of the investor discount rate.

Figure 4.14 uses the knowledge-building loop introduced in Chapter 2 to illustrate a process that has been in use for decades to improve the components of the life-cycle valuation model. The key criterion is to improve the historical tracking of a firm's warranted values versus actual stock prices. A result of this process is that estimates of the investor discount rate improve over time principally due to better estimates of future net cash receipts for firms in the global database.

The *purpose* is to improve the life-cycle track records for individual firms and the calculation routines that implement the life-cycle valuation model, as well as to gain insights in general about how firms create or dissipate value. The *worldview* employed relies on the life-cycle framework. *Perceptions* consist of observations of life-cycle track records and value charts. Tracking of warranted values (via the life-cycle valuation model) versus actual stock prices is enabled by the value charts, which plot actual stock prices versus warranted values using standardized fade forecasts based on

FIGURE 4.14 **Knowledge building and the life-cycle framework**

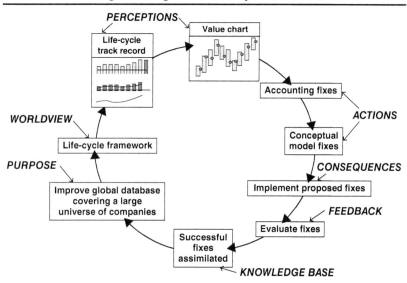

known firm characteristics at points in time. The resulting deviations, when significant and persistent, signal a problem to be investigated, especially if a group of firms (typically in the same industry) all experience either a similar overtracking or undertracking.

For example, in the early Callard Madden work, warranted values of firms with accelerated depreciation were consistently well below actual stock prices. This problem was easy to fix. The CFROIs were too low because the asset life utilized in the CFROI calculation was too short. The economic fix was to use straight-line-depreciation life. A problem addressed later was the appropriate treatment of firms with high R&D expenditures. This resulted in a conceptual model fix, that is, capitalize R&D as part of the firm's asset base, thereby improving both CFROIs and reinvestment rates. Problems are the source of improvements to the valuation system (model). The *actions* of developing solutions to perceived problems have *consequences* (i.e., implementation of proposed fixes). Finally, *feedback* from evaluating the extent of improvement in actual versus warranted values and the soundness of the economic logic will determine if the proposed fixes are adopted as part of the *knowledge base.*

On the issue of estimating discount rates, the objective is to quantify the investor discount rate for firms with specified characteristics. A plausible approach is to construct a regression equation where the dependent variable is a firm's market-implied discount rate that equates its total market value to the present value of forecasted net cash receipts. Note that the net cash receipts are driven by CFROIs, which use after-tax cash flows that benefit from interest payments being tax deductible. Hence, the market-derived discount rate represents a total firm cost of capital like the traditional WACC (weighted average cost of capital), but differs from conventional WACC, which puts the benefit of the interest payment tax deductibility into a lower debt cost.

The HOLT regression equation uses financial leverage as an independent variable to reflect the increased chances of financial distress at higher debt loads that are not reflected in the net cash receipt forecast. In addition, the smaller the firm, the higher the transactions costs to accumulate an ownership position. To compensate investors (especially institutional money management firms that buy large positions), it is reasonable that they should demand a higher return. So, firm size is also an independent variable. One could argue that the stability of larger firms is not fully expressed by the fade forecasts and is reflected in the size variable. This regression equation was applied to the Credit Suisse HOLT global database and generated the investor discount rate data displayed in Figure 4.9. This chart reflects a standard firm (i.e., a medium-sized, industrial firm with typical financial leverage).

Although this approach keyed to financial leverage and size has proven useful for many years, it certainly will be improved with further research.[33] For example, research that provides a deeper understanding of the interplay between net cash receipts and demanded returns may well lead to a reconfiguration of the independent variables. The key point is that the forecasting procedure for net cash receipts is intimately involved with estimating market-implied discount rates. A fruitful path to improve estimates of the investor discount rate is to *improve the forecasts of future net cash receipts to better reflect investor expectations,* instead of relying solely on advanced econometric techniques applied to readily available historical financial data.

The next chapter addresses critical issues concerning intangibles, including brand values. In addition, the advantages of the life-cycle framework are shown for dealing with the root causes of long-term shareholder returns that are significantly greater than, or less than, the general market.

---

[33] Bryant Matthews of Credit Suisse HOLT has hypothesized that the financial leverage variable is a useful proxy for a firm's life-cycle stage and its associated risk The chief aspects of this risk are technological obsolescence and financial distress. Late-stage firms (see the mature and failing business model stages illustrated in Figure 4.2) have higher financial leverage and less viable long-term business prospects compared to early-stage firms earning above-cost-of-capital economic returns. This is arguably a non-diversifiable risk.

5

INTANGIBLE ASSETS, BRANDS, AND SHAREHOLDER RETURNS

The failure of the accounting system to reflect the value of these [intangible] assets in financial reports, to properly account for their impact on firms' operations, and to provide investors with information about the exposure of these assets to threats of infringement and disruption, is a major cause of accounting's relevance lost. How ironic (or sad) that largely irrelevant assets to companies' growth and competitive edge—like inventory, accounts receivable, or plant and machinery—remain prominently displayed on corporate balance sheets, whereas patents, brands, IT, or unique business processes are accounting MIAs.

—Baruch Lev and Feng Gu[1]

Brands build resonance through a hierarchy of meaning that roughly parallels Maslow's hierarchy of needs: functional, emotional, social, and cultural. Unless a brand can ensure that it is conveying the lower levels of meaning, it will fail to achieve the higher levels. ... If a brand is intended to

[1] Baruch Lev and Feng Gu, 2015, *The End of Accounting and the Path Forward for Investors and Managers.* Hoboken, NJ: John Wiley & Sons, p. 81.

create sustainable competitive advantage, then that brand had better be well differentiated. … Think about the brands that are typically cited by marketers as the ones they admire: Apple, Virgin, Facebook, Disney, Coke, Audi, Jack Daniel's. These brands are all well differentiated; they set the trends for their category or transcend it, and they act differently and stand out from the competition.

—Nigel Hollis[2]

This chapter extends the life-cycle framework to provide a logical and intuitive understanding of the relationship between shareholder returns (see Figure 5.1) and the market over the long term. However, a prerequisite to analyzing shareholder returns in today's New Economy is an insightful understanding of connectivity-enabled innovation, networks, platforms, and the increased importance of intangible assets (e.g., brands).

When expenditures are incurred that yield benefits beyond the accounting period being measured, these outlays represent intangible assets. Examples include expenditures for R&D, building a brand, supply

FIGURE 5.1 **Shareholder returns**

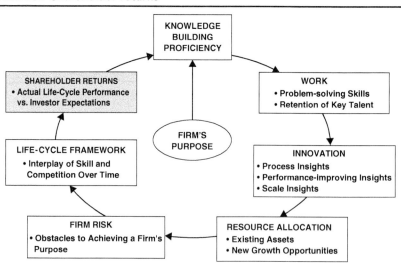

[2]Nigel Hollis, 2013, *Brand Premium: How Smart Brands Make More Money*. New York: Palgrave Macmillan. pp. 95 and 105–106.

chain software, customer recommendation algorithms used by Amazon and Netflix, expansion of lean manufacturing expertise, platforms that greatly expand their value as more users join, and much more. The measurement challenge is in estimating the useful life over which benefits accrue from the intangible expenditure.

Intangibles play an important role in the generation of a firm's life-cycle performance. When the actual life-cycle performance is significantly higher (lower) than investor expectations, the result is excess positive (negative) shareholder returns as noted in Figure 5.1.

THE NEW ECONOMY AND CONNECTIVITY-ENABLED BUSINESS MODELS

We begin by focusing on what is fundamentally the same principle for economic growth in the New Economy as it was in the Old Economy: value creation depends upon the quality of ideas. Investing in noninnovative ways, such as building more horse-drawn carriages, did little to improve the standard of living and job creation compared to the development of the automobile. Another example is building houses with electricity, lights, heating and air conditioning compared to building houses containing nothing more than a roof, walls, and a fireplace. In both instances, the builders committed resources that might have alternatively been used for immediate consumption and instead made a capital investment in order to receive greater benefits in the future. But the quality of the ideas incorporated in the modern house is the critical difference that spurs innovation-induced economic growth and a rising standard of living. This resonates with this book's theme that a firm's knowledge-building proficiency—its competency in generating high-quality ideas of practical use in creating value—is the dominant determinant of its long-term survival and prosperity.

Economists and accountants would conclude that a capital asset was created with both the primitive house and the modern house. On one hand, it is easy to visualize the important ideas incorporated in the modern house. On the other hand, the primitive house also incorporated important ideas about transforming trees into usable lumber and creating and using nails and hammers in order to build a structure that offers shelter. This way of looking at investment suggests that, fundamentally, capital is embedded ideas. Ideas are no less important in the Old Economy as the New Economy.

Accountants calculate balance sheets and income statements using rules to compute assets and then deduct liabilities to determine what remains for the firm's capital owners (debt and equity). In the Old Economy ideas principally were used to create tangible assets such as oil reserves (note that ideas for internal combustion engines enabled oil reserves to become valuable), machinery and related equipment in factories, and so on. These assets had verifiable useful lives and the accountants could deduct depreciation expenses on the income statement and directly compute net assets (net of accumulated depreciation) on the balance sheet. The accounting objective is to match revenues with related expenses over time, yielding a reliable measure of earnings and assets. In the Old Economy most assets were tangible with verifiable useful lives and could be depreciated accordingly. But in the New Economy, mostly intangible assets are critical for value creation and, as previously noted, estimated useful lives for these intangibles are exceedingly difficult to estimate. The result is big problems not only for the accounting rule-makers who require verifiable data, but also for managers and investors who use accounting data for decision-making.

The above discussion on the fundamental role of ideas in economic growth connects to Paul Romer's thinking highlighted in Chapter 1. Romer points out that physical stuff is limited but ideas are limitless and most (nonpatented) ideas can be distributed at essentially zero cost, which is not fully appreciated by neoclassical economics. Sharing ideas is an important part of the New Economy. In addition, the Internet and related connectivity technology offer new opportunities to create value which were unavailable in the Old (pre-Internet) Economy. Some of these opportunities disrupt Old Economy firms and create substantial market value for the disruptor firms accompanied by shareholder returns that greatly exceed the general market.

A particularly important way to create significant value in the New Economy is winning the competitive battle to secure a dominant platform that efficiently makes connections that were previously either unavailable or expensive in time and money. Internet search via Google's search engine (platform) connects the users with information. Ebay's platform connects buyers and sellers. Amazon's platform connects consumers to products that previously required visits to physical stores.

Platforms facilitate network connections. The two primary network effects are: (1) incremental benefit to existing users for each new user joining the network, and (2) diminishing marginal costs to serve new customers. In contrast to a linear business model (i.e., one where a linear supply chain is used), a successful platform/network business scales more efficiently since revenues can rise faster than costs for an extended time period.

> When a linear business gains a customer, it adds only one new relationship—one buyer of products or services. When a platform adds a new user, that person doesn't add just a single relationship but rather a potential relationship with all of the platform's users. In other words, platforms grow exponentially rather than linearly. As a result, platform business models are far more cost-effective and higher scale than the old, linear models they are replacing ... it's still possible to build a valuable linear business, but its competitive advantage often evaporates quickly as products get commoditized and competitors copy features—leaving the originator continually scrambling to replace those strengths. Features are easy to emulate; networks aren't. Products get commoditized, platforms don't.[3]

In the Old Economy, firms created the most value by controlling physical resources and/or supply chains with factories that made products that were then distributed to other firms that sold to the end customers. Leading Old Economy firms scaled physical assets to gain efficiency and market share.

---

[3] Alex Moazed and Nicholas L. Johnson, 2016, *Modern Monopolies: What It Takes to Dominate the 21st Century Economy*. New York: St. Martin's Press, pp. 31 and 212.

In the New Economy, leading firms scale up their platforms by connecting more and more users.

For instance, the value of Facebook's platform to its users increases exponentially as the number of Facebook users increase. The more drivers who sign up with Uber, the more valuable its platform is to consumers needing to connect with a driver. Uber's efficiency relates to its avoidance of owning tangible assets, since drivers own their vehicles. The market value of Uber depends upon satisfying customers in need of a ride, that is, scaling up both its drivers and the consumers who automatically use the Uber driver app on their cellphones. More and more firms create value, like Uber, through their intangible assets.

EMPIRICAL EVIDENCE ABOUT INTANGIBLE ASSETS

There is less uncertainty about achieving benefits over the economic life of *tangible* assets such as machinery. However, *intangible* assets typically involve considerable uncertainty as to both the magnitude and duration (life) of future benefits. The DNA of accounting rule-makers compels them to require verifiable amounts on accounting statements, which helps to explain the exceptionally slow pace of adoption of rules to capitalize and amortize intangibles.

In the United States, the Financial Accounting Standards Board (FASB) ruled that technologically proven software development costs should be capitalized. Interestingly, acquired R&D (verified transaction) becomes an intangible asset recorded on the balance sheet; yet, similar internally developed R&D must be expensed. Outside the United States, the International Accounting Standards Board (IASB) controls the IFRS (International Financial Reporting Standards) standards which currently allow capitalization of the "D" part of R&D expenditures given certain conditions (IAS 38).

It is informative to briefly summarize empirical research about the importance of intangibles for the firm's financial performance and valuation. The bottom line is that a compelling logical rationale exists for capitalizing and amortizing these expenditures when the assigned economic lives are defensible. Decades of empirical studies (briefly summarized below) conclude that future benefits accrue from expenditures for intangibles and that the stock market rewards these types of investments. Of considerable importance to investors analyzing a firm's track record of financial performance is that full expensing for firms with substantial expenditures for intangibles yields return-on-capital metrics that are biased in complex ways.[4] (This is why R&D is capitalized for the calculation of CFROIs, as noted in Chapter 4.) In addition to capitalization and amortization of intangibles, valuable information can be presented by management via supplementary disclosure; for example, information about the potential scalability of a firm's intangible assets is critical for investors analyzing the risk and reward from investing in intangibles-intensive firms.

Academic research has documented the economically consequential link between profitability and market valuation with intangible assets.[5] Early academic research found that

> brands impact a firm's market value; R&D, and patents in particular, are useful predictors of future shareholder returns; asymmetric knowledge (insiders versus outside investors) about a firm's intangibles leads to substantial insider trading profits and higher costs of capital (all else equal, higher bid-ask spreads for trading stocks) for intangibles-intensive firms.[6]

Reviewing empirical studies on intangibles leaves the distinct impression that the researchers are formulating hypotheses that logically mirror common sense. For example, especially large increases in R&D expenditures subsequently tended to lead to profitability gains and positive

---

[4] Baruch Lev, Bharat Sarath, and Theodore Sougiannis, 2005, "R&D Reporting Biases and Their Consequences," *Contemporary Accounting Research* 22(4): 977–1026.

[5] Anne Wyatt, 2008, "What Financial and Non-financial Information on Intangibles Is Value Relevant? A Review of the Evidence," *Accounting and Business Research* 38(3): 217–256. For a particularly comprehensive review, see Daniel Zeghal and Anis Maaloul, 2011, "The Accounting Treatment of Intangibles—A Critical Review of the Literature," *Accounting Forum* (35): 262–274. The importance of accounting for scale in regression studies focused on the value relevance of intangibles was demonstrated in Mustafa Ciftci, Masako Darrough, and Raj Mashruwala, 2014, "Value Relevance of Accounting Information for Intangible-Intensive Industries and the Impact of Scale: The U.S. Evidence," *European Accounting Review* 23(2): 199–226.

[6] These findings are taken from John Hand and Baruch Lev, eds., 2003, *Intangible Assets: Values, Measures, and Risks.* Oxford: Oxford University Press.

above-market returns to shareholders.[7] Organizational (intangible) capital developed by talented employees tends to be reflected in efficient business processes and is associated with significant excess shareholder returns.[8]

As to employee satisfaction, management can expect to retain key employees when they work in a culture that supports win-win partnerships enabling employees to directly connect their efforts to deliver value to customers and to making the world a better place. With such a culture, job satisfaction can offer more motivation than monetary compensation. Using a large-scale proprietary database of employees' compensation and employment duration at specific firms, research has shown that when "pivotal" employees (measured by percentage pay progression) leave firms at a fast pace, a firm's CFROIs (cash-flow-return-on-investment) subsequently decline, whereas high retention rates of pivotal employees subsequently led to higher CFROIs.[9] Talented employees are an exceedingly important intangible asset.[10]

Intangibles research clarifies stock market valuations for many types of firms. The high market-to-book ratios of firms in the wireless communications industry are influenced by advertising and especially radio spectrum licenses (intangible asset).[11] Consider firms with large information technology (IT) outlays. The performance of these IT-intensive firms

---

[7] Allan C. Eberhart, William F. Maxwell, and Akhtar R. Siddique, 2004, "An Examination of Long-Term Abnormal Stock Returns and Operating Performance Following R&D Increases," *Journal of Finance* 59(2): 623–650.

[8] Andrea L. Eisfeldt and Dimitris Papanikolaou, 2013, "Organization Capital and the Cross-section of Expected Returns," *Journal of Finance* 68(4): 1365–1406.

[9] Mark C. Ubelhart, 2009, "An Economic View of the Impact of Human Capital on Firm Performance and Valuation." In Rawley Thomas and Benton Gup, eds., 2009, *The Valuation Handbook: Valuation Techniques from Today's Top Practitioners.* Hoboken, NJ: John Wiley & Sons. This research is discussed in Mark L. Frigo and Mark C. Ubelhart, 2015, "CFO+CHRO=POWER PAIR." *Strategic Finance*, November 2015. For a comprehensive literature review of how human capital impacts firm performance see Aaron Bernstein and Larry Beeferman, 2015, "The Materiality of Human Capital to Corporate Financial Performance." New York: IIRC Institute.

[10] A study addressed this question: Are differences in inventor productivity due to differences in inventors' skills or differences in the capabilities of the firms where they were employed? The conclusion was: "Our estimates suggest human capital is 4 to 5 times more important than firm capabilities for explaining the variance in inventor productivity." Ajay Bhaskarbhatla, Deepak Hegde, and Thomas Peeters, 2017, "Human Capital, Firm Capabilities, and Innovation." SSRN working paper abstract=3081933.

[11] Mark Klock and Pamela Megna, 2000, "Measuring and Valuing Intangible Capital in the Wireless Communications Industry," *Quarterly Review of Economics and Finance* 40(4): 519–532.

was impacted by the degree of alignment between IT outlays and IT capabilities.[12] In addition, explanatory details about the customer base for subscription-based firms helps explain market valuations.[13]

Outside of R&D expenditures, the main source of investments in intangible assets is specific components to a firm's selling, general, and administrative (SG&A) expenditures. The predictability of future earnings and shareholder returns is improved by dissecting SG&A expenditures into pure operating expenses versus outlays for intangibles.[14] Interestingly, after management received long-term equity incentives, increases soon followed in those SG&A components tied to future economic benefits.[15]

An important conclusion from this summary of intangibles empirical research is that in the New Economy, competitive advantage, and excess shareholder returns depend on hard-to-duplicate intangible assets. One example of a hard-to-duplicate, and highly valuable, intangible asset is a firm's unique brand that ideally makes an emotional connection with consumers.

BRANDS IMPACT A FIRM'S MARKET VALUE

Research on brands ranges from exploring a conviction that brands are best viewed as existing in the minds of consumers to explicit quantitative estimates of point-in-time values for brands. As an example, Starbucks sold to Nestle the right to use the Starbucks name on Nestle coffee products for $7 billion, which strongly suggests that the Starbucks brand is a uniquely valuable asset owned by Starbucks. To be sure, a brand does not have the

---

[12] Sinan Aral and Peter Weil, 2007, "IT Assets, Organizational Capabilities, and Firm Performance: How Resource Allocations and Organizational Differences Explain Performance Variation," *Organization Science* 18(5): 763–780.

[13] Massimiliano Bonacchi, Kalin Kolev, and Baruch Lev, 2013, "Customer Franchise—A Hidden, Yet Crucial Asset," *Contemporary Accounting Research* 32(3): 1024–1393.

[14] Luminita Enache and Anup Srivastava, 2018, "Should Intangible Investments Be Reported Separately or Commingled with Operating Expenses? New Evidence," *Management Science* 64(7): 3446–3468 and Annete Ptok, Rupinder P. Jindal, and Werner Reinartz, 2018, "Selling, General, and Administrative (SG&A) Expense-based Metrics in Marketing: Conceptual and Measurement Challenges," *Journal of Academy of Marketing Science* 46(6): 987–1011.

[15] Ragiv Banker, Rong Huang, and Ram Natarajan, 2011, "Equity Incentives and Long-term Value Created by SG&A Expenditures," *Contemporary Accounting Research* 28(3): 794–830.

easily measured value of cash on the balance sheet. However, a brand value is assigned when a firm acquires a brand as part of an acquisition. Nevertheless, accounting rules currently prohibit internally developed brands from being recorded as intangible assets thereby distorting the cross-comparison of performance metrics that use as-reported balance sheets of firms with significant brands.

On February 22, 2019, Kraft Heinz's stock price dropped 27% as investors reacted to management's lowering of expectations of future earnings, and especially, the news that the firm incurred a $15 billion goodwill impairment charge related to the perceived values of Kraft and Oscar Mayer brands. Noteworthy, Kraft Heinz management had been significantly reducing investment outlays for its brands while consumers were moving away from highly processed products and toward fresh food. Brands impact a firm's market value. Brands are important intangible assets.

What is a brand? A brand consists of one or more assumptions held by consumers about the rewards from buying the product. The stronger the assumptions and the higher the anticipated rewards, the more valuable is the brand. Consumer assumptions influence how the product is perceived by consumers and the premium they are willing to pay. With the most valuable brands, consumers emotionally bond with the product, believing that it excels in delivering what is important to them. Noteworthy was Frank Sinatra's instructions to be buried with a bottle of Jack Daniel's whiskey. Brown-Forman, the firm that owns the Jack Daniel's brand, subsequently created a new whiskey, Sinatra Select. Brown-Forman management has successfully spread its brand message—"Charcoal mellowed. Drop by drop." They have nurtured a wide consumer franchise from bankers to bikers, affirmed in a notable advertisement: "Jack Daniel's—served in fine establishments and questionable joints."

The energy drink Red Bull was launched in 1987 and targeted consumers who needed an energy pickup to stay sharp and on task. The Austrian firm Red Bull GmbH pioneered the energy drink market and built the brand by linking Red Bull to extreme sports that require high energy and a sharp mind. The brand slogan is: "Red Bull gives you wings." This product illustrates a hugely successful marketing innovation focused on building an enduring connection (a bond) with highly specific consumers across countries and cultures.

> You cannot create passion by appealing to all people equally. If you stand for something, some people will love you and some will hate you, but the ones who love you will buy your brand and pay a premium for it. This no-compromise attitude extends to the Red Bull business model. Their focus is single-minded: no diversification, no licensing, no brand merchandising, and no umbrella branding. How many brands can you think of that lost their way by trying to spread beyond their core positioning and target group? I suspect Red Bull is one of the very few not to try.[16]

Building a stellar brand name such as Jack Daniel's or Red Bull entails much more than simply a recognizable name. Who gets inspired by Yahoo or General Motors?

But at one time, countless American consumers aspired to be part of the GM family and work their way up the ladder of GM brand choices, starting with the value-conscious Chevrolet, the higher quality Oldsmobile, and on to the luxurious Cadillac and its image of well-heeled prosperity. Clearly, maintaining a brand is just as difficult as building one. A reasonable question now is: What do these GM brands stand for in the eyes of consumers?

On one hand, when firms with highly valued brands miss a major technological change, their brands can easily lose their emotional connection to consumers. Blockbuster, BlackBerry, and Kodak are prime examples. On the other hand, when a firm originates a new experience that clearly fulfills consumer needs, it has an opportunity to create a brand that suggests this firm "owns this space." Such an opportunity was seized by Peloton Interactive, the home exercise equipment firm that brought consumers a digitally connected stationary bike. Their brand name cleverly refers to those cyclists

---

[16]Nigel Hollis, 2008, *The Global Brand: How to Create and Develop Lasting Brand Value in the World Market*. New York: Palgrave Macmillan, p. 38

at the front of the pack known as "peloton." Users of Peloton bikes are digitally connected to a "virtual pack" and the brand name resonates with the community experience of riding (and competing) with other cyclists, not just solo exercising.

Brands and R&D have similar measurement challenges given their characteristics as intangible assets. Recall in Chapter 4 the emphasis on the importance of capitalization and amortization of R&D for R&D-intensive firms (e.g., biopharmaceutical firms). Capitalization of R&D is needed to improve one's understanding of a firm's track record, specifically its economic returns, which become biased in complex ways when substantial investments in intangible assets are ignored. In addition, past reinvestment rates (asset growth rates) are misleading when calculated using unadjusted accounting data.

There is considerable current interest in the inclusion of brand "values" on balance sheets. This is partly due to the recognizable impact of brands on a firm's market value. But note that brands are an *integral part of a business system that generates future cash flows*. An explicit estimate of a brand value can falsely imply a stand-alone value that can be monetized independently of the firm currently using the brand. For example, all else equal, a firm with highly skilled management will utilize a brand better than a much-less-skilled management and generate higher future cash flows. Nevertheless, supplementary information about brands can help investors make long-term forecasts of the firm as a total system in order to calculate warranted valuations.

Consider the ubiquitous automobile brand Chrysler. Daimler-Benz and Chrysler managements announced a "merger of equals" in 1998, although in reality Daimler-Benz actually acquired Chrysler and controlled the new firm. This combination proved to be a financial disaster and illustrates the lack of skill by Daimler-Benz management in both planning and execution. They failed to effectively use the Chrysler brand and sold Chrysler in 2007.

The next section provides a conceptual roadmap for handling intangible assets such as brands, which benefit over time from outlays that are expensed even though they yield future benefits.

A CONCEPTUAL ROADMAP FOR HANDLING INTANGIBLE ASSETS

There is substantial ongoing intellectual effort focused on intangibles in general, and R&D and brands in particular. Nevertheless, after decades of research documenting the value-relevancy of intangibles, very little has been accomplished by way of useful accounting rules. In fact, the FASB's rule that mandated expensing of R&D was shown to negatively impact market valuations of R&D intensive firms.[17] It is time for the accounting rule-makers to think differently and adopt a more holistic perspective. Let's begin with what different constituents (i.e., accounting rule-makers, management, and investors) ideally want.

The primary objectives of accounting rule-makers are:

- Match revenues with expenses so that "true" earnings can be calculated.
- Provide useful and reliable information to users of accounting statements.

Managements seeking to optimize long-term value creation should want to:

- Avoid business-as-usual, automatic funding of business units and related projects and be vigilant for the need to adapt to a changing environment in order to at least earn the cost of capital over the long term.
- Improve decision making by adjusting, as needed, accounting-based performance metrics to reflect the economic reality of long-term benefits from R&D expenditures and selected selling, general, and administrative (SG&A) expenditures.
- Disproportionately direct investment outlays to the most compelling value-creation opportunities.

---

[17] Urooj Khan, Bin Li, Shivaram Rajgopal, and Mohan Venkatachalam, 2018, "Do the FASB's Standards Add Shareholder Value?" *Accounting Review* 93(2): 209–247.

The primary objectives of knowledgeable investors, including active (as opposed to passive index investors) money managers, are:

- For a firm of interest, articulate a range of plausible forecasts of future performance that links to valuation (e.g., optimistic, most likely, and pessimistic).
- Compare these forecasts to market expectations implied in a firm's current stock price.
- Evaluate a firm's upside potential and the downside risk in order to make buy/hold/sell decisions.

While the above objectives may seem highly attuned to the specific needs of each constituent, there are five principles that can be applied to the mutual benefit of rule-makers, managements, and investors:

1. A firm's key financial performance metric is its ROI (return-on-investment) versus the cost of capital.
2. An ROI compares what is given up (the *historical cost* of resources consumed) to what is received (cash inflows).
3. The historical cost of assets should be preserved on a firm's balance sheet.
4. An asset's (e.g., a brand's) estimated market value or relevant data for estimating an asset's contribution to future cash flows should be supplementary disclosure that complements the historical-cost-based balance sheets.
5. For practical purposes, the usefulness of accounting data depends upon how well it assists analyzing the warranted value of a firm or a business unit. This necessarily involves a valuation model and a related track record.

The above five principles are offered as a beginning point in developing a conceptual roadmap for intangibles. Furthermore, we should constructively challenge two subtle assumptions that rarely are questioned. First is that intangibles are an accounting problem and the complete solution needs to be provided by the accounting rule-makers. Actually, it is a problem involving accounting and valuation, which are inextricably connected. Second is the assumption that the handling of intangibles should be strictly guided by the goal of true earnings wherein revenues match expenses. Adherence to true earnings as the ultimate goal constricts the array of other mechanisms for handling intangibles, such as adjustments to forecast fade rates.

Before delving into discussing a way forward, let's look at the past and understand why so little has been accomplished for handling intangibles. Baruch Lev and his coauthors have published a large number of empirical studies that yield genuine insights about intangibles. He makes the following astute observations:

> I believe that the major obstacle for an accounting-for-intangibles change is the absence of change-incentives of the two major accounting constituents, or "influencers": corporate managers and public accountants. … My sense is that executives' opposition to intangibles' capitalization reflects their reluctance to present on the balance sheet assets (capitalized intangibles) whose value can be impaired, or even vanish when disrupted by new technologies. Investors' consequent questions about why the intangibles were not properly protected against disruption, or even why the investments were made in the first place will surely be embarrassing. Better, from managers' perspective, to expense all intangibles immediately, thereby leaving no trace of them in the financial reports. … Public accountants too seem unenthusiastic about changing the accounting for intangibles. … With intangibles' capitalization, auditors will have to periodically assess the viability of the capitalized intangibles and whether they were impaired, thereby enhancing their responsibility for these hard-to-value assets. Why create additional liability concerns?[18]

The above reality check suggests that supplementary disclosure will likely play an important role in the future regarding more extensive handling of intangibles.

---

[18] Baruch Lev, 2018, "Ending the Accounting-for-Intangibles Status Quo," *European Accounting Review*, http://doi.org/10.1080/09638180.2018.152165 28(1): 1–24.

It is worthwhile to review an episode of the rule-makers, in this case the U.S. Securities and Exchange Commission (SEC), aggressively implementing rules to compel management to report more "relevant" information. During the high-inflation environment of the 1970s, the SEC mandated that 1,000 of the largest U.S. firms estimate how much it would cost to replace their assets, and then compute depreciation charges based on replacement cost. The logic was that this would be more informative to investors than historical cost accounting. This proved to be a hugely expensive mistake. Why?

Returning to the life-cycle valuation model reviewed in Chapter 4, the value of the firm is comprised of the value of its existing assets and its future investments. Management should seek the best opportunities for future investments, which may or may not be reinvestment in existing assets. Neglecting this management guidepost leads one to conclude that depreciation charges are automatically reinvested in order to maintain the firm as a "going concern." With this view, it seemed logical to the SEC that the high-inflation environment necessitated depreciation charges to be estimated based on higher replacement cost.

The SEC made two major mistakes. One concerns economic performance measurement and the other concerns valuation. First, from the *investors' perspective* the "real" or inflation-adjusted economic return of an investment uses cash outflows and cash inflows that actually occurred, and adjusts them into units of constant purchasing power via the GDP Deflator. Estimated replacement costs are unnecessary. Second, knowledgeable investors forecast future net cash receipts, and many are assisted by using life-cycle-based forecasts of economic returns and reinvestment rates. Such forecasts should anticipate how management will adapt to change, including the pernicious effects of inflation. The role of accounting data is to provide useful information and not to make assumptions about management's future investment decisions. For example, with the accelerating use of battery-powered electric vehicles today, is it not misleading to assume gas stations will be replaced in their current configuration. The key point is that the strict adherence to a notion of "true earnings" blinds accounting rule-makers from developing a holistic perspective that would include the role of investors in forecasting future cash flows.

A holistic or systems perspective suggests that the preferred way forward will involve experimentation and learning that should be facilitated by, and also inform, the accounting rule-makers. Figure 5.2 outlines an evolution-ary path that exploits the usefulness of experimentation and feedback. This process returns full circle to the knowledge-building loop of Figure 2.1, which is central to every chapter in this book.

As shown in Figure 5.2, SG&A and R&D expenditures that qualify as intangible assets should be classified into two groups. The first group includes expenditures that involve economic lives that can reasonably be estimated and these expenditures should be capitalized. Such intangibles confer ownership rights to the firm and are expected to generate future benefits. Consequently, their estimated economic lives can be defended

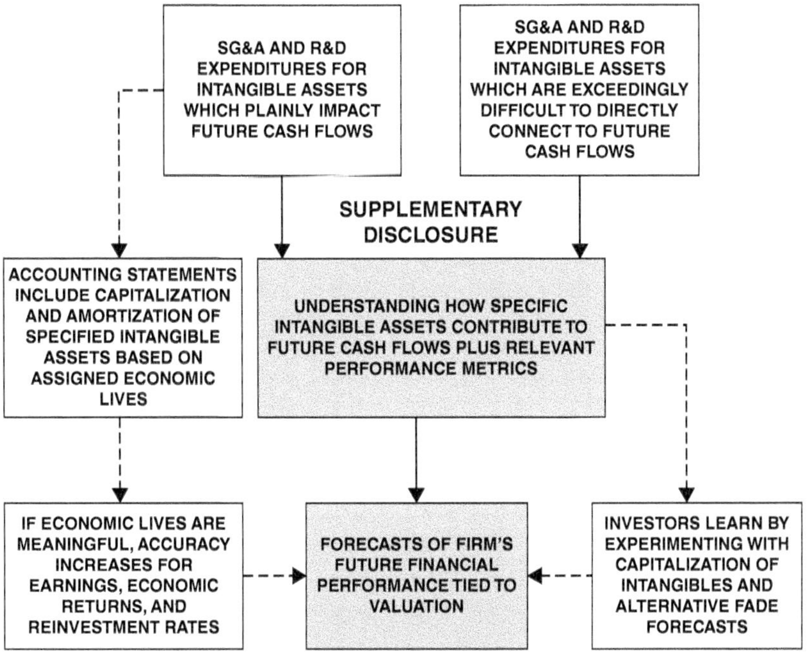

FIGURE 5.2 An evolutionary path for quantifying the value of intangibles

as reasonable attempts to add relevance to the accounting data. Their capitalization and amortization would incorporate management's intimate knowledge of these assets, leading to more accurate calculations of earnings, economic returns, and reinvestment rates. The second group includes the remaining expenditures that would not be capitalized but rather expensed. Both groups of intangibles warrant supplementary disclosure that assists investors in analyzing firms' track records and making forecasts that help to quantify the value effect from scenarios ranging from optimistic and most likely to pessimistic. Importantly, investors could experiment with capitalization and also adjust their *long-term fade forecasts* of economic returns and reinvestment rates to incorporate their overall assessment of a firm's prospects, including its intangible assets such as brands. Figure 5.3 highlights this process. This notion of investor experimentation is not an abstract idea. Rather, professional money management organizations, including those that subscribe to the Credit Suisse HOLT global database that provides the data for the life-cycle track records in this book, are well equipped to both experiment with capitalization and related economic life assumptions and translate their research analyses into fade forecasts for firms. Increased supplementary disclosure would further boost such efforts.

FIGURE 5.3 Intangible assets and fade rates

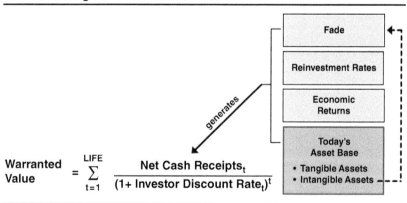

$$\text{Warranted Value} = \sum_{t=1}^{\text{LIFE}} \frac{\text{Net Cash Receipts}_t}{(1+ \text{Investor Discount Rate}_t)^t}$$

The benefits of experimentation for handling intangibles extend to management. The next section describes how this can be accomplished.

INTEGRATED REPORTS, LIFE-CYCLE REVIEWS, AND INTANGIBLES

There is an accelerating trend for firms to publish Integrated Reports that recognize that, over the long term, shareholder interests should be aligned with other stakeholders. This is consistent with the four-part definition of the purpose of the firm discussed in Chapter 1. "Integrated Reports," as explained by Robert Eccles and Michael Krzus:

> is, at its core, a social movement. When put into practice by companies and used by the audience of report consumers, it can transform the way resource allocation decisions are made inside companies and markets across the globe. Its social goal is to use corporate reporting as a means to influence companies and investors such that they incorporate the consequences of the positive and negative externalities of corporate decisions (most typically referred to as "sustainability" regarding social and environmental issues) and the increasing importance of intangible assets. ... The litmus test for both advocates and skeptics is whether integrated reporting leads to better corporate performance through integrated thinking, all of which should be *ultimately reflected in a company's stock price.*[19] (italics added)

Integrated Reports focus attention on a holistic view of organizations that includes social and environmental issues. Referring to the four-part purpose again, recall how it emphasizes that nothing works long term if a firm consistently fails to earn its cost of capital. Said differently, a firm with high marks for social and environmental issues that fails to earn the cost of capital is *unsustainable*. As reviewed in Chapter 1, a sustainable firm fulfills its four-part purpose: (1) a vision to make the world a better place, (2) survive and prosper through continual gains in efficiency and innovation,

---

[19] Robert G. Eccles and Michael P. Krzus, 2015, *The Integrated Reporting Movement: Meaning, Momentum, Motives, and Materiality.* Hoboken, NJ: John Wiley & Sons, pp. 59 and 99.

(3) sustain win-win relationships with all of the firm's stakeholders, and (4) take care of future generations. Sustainability is rooted in achieving a sound and inspiring purpose that creates genuine value.

As to the practical tasks of value creation, it is imperative for management and the board of directors to widely implement a *common valuation language* that is focused on return on investment and the cost of capital, that is, long-term value creation, and explicitly apply value-creation thinking to the firm's business units. A systematic application of this value-creation language could take the form of a *Life-Cycle Review* focused on a firm's business units.[20] Life-Cycle Reviews would improve resource allocation decisions and help management engage in a dialogue with the very investors they would want in their shareholder base—highly knowledgeable investors seeking to own firms for the long term.

A Life-Cycle Review focuses on the firm as a whole plus its individual business units and has three components. It details past life-cycle track records; highlights key value-creation issues; and guides strategic resource allocation decisions. Some have voiced concern that the life-cycle track records for business units would reveal too much information that could be useful to a firm's competitors. On the other hand, the comprehensiveness, transparency, and rigor of the information is well suited to transitioning investor communications away from short-term myopia to long-term fundamentals. A decision to not publicly display perceived sensitive information should not deter managements and boards from internal use and gaining insights not otherwise available. The three components are described below.

1. **Value-relevant track records.** Management would display the top two panels of life-cycle charts (e.g., Figures 4.4 and 4.5)—economic returns versus cost of capital and reinvestment rates—for their firm and individual business units. The

---

[20]The concept of a Life-Cycle Review was first proposed in Bartley J. Madden, 2007, "For Better Corporate Governance, the Shareholder Value Review," *Journal of Applied Corporate Finance.* 19 no. 1 (Winter): 102–114. See also Bartley J. Madden, 2007, "Guidepost to Wealth Creation: Value-Relevant Track Records," *Journal of Applied Finance* 17(2): 119–130.

necessary calculations involve a tradeoff between accuracy and simplicity, such as how R&D is capitalized and amortized. Reinvestment rates should be decomposed into organic growth and the growth impact of any acquisitions or divestitures.

2. **Strategy and reinvestment.** In the *context* of a business unit's track record of economic returns in relation to the cost of capital and its reinvestment rates, management's strategy is explained. By positioning a business at a point in time in its life-cycle, relevant issues are raised. For example, there is a compelling strategic logic for mature business units that have steadfastly been earning approximately the cost of capital to raise their economic returns instead of chasing asset growth. This is especially true for an ongoing business unit (not a startup) that has been unable to earn the cost of capital.

3. **Intangibles.** Management provides an overview of how intangible assets are used to improve long-term financial performance. This overview represents work-in-progress and a learning experience for those who prepare the adjusted data to better measure economic returns and reinvestment rates, and for those who use the information for their own analysis. Chief financial officers and their staffs would play a vital role in leading this learning experience. They probably would be much more enthused about participating in this innovative and highly useful work versus providing voluminous 10-K data that few investors find useful or even read.

In addition to improving decision making inside the firm there are three other reasons for implementation of Life-Cycle Reviews. First, their preparation enables management to gain deep knowledge about the most useful information to include in the Supplementary Disclosure section of their annual report. Second, Life-Cycle Reviews provide insights for connecting financial performance to the broader stakeholder concerns addressed by Integrated Reports.

Third, consider the following thought experiment. You won a prize that entitled you to select one stock from a group of stocks about which you have very limited information. The prize is $50,000 worth of shares of stock in one of the firms in the group, and you must hold that stock for a minimum of five years. The information you receive is that all firms are in the same industry and have been in business for at least twenty years. In addition, the CEO of every firm will soon announce that a major investment initiative has begun that will depress near-term quarterly earnings, although management forecasts significant long-term value creation.

You must specify one criterion to be applied to all firms in the group and this will determine which stock you own. In all likelihood you give serious thought to what is the most important characteristic of a firm that is straightforward to measure; is highly predictive of success in the future; and can potentially convince investors not to sell their shares due to management's purposeful depressing of near-term quarterly earnings. A reader of this book who embraces its ideas would likely choose this criterion: "Demonstrated long-term track record of significant value creation by management."

Put differently, management needs to earn the right to reduce quarterly earnings in order to make large investments. In Chapter 4 we noted that Jeff Bezos, Amazon's CEO, has repeatedly made large investments that, on average, proved exceedingly rewarding to patient shareholders. To no surprise, in the past Amazon's stock price has risen in the face of quarterly "shortfalls" that were part of big investment outlays. One reason for writing this book is to support the transition for publicly traded firms to minimize quarterly report myopia and manage for long-term value creation, similar to how highly successful, privately held firms are managed. In summary, Life-Cycle Reviews can advance value creation by putting planned future investments in the context of past results.

The next three sections analyze value creation via the long-term histories of three companies with exceptionally well-known brands.

EXPECT MORE THAN COFFEE—STARBUCKS

Innovative business models do not require a revolutionary idea new to humankind. Rather, one can make observations and new connections that lead to genuine value creation, such as when Howard Schultz observed the intense relationship that Italians had with drinking their coffee at neighborhood coffee bars. He intuitively knew that this social type of coffee drinking could flourish in the United States. That was 1983. Schultz became CEO of Starbucks in 1987, and today the company has over 30,000 worldwide stores.

Schultz orchestrated an authentic win-win relationship with employees and an emotional connection with customers resulting in the uniquely valuable Starbucks brand. The life-cycle track record in Figure 5.4 attests to a superior-performing company that was built over decades outperforming the S&P 500 more than 10-fold (see lower panel of Figure 5.4) from 1992 to 2018. CFROIs were depressed in the early years due to an exceptionally rapid expansion of stores.

As to the culture driving this performance, Schultz noted:

> But the story of Starbucks is not just a record of growth and success. ... It's living proof that a company can lead with its heart and nurture its soul and still make money. It shows that a company can provide long-term value for shareholders without sacrificing its core belief in treating its employees with respect and dignity, both because we have a team of leaders who believe it's right and because it's the best way to do business.
> ... a comprehensive health-care program, even for part-timers, and stock options that provide ownership for everyone. We treat warehouse workers and entry-level retail people with the kind of respect most companies show for only high executives.
> If people relate to the company they work for, if they form an emotional tie to it and buy into its dreams, they will pour their heart into making it better. When employees have self-esteem and self-respect they can contribute so much more to their company, to their family, to the world.[21]

---

[21] Howard Schultz, 1997, *Pour Your Heart into It: How Starbucks Built a Company One Cup at a Time.* New York: Hyperion, pp. 5–6.

FIGURE 5.4 **Starbucks 1992 to 2018**

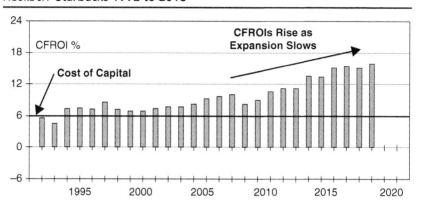

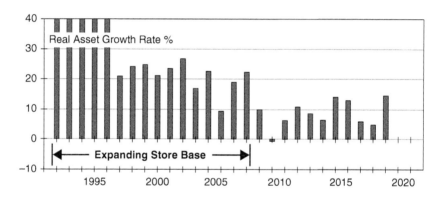

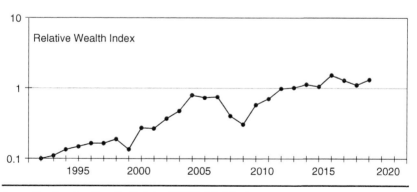

Source: Based on data from Credit Suisse HOLT global database.

Schultz relinquished the CEO reins in 2000 and became Starbucks chairman focusing on global strategy and expansion. Large-scale store expansion (see middle panel of Figure 5.4) was a top priority, which, however, resulted in operating problems culminating in a sharp drop in profits in 2008. Keep in mind that the natural tendency for companies with substantial growth for decades, and becoming large organizations, is to encounter heightened competition which hastens the transition into the mature life-cycle stage. To avoid this competitive decline, Schultz returned as CEO in 2008 intent on reigniting the emotional connection to consumers in order to improve profitability. Schultz penned a memo that reflected a hard-nosed reality check (feedback) about the business situation:

> Over the past 10 years, in order to achieve the growth, development and scale necessary to go from less than 1,000 stores to 13,000 stores and beyond, we have had to make a series of decisions that, in retrospect, have led to the watering down of the Starbucks Experience, and what some might call the commoditization of our brand.
>
> Many of these decisions were probably right at the time, and on their own merit would not have created the dilution of the experience; but in this case, the sum is much greater and, unfortunately, much more damaging than the individual pieces.[22]

The renewal of Starbucks was successful as depicted in the rising CFROIs (top panel Figure 5.4) well in excess of the cost of capital.

COSTCO STARTS BY CARING FOR ITS EMPLOYEES

A firm admired for consistent superior financial performance in the retail industry is Costco. Similar to Starbuck's recent performance, Costco has delivered sustained CFROIs well in excess of the cost of capital. It is a multinational corporation operating membership-only warehouse clubs with a well-deserved reputation for selling quality merchandise at low prices. Large-scale efficiency is the hallmark of Costco.

---

[22] Howard Schultz, 2011, *Onward: How Starbucks Fought for Its Life without Losing Its Soul.* New York: Rodale, p. 23.

Notably, Costco employees are much higher compensated (salary and benefits) compared to competitors, such as Walmart's Sam's Club. Unsurprisingly, the annual turnover of Costco's highly motivated employees is a fraction of the turnover of its competitors. James Sinegal, Costco's cofounder and CEO from 1983 to 2011, explains:

> Paying your employees well is not only the right thing to do but it makes for good business. In the final analysis, you get what you pay for. Paying rock-bottom wages is wrong. ... It doesn't keep employees happy. It keeps them looking for other jobs. Plus, managers spend all their time hiring replacements rather than running your business. ... When employees are happy, they are your very best ambassadors. ... If we take care of the business and keep our eye on the goal line, the stock price will take care of itself.[23]

Costco's life-cycle track record in Figure 5.5 shows sustained value-creating CFROIs with recent asset growth slowing as the firm grows larger. Although, as I write this chapter, Costco's first store opened in China, and the stampede of new Chinese Costco members forced the store to close early on opening day.

At times, analysts have criticized Costco's generous (by industry standards) employee compensation packages. Sinegal responds:

> You have to take the shit with the sugar, I guess. We think when you take care of your customer and your employees, your shareholders are going to be rewarded in the long run. And I'm one of them [the shareholders]; I care about the stock price. But we're not going to do something for the sake of one quarter that's going to destroy the fabric of the company and what we stand for.[24]

A Costco warehouse has a limited selection of about 4,000 items with about 75% being consumer staples and the remainder special items which frequently change and add adventure to a Costco shopping experience. In

---

[23]Rajendra S. Sisodia, David B. Wolfe, and Jagdish N. Sheth, 2007, *Firms of Endearment: How World-Class Companies Profit from Passion and Purpose.* Upper Saddle River, NJ: Wharton School Publishing, p. 34.
[24]John Heylar and Ann Harrington, November 24, 2003, "The Only Company Walmart Fears," *Fortune.*

FIGURE 5.5 Costco 1993 to 2018

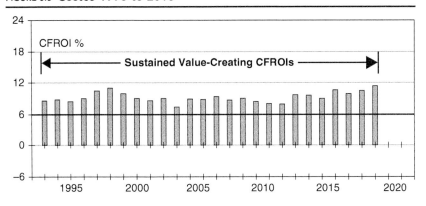

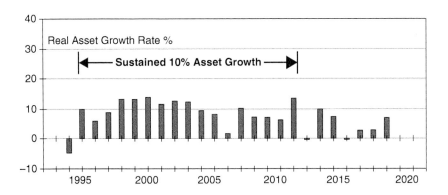

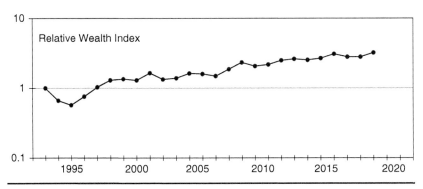

Source: Based on data from Credit Suisse HOLT global database.

addition, Costco's Kirkland Signature brand covers a wide range of products from nuts to dress shirts to golf balls. The common denominator is high quality at a price significantly lower than competing brands. To sum up, this is a formidable business model which is exceedingly difficult to compete against due to Costco's scale advantages.

Costco as a company is a valuable brand in addition to its Kirkland signature brand. However, technology changes and new competitors arrive that can significantly dilute a once valuable brand. The BlackBerry smartphone brand suffered this fate with the arrival of the Apple iPhone. Avon is another once highly valuable brand that became decidedly less valuable as the world changed.

RINGING DOORBELLS AND CHANGING TIMES—AVON

Avon began in 1886 when David McConnell decided to switch from selling books door-to-door to perfumes. The firm grew to hold the dominant position in door-to-door selling of beauty products. As I write about the company in late 2019, Avon is likely to be acquired by Natura, a Brazilian cosmetics firm with a similar business model as Avon's. Brazil is now Avon's largest market. The acquisition purchase price is about $2 billion, which compares to an equity market value of about $20 billion two decades earlier.

The beginning of the life-cycle track record for Avon (Figure 5.6) shows a successful business model keyed to the widely recognized Avon brand that resulted in high CFROIs (top panel) and high asset growth (middle panel) from 1960 to the early 1970s. Competitive fade occurred as CFROIs then declined to the mid-1980s.

Hicks Waldron became CEO in 1983 after Avon's CFROIs and stock price had sharply fallen from their peak in the early 1970s. Under his watch, the core business of direct selling was deemphasized, and a series of failed health care acquisitions soon followed. In his 1985 letter to shareholders, Waldron wrote these uninspiring words: "This is an exciting time at Avon,

FIGURE 5.6 Avon 1960 to 2018

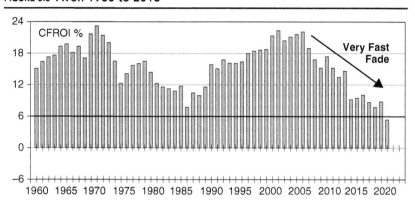

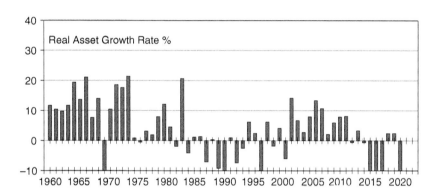

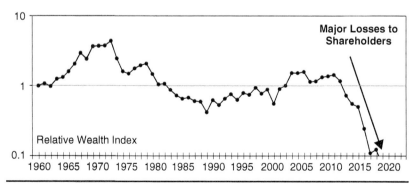

Source: Based on data from Credit Suisse HOLT global database.

and I am pleased to be a part of it. ... This is also an awkward time. We are not what we have been. Neither are we what we will be."

In 1988, James Preston became CEO and announced the obvious that the health care diversification strategy was ill-conceived and value-dissipating. Furthermore, he stated that Avon's core beauty and direct selling business was the future. Preston immediately focused on curtailing Avon's free-spending habits in order to generate cash flow to handle the debt load incurred by his predecessor's debt-financed acquisitions.

In Preston's 1992 letter to shareholders, he crafted a new vision for Avon: "To be the company that best understands and satisfies the product, service, and self-fulfillment needs of women— globally."

In 1999, Andrea Jung became Avon's first female CEO and held that position until 2012. As the top panel of Figure 5.6 displays, after early success, a fast fade of CFROIs took place under her leadership. Not only was Avon executing poorly, but the firm faced heightened competition from physical retail stores and online Internet stores; meanwhile costly corruption charges in China took years to resolve. Also, more women were working and not at home for easy access by Avon's sales representatives. Sheri Cox became the next CEO, and the firm continued to falter with severe losses to shareholders (bottom panel of Figure 5.6).

WHY DID ILLUMINA OUTPERFORM THE STOCK MARKET 18-FOLD FROM 2004 TO 2014?

Illumina is today's leader in instrumentation tools for large-scale analysis of genetic variation and function. Figure 5.7 plots monthly stock prices for Illumina beginning at year-end 2004. From this point to year-end 2014, Illumina's stock outperformed the S&P 500 18-fold. Why?

To answer the question of excess return, either positive or negative, one needs to quantify investor expectations of financial performance at the beginning of the period and compare these expectations to subsequent financial performance. The life-cycle framework is ideally suited for this task. Illumina's life-cycle track record (Figure 5.8) identifies the period 2000 to 2004 as startup years with repetitive negative CFROIs (top panel).

FIGURE 5.7 Illumina stock price 2005 to 2019

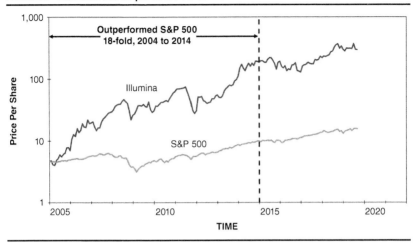

Source: Based on data from Credit Suisse HOLT global database.

FIGURE 5.8 Illumina life-cycle expectations year-end 2004

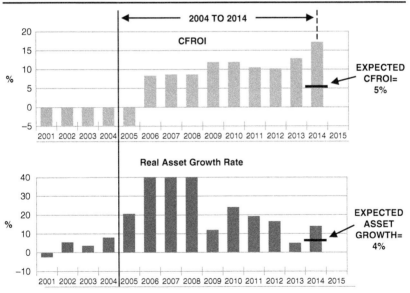

Actual life-cycle performance relative to expectations drives excess shareholder returns.

The life-cycle valuation model described earlier (Figure 4.6) in Chapter 4 was used with data from the HOLT global database to quantify expectations implied in Illumina's stock price at year-end 2004. Given the estimated investor discount rate for Illumina at that time and the known market value of the company, the implied net cash receipt stream was calculated and expressed in life-cycle language. The expectations were that CFROIs would only improve to about 5% in 2014 coupled with asset growth of approximately 4% as shown above. In other words, investors did not expect what actually happened with Illumina dominating the genetic instrumentation market with rising CFROIs well above the cost of capital and high asset growth. As this stellar life-cycle performance unfolded during this 10-year period investors continually revised their expectations upward, which generated the 18-fold outperformance of the S&P 500 Index.

At one level of analysis, we have answered the question of why the outperformance occurred. But at a deeper and more holistic level, what caused this superior financial performance? The cause of Illumina's excess return from 2004 to 2014 was a superior knowledge-building culture reflected in both the strategic acquisitions made and the management of employees.

Jay Flatley, CEO from 1999 to 2016, excelled at knowledge building. His feedback about the external environment pinpointed where Illumina's technology was lagging in the fast-moving environment of DNA sequencing. Consequently, he made a series of acquisitions to expand Illumina's technology expertise, including a critically important 2007 acquisition of Solexa. As to his managerial approach, Flatley noted:

> One of the really important things we did, early on, was structured our product development process in a way where we could very efficiently run a large number of projects simultaneously. This is what has given us the ability to scale, in size and complexity and number of products, and still be able to manage with a limited number of top executives. That's because of how we empower our teams to go

off and do great things. They only have to come back to us under a very fixed set of circumstances. We [in management] can set the strategy and direction and talk about specifications. They can do the execution, which they are really good at.[25]

The Illumina example illustrates how cause and effect analysis improves understanding, which is a topic discussed further in the next section.

THE EFFICIENT MARKET HYPOTHESIS AND THE FACTOR ZOO

This chapter began with a review of intangibles as a prerequisite to analyzing the process of generating excess (positive/negative) shareholder returns. Empirical studies summarized the influence of intangibles on both firms' financial performance and their shareholder returns. The implicit logic of this research is that since intangibles are important, they also impact shareholder returns.

When researchers find that variable X is important for the successful management of firms, expect them to formulate a hypothesis that high/low values of X contribute to high/low shareholder returns. For example, corporate culture is generally acknowledged as an important variable impacting firm performance.[26] Using employees' personal evaluations of firms as a favorable place to work as a proxy for a value-creation culture favorable to business success, data indicates that a value-weighted portfolio of the "100 Best Companies to Work for in America" earned a four-factor alpha of 0.29% per month from 1984 to 2009, or 3.5% per year.[27]

---

[25]Luke Timmerman, April 29, 2015, "DNA Sequencing Market Will Exceed $20 Billion, Says Illumina CEO Jay Flatley," *Forbes*.

[26]Luigi Guiso, Paola Sapienza, and Luigi Zingales, 2015, "The Value of Corporate Culture," *Journal of Financial Economics* 117(1): 60–76.

[27]Alex Edmans, 2011, "Does the Stock Market Fully Value Intangibles? Employee Satisfaction and Equity Prices," *Journal of Financial Economics* 101(3): 621–640. See also James K. Harter, Frank L. Schmidt, and Theodore L. Hayes, 2002, "Business-Unit-Level Relationship between Employee Satisfaction, Employee Engagement, and Business Outcomes: A Meta-Analysis," *Journal of Applied Psychology* 87(2): 268–279.

Environmental, social, and governance (ESG) practices are increasingly viewed not as optional "do good" initiatives but as an integral component to firms *sustaining* long-term success. A study of high sustainability companies with highly-rated ESG practices versus a matched sample of low sustainability companies documented that the former outperformed the latter over the long term both in terms of investor returns and accounting-based performance.[28] In an influential report, *From the Stockholders to the Stakeholders,* Omar Selim summarized research on ESG:

> In this enhanced meta-study we categorize more than 200 different sources. Within it, we find a remarkable correlation between diligent sustainability business practices and economic performance. The first part of the report explores this thesis from a strategic management perspective, with remarkable results: 88% of reviewed sources find that companies with robust sustainability practices demonstrate better operational performance, which ultimately translates into cash flows. The second part of the report builds on this, where 80% of the reviewed studies demonstrate that prudent sustainability practices have a positive influence on investment performance.
>
> This report ultimately demonstrates that responsibility and profitability are not incompatible, but in fact wholly complementary. When investors and asset owners replace the question "how much return?" with "how much sustainable return?," then they have evolved from a stockholder to a stakeholder.[29]

However, there is a danger that some managements will conclude that any outlay that improves their ESG rating is worthwhile. This becomes all the more tempting as money management firms gather assets earmarked for investment in firms that are highly rated as to ESG practices. Importantly, ESG outlays should be an integral part of managing to create value; for example, effective corporate governance practices result in resources

---

[28] Robert G. Eccles, Ionnis Ioannou, and George Serafeim, 2014, "The Impact of Corporate Sustainability on Organizational Processes and Performance," *Management Science* 60(11): 2835–2857.

[29] Gordon L. Clark, Andreas Feiner, and Michael Viehs, 2015,.\ *From the Stockholder to the Stakeholder.* Smith School of Enterprise and the Environment and Arabesque Partners. Similar conclusions are contained in Gunnar Friede, Timo Busch, and Alexander Bassen, 2015, "ESG and Financial Performance: Aggregated Evidence from More Than 2000 Empirical Studies," *Journal of Sustainable Finance & Investment* 5(4): 210–233.

being allocated to their most likely best uses. Successful ESG outlays meaningfully contribute to a firm sustaining its long-term ability to at least earn the cost of capital.

As to investor returns, the number of finance articles devoted to empirical tests of the degree of market efficiency is extraordinarily large and seemingly never ending. This is not surprising since the heart of modern finance seeks to connect risk and return within an equilibrium setting of market efficiency. The workhorse model first used to test market efficiency was CAPM, using Beta as a one-factor model. In his Nobel lecture, Gene Fama summarized his extensive contributions to finance research, noting:

> It was clear from the beginning that the central question is whether asset prices reflect all available information—what I labeled the efficient market hypothesis. ... The difficulty is making the hypothesis testable. We can't test whether the market does what it is supposed to do unless we specify what it is supposed to do. In other words, we need an asset pricing model, a model that specifies the characteristics of rational expected asset returns in a market equilibrium. Tests of efficiency basically test whether the properties of expected returns implied by the assumed model of market equilibrium are observed in actual returns. If the tests reject, we don't know whether the problem is an inefficient market or a bad model of market equilibrium. ... The [CAPM] model is an elegantly simple and intuitively appealing *tour de force* that lays the foundations of asset pricing theory, but its major prediction that market B [Beta] suffices to explain the cross section of expected returns seems to be violated in many ways.[30]

Fama and French subsequently developed a three-factor model which, in addition to Beta, added size measured by a firm's market capitalizations (smaller size yields higher returns) and value measured by book-to-market ratios (higher ratios outperform) as proxies for risk not captured by Beta.[31] That started an outpouring of factor studies that has lasted for decades with no sign of fatigue. To date, more than 300 factors have been reported in academic articles, prompting this research to be characterized as a

---

[30] Eugene F. Fama, 2014, "Two Pillars of Asset Pricing,.\" *American Economic Review* 104(6): 1467–1485.

[31] E. F. Fama and K. R. French, 1992,.\ "The Cross-Section of Expected Stock Returns," *Journal of Finance* 47(2): 427–465.

"factor zoo."[32] Fama and French added profitability (higher leads to higher investor returns) and asset growth (lower leads to higher investor returns) to produce a five-factor model.[33] Some contend that these additional factors reflect risk not captured by Beta. Others point out the implausibility of labeling some factors as a proxy for risk such as price momentum after a firm delivers surprisingly favorable quarterly operating performance.

The process by which the prices of assets, such as a firm's stock price, move to incorporate new information to better estimate a "rationally" determined price ("the price is right") is important. Asset prices drive decentralized decision making, including resource allocations, and therefore are critical to a free (decentralized) market economy. An efficient market implies prices that incorporate all available value-relevant information with the result that there is no easy way to earn excess returns after transaction costs. This idea is simple enough.

However, researchers then confront the joint hypothesis problem articulated by Fama whereby abnormal returns may compensate for one or more unknown risk factors (deficient asset pricing model).[34] If markets are efficient in the sense that the price is right, then the price likely reflects knowledgeable investors' forecasts of future net cash receipts translated to a present value using the investors' discount rate (Figure 4.6). Periods of high volatility can be due to variation in expected net cash receipts and/or changes in the investor discount rate. The latter point is referred to as time-varying expected returns and is corroborated by the time series discount rate data displayed in Figure 4.9.

What is the end game for research searching for factors that attempt to parsimoniously explain many investor return anomalies? What value is delivered and to whom?

[32] Harvey, Campbell R. and Yan Liu, 2018, "Lucky Factors." SSRN working paper. https://ssrn.com/abstract=2528780.
[33] Eugene F. Fama and Kenneth R. French, 2015, "A Five-Factor Asset Pricing Model," *Journal of Financial Economics* 116(1): 1–22.
[34] For an empirically based argument that risk is misunderstood by efficient-market proponents, see Eric Falkenstein, 2012,. *The Missing Risk Premium: Why Low Volatility Investing Works.* Hoboken, NJ: John Wiley & Sons.

The evidence on the predictability of stock returns is increasingly more difficult to reconcile with the efficient market framework. ... We find particularly compelling the evidence that *healthier* and *safer* firms, as measured by various measures of risk or fundamentals, often earn higher subsequent returns. Firms with lower Beta, lower volatility, lower distress risk, lower leverage, and superior measures of profitability and growth, all earn higher [investor] returns. ... If these firms are riskier, it is odd that they should exhibit future operating and return characteristics that suggest the opposite.[35]

There is a persuasive logical argument that markets may be efficient in the sense of no easy way to earn abnormal profits after transactions costs, yet actual prices may deviate from the rationally determined DCF (discounted cash flow) warranted valuations made by knowledgeable investors participating in setting the price.[36] Consistent with this line of thinking, serious investors equipped to do DCF analysis on firms should always be skeptical of market prices; monitor investor expectations implied in stock prices; and also monitor their upside, most likely, and pessimistic forecasts for plausibility as new information is received. Such a skeptical mindset and a well-grounded willingness to disagree with the market is facilitated by forecasts expressed in life-cycle terms and expectations implied in current stock prices articulated in life-cycle terms (i.e., economic returns and reinvestment rates).

EXCESS SHAREHOLDER RETURNS AND THREE LEVELS OF CAUSE-AND-EFFECT LOGIC

The previous section focused on tests of market efficiency and highlighted statistical studies that have produced a factor zoo. Let's pause for a moment and seriously question the research process at work. Specifically, the beginning point is the CAPM that elegantly connects risk and return in an environment of equilibrium coupled to the efficient market hypothesis.

---

[35]Charles M. C. Lee and Eric So, 2014, "Alphanomics: The Informational Underpinnings of Market Efficiency," *Foundations and Trends in Accounting* 9(2-3): 59–258.
[36]Robert Shiller, 1984, "Stock Prices and Social Dynamics," *Brookings Papers on Economic Activity* 2: 457–510.

This framework led to statistical studies using regression equations to measure correlations of variables with excess return. But these studies, for the most part, lack a *cause-and-effect logic as to what drives a firm's market valuation.*[37] This should be no surprise since in equilibrium an efficient market means that it is futile to seek excess risk-adjusted returns by analyzing how firms create value and calculating warranted valuations. This is because all available value-relevant information is assumed to be assimilated in the current price.

One way to think about empirical research on the topic of excess shareholder returns is to divide this research into three levels according to the type of cause-and-effect logic employed. Level 1, described above, is essentially a search for correlations between readily available computerized financial data on firms and excess returns. These studies address both market efficiency and candidate variables (factors) to improve upon the one-factor (Beta) CAPM. Little attention is given to a deeper understanding of life-cycle-type analysis and the role of a firm's knowledge-building proficiency. However, the life-cycle lens can provide insights that lead to groupings of firms that behave in predictable ways totally missed by data analysis that ignores life-cycle stages (Figure 4.2). For example, asset growth rates have been shown to be correlated with excess returns, that is, low asset growth firms exhibit higher shareholder returns, on average, than high asset growth firms.[38] But attention to causality suggests that we consider the relationships of all the variables in the life-cycle valuation model, not merely isolate on asset growth.[39] Should we not employ a more fine-grained analysis that segments the aggregated data to focus on the impact of knowledge building in sustaining a firm's profitability at high levels? In these situations, big reinvestment rates (asset growth) coupled to high and sustained CFROIs can easily produce positive excess returns—the opposite

---

[37] Ian D. Gow, David F. Larcker, and Peter C. Reiss, 2016, "Causal Inference in Accounting Research," *Journal of Accounting Research* 54(2): 477–523.

[38] Cooper, Michael J., Huseylin Gulen, and Michael J. Schill, 2008, "Asset Growth and the Cross-Section of Stock Returns," *Journal of Finance* 63(4): 1609–1651.

[39] For an insightful and comprehensive discussion of causality and data analysis, see Judea Pearl and Dana Mackenzie, 2018, *The Book of Why: The New Science of Cause and Effect.* New York: Basic Books.

of the reported relationship for asset growth.[40] Also, we could observe the type of firms recording high asset growth due to repeated acquisitions. Consider grouping firms earning high CFROIs due to demonstrated skill in consolidating industries or improving the operations of acquired firms (e.g., Danaher). This group differs from less skilled acquisitive firms, some of which may be earning low CFROIs and in need of restructuring rather than empire-building acquisitions. These "skilled" acquirers who exhibit high asset growth may perform quite differently than the aggregated data and deliver, on average, positive excess shareholder returns.

Many Level 1 studies can be criticized for ignoring the increasing importance of intangibles (not yet a meaningful part of accounting data) in the New Economy. Reported accounting numbers for book values lose meaning in more recent years compared to historical years when tangible assets dominated. The often-tested book-to-market ratio is clearly a problematic variable as to its predictability for excess returns in future years. Moreover, in the Old Economy entrepreneurial small firms led the innovation charge while large firms were faced with saturated markets for their products. However, in the New Economy firms with successful platforms quickly get large and then begin an extended period of value creation. So, size in the future may not be a predictive factor for excess returns, which would be contrary to findings based on historical data. Many successful startup firms in the New Economy do an IPO at a valuation that makes them a large company. These are examples of potential problems when correlations using financial variables are divorced from causality and changing context.

Compared to Level 1, Level 2 thinking uses more straightforward cause-and-effect logic between a variable and its perceived impact on firm performance. The idea is that investors may not fully appreciate the variable's importance and, as firm performance unfolds over time,

---

[40] Similar thinking suggests that high asset growth may be related to positive excess returns for firms with demonstrated innovation skill as measured by securing patents. This is, in fact, supported by Kumar, Praveen and Dongmei Li, 2016, "Capital Investment, Innovative Capacity, and Stock Returns," *Journal of Finance* 71(5): 2059–2094. For a discussion of how Walmart's sustained 20% plus asset growth rates from 1979 to 1989 contributed to its stock outperforming the market 13-fold see Bartley J. Madden, 2016, *Value Creation Thinking*. Naperville, IL: LearningWhatWorks, pp. 131–133.

investors react and the result is excess shareholder returns. Three variables discussed earlier in this chapter are representative of Level 2 thinking. First, environmental, social, and governance (ESG) research was summarized that affirmed a correlation with firm performance and excess shareholder returns. Keep in mind that successful (and therefore) profitable firms have available cash to fund increased ESG expenditures and consequently one needs to be careful about cause and effect as to how much of a firm's success was directly due to ESG expenditures. Second, as previously noted, the impact on firm performance and excess investor returns was documented due to a firm's value creation culture. Third, a similar finding was documented for a wide range of studies focused on intangibles. Importantly, Level 2 research more closely connects causal variables to life-cycle performance and investor returns compared to the myriad correlations and inferences about not-yet-specified risk variables encountered in Level 1 research. Recall the example of Illumina whereby the life-cycle valuation model was used to calculate investor expectations at year-end 2004 for the next 10 years. The subsequent actual economic returns and reinvestment rates significantly exceeded these expectations generating an investor return that outperformed the S&P 500 Index 18-fold. This kind of analysis represents a much stronger cause-and-effect logic versus Level 1 research.

Level 3 thinking emphasizes the primary importance of a firm's knowledge-building proficiency (i.e., the pragmatic theory of the firm). Put differently, top management skilled in knowledge building will most likely appreciate that value creation requires the development of intangible assets, the "right" culture, and a firm's purpose that motivates ESG initiatives that support value creation for all stakeholders (see Figure 5.9). In this sense, *the fundamental cause of what shows up as long-term shareholder returns is rooted in a firm's knowledge-building proficiency*. At bedrock, this causality is what the pragmatic theory of the firm explains in detail.

A similar bedrock causality was addressed in Chapter 2 concerning Christensen's Theory of Jobs to Be Done. Of course, consumers hire a product to get a specific job done—so obvious once the idea is explained and it fully sinks in. Useful theories do not require elegant mathematical

FIGURE 5.9 Cause-and-effect logic applied to shareholder returns

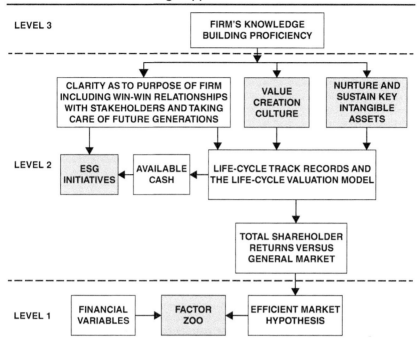

expressions, just powerful connections that explain causality. Application of the Jobs Theory helps explain why certain product innovations do poorly while others do well. Similarly, application of the pragmatic theory of the firm helps explain long-term shareholder returns as caused by life-cycle performance, which is driven by a firm's knowledge-building proficiency.

The above discussion about the three different levels of cause-and-effect logic is summarized in Figure 5.9.

The difference between Level 2 thinking and Level 3 thinking is revealed by answering questions like the following, which involve drilling down to root causes:

- Why did Nucor's stock outperform the market 10-fold from 1975 to 1995? This is a steel company in a notoriously low return cyclical industry. Importantly, Nucor's life-cycle track record shows economic returns that were cyclical but averaging well above the cost of capital and substantially greater than its industry peers during this time period.

- What caused this financial performance? Many point to Nucor's innovation of especially productive mini-mills that use electric arc furnaces and high bonuses paid to its exceptionally productive employees.
- What caused this productivity? The answer is Nucor's knowledge-building proficiency orchestrated by Ken Iverson, its longtime CEO who retired in 1996. Iverson was the root cause of Nucor's value-creation culture that produced industry-leading technology and the industry's highest productive employees. In Iverson's words:

> My way of thinking … Instead of telling people what to do and then hounding them to do it, our managers focus on shaping an environment that frees employees to determine what they can do and should do, to the benefit of themselves and the business.
> I recall that we started a crew on a straightener machine—which straightens steel angles to meet our customers' requirements—at a production bonus of eight tons per hour. The rated capacity of the machine was ten tons per hour. Well, that crew kept tinkering and experimenting. They installed a larger motor, fed the angles into the machine in various ways, and so on. Within a year, their production was up to twenty tons an hour, twice that machine's rated capacity. Perhaps the engineers who calculate a machine's capacity should come up with a new formula, one that estimates the capacity of machines run by people who earn according to what they produce.[41]

Level 2 puts a spotlight on hypothesized causes of a firm's life-cycle track record. Life-cycle track records decompose a firm's financial performance showing the results of key strategic choices and management's skill in adapting to change. To my knowledge, empirical studies in the top academic journals to-date have not used the life-cycle framework similar to

---

[41] Ken Iverson, 1998, *Plain Talk: Lessons from a Business Maverick*. Hoboken, NJ: John Wiley & Sons, pp. 98 and 105–106.

the Illumina example even though this yields a far greater understanding of cause and effect versus Level 1 correlation studies.

Occasionally a study addresses Level 3 thinking and focuses on "smart" management (highly rated as to knowledge-building proficiency) and hypothesizes that smart management is more likely to create significant future value compared to less skilled management. A study by Lauren Cohen, Karl Diether, and Christopher Malloy represents Level 3 thinking. The authors gauge a firm's knowledge-building proficiency according to its *track record* of translating R&D expenditures into sales.

> Our approach is based on the simple idea that some firms are likely to be skilled at certain activities, and some are not, and this skill may be persistent over time. ... We show that ... substantial return predictability exists by exploiting the information in these firm-level track records. We find that a long-short portfolio strategy that takes advantage of the information in past track records yields abnormal returns of 11 percent per annum. ... We show that the firms we classify as high ability based on their past track records also produce tangible results with their research and development efforts. In particular, R&D spending by high ability firms leads to increased numbers of patents, patent citations, and new product innovations by these firms in the future. The same level of R&D investment by low ability firms does not.[42]

Here is one more example of Level 3 thinking regarding knowledge building and firm performance. A creative study was done that focused on an exogenous shock to a group of medical device firms which caused the firms to lose, for a period of time, the knowledge-building contribution from nonemployee physicians, and this negatively impacted firm performance.

> In 2005, the U.S. Department of Justice (DOJ) investigated the five leading orthopedic device companies regarding their close relationships with physicians. We ... find evidence of a large decline

---

[42] Lauren Cohen, Karl Diether, and Christopher Malloy, 2013, "Misvaluing Innovation," *Review of Financial Studies* 26(3): 635–666.

in FDA-approved products for the firms under investigation. ... We find the largest decreases in both the number and average quality of inventions in the technology areas where physician knowledge is most important and the largest decreases in the number of FDA-approved products in areas related to prosthesis and spine, where physician collaboration is crucial.[43]

A transition to Level 3 research entails significant creativity and willingness to gather data that is not so easy to obtain compared to the computerized financial data typically used in Level 1 research.

USEFUL IDEAS FOR INVESTORS, MANAGEMENTS, AND ACADEMIC RESEARCHERS

Investors

I have had a long career working with the life-cycle framework applied to corporate consulting and especially money management. Here are key observations about the worldview of successful money managers who have committed to the life-cycle framework for analyzing companies and guiding their buy/hold/sell decisions.

- Stock prices, on average, represent extraordinarily astute forecasts of a firm's future life-cycle performance. There is no easy way, on a sustained basis, to earn excess investor returns after transactions costs when managing a sizable portfolio.
- The long-term success of active portfolio managers depends upon their valuation model and their skill in forecasting variables such as fade rates and their discipline in waiting for opportunities. An opportunity represents exploitable mispricing because of their specific company insights and cognizance of why a company's

[43] Aaron K. Chatterji and Kira R. Fabrizio, 2016, "Does the Market for Ideas Influence the Rate and Direction of Innovative Activity? Evidence from the Medical Device Industry," *Strategic Management Journal* 37(3): 447–465.

stock price trades as it does. These successful active managers recognize that most stocks most of the time offer no exploitable mispricing.

- Life-cycle track records need to use accounting data that has been adjusted by capitalizing and amortizing intangibles for which economic lives can be approximated to a reasonable degree. The resulting time series of economic returns and reinvestment rates help explain why a stock has outperformed or underperformed the market over longer periods of time.

- Life-cycle track records enable one to understand a company's history in an economically meaningful way. To judge the plausibility of a forecast, it helps to juxtapose a firm's forecasted *future* life-cycle performance next to its *past* life-cycle performance and also compare to track records of competitors.

- Display one's optimistic, most likely, and pessimistic long-term forecasts as economic returns and reinvestment rates that *fade* over time. A uniquely valuable skill for investors is in forecasting future fade rates which incorporate the likely contribution of intangible assets.

- Invest for the long term.[44] Patiently wait for the occasional opportunity to disagree, via a well-grounded analysis, with the investor expectations implied in current stock prices.

- Knowing why current investor expectations differ from one's most likely forecast is especially useful. Is this due to a short-term situation that does not fundamentally alter one's long-term forecast? Or, is the market possibly seeing around a corner and one's current assessment of a firm's future will be proved wrong?

---

[44]Martijn Cremers and Ankur Pareek, 2016, "Patient Capital Outperformance: The Investment Skill of High Active Share Managers Who Trade Infrequently," *Journal of Financial Economics* 122 (2): 288–306. See also Brad M. Barber and Terrance Odean, 2000, "Trading Is Hazardous to Your Wealth: The Common Stock Investment Performance of Individual Investors," *Journal of Finance* 55(2): 773–806.

Managements

Management is about value creation. Experience communicating to management and boards concerning the basic fundamentals about value creation and how the stock market works suggests the following key points.[45]

- Top management, board members, and other groups within the firm typically have strong opinions about competitors and can easily rank competing firms high to low on skill in efficiently creating value for customers.
- When the life-cycle track records of these competitors are presented, invariably these financial performance scorecards correlate closely with the ranking of companies by skill. In addition, it is straightforward to demonstrate that the life-cycle framework does a significantly better job than P/E multiples and earnings growth rates in explaining investor expectations implied in stock prices.
- Value is created by earning economic returns above the cost of capital and high reinvestment in these businesses is warranted; investing in cost-of-capital businesses represents getting bigger but not creating incremental value; and those businesses (not startups) that steadfastly fail to earn the cost of capital need to purge business-as-usual reinvestment and restructure.
- The logical next step is to construct life-cycle track records for a firm's business units. At this point, the handling of intangible assets is no longer an abstract accounting issue but an important measurement challenge that needs to be addressed. There is a tradeoff between accuracy and simplicity. Begin with conventional RONA (return-on-net assets) and experiment with more accurate calculations along the lines of the CFROI. As previously

---

[45] For many years at Callard Madden & Associates I worked with Bob Hendricks on corporate consulting assignments, and later joined Bob at HOLT Value Associates prior to the firm being acquired by Credit Suisse. Bob was a master communicator and especially skilled at explaining corporate performance and valuation issues to top managements and boards of directors.

noted, when substantial intangibles are capitalized and amortized, more accurate track records result.[46]

- In the spirit of the Life-Cycle Review discussed earlier, management and the board are better equipped to debate strategy and resource allocation when business unit performance is put in the context of life-cycle track records.

Academic Researchers

Finance, accounting, and management researchers would benefit from fresh thinking about the Efficient Market Hypothesis, related factor models, and the information needs of management in the New Economy. The following points are relevant:

- As previously noted, knowledgeable investors agree that there is no easy way to make money, after transactions costs, in publicly traded markets on a sustained basis, and especially with larger assets being managed.[47]
- Finance researchers should reassess the rationale for continually enlarging the factor zoo. As to research on investor returns, a transition from Level 1 thinking to Level 2 and especially Level 3 thinking may generate new insights connecting a firm's financial performance to its investor returns.
- Simulations, such as the display in Figure 4.11, that connect known economic scenarios (e.g., cash-out and cash-in time series for modeled firms) to the resulting accounting data are a fertile field that has not yet been meaningfully plowed and could

---

[46]Christopher D. Ittner, 2008, "Does Measuring Intangibles for Management Purposes Improve Performance? A Review of the Evidence," *Accounting and Business Research* 38(3): 261–272.

[47]That most reported accounting-based return anomalies are spurious was documented in Juhani T. Linnainmaa and Michael R. Roberts, 2016, "The History of the Cross Section of Stock Returns." NBER Working Paper 22894, http://www.nber.org/papers/w22894. See also Campbell R. Harvey, Yan Liu, and Heqing Zhu, 2015, " … and the Cross-Section of the Expected Returns," *Review of Financial Studies* 29(1): 5–68.

lead to innovative breakthroughs in accounting for intangibles to the benefit of management, investors, and the accounting rule-makers.[48]

- Historical studies of firms would benefit from the inclusion of life-cycle track records that sharpen the link between management behavior and financial performance.

- Finance, accounting, and management researchers should jointly work on the information needs of management to improve firm performance. A useful starting point is the six critical questions outlined in the next section.

SYSTEM PRINCIPLES AND EFFECTIVE LANGUAGE

Keep in mind that a useful theory brings a deeper understanding of the phenomena of interest, makes important predictions, and also *reveals problems* that otherwise remain unnoticed. Specifically, a major thrust of Lean Thinking is problem solving to yield continual process improvements. Employees should be motivated to develop, and be compensated for, continual process improvements. But, at higher organizational levels of most firms, management uses accounting-based reports to measure business unit performance. Tom Johnson summarizes the situation:

> No company that talks about improving performance can know what it is doing if its primary window on results is financial [accounting] information and not system principles. ... The dilemma facing all companies that intend to become "lean" is that they can follow a truly systemic path to lean or they can continue to use management accounting "levers of control." They can't do both.[49]

---

[48] Chapter 7 of Bartley J. Madden, 2016, *Value Creation Thinking*. Naperville, IL: LearningWhatWorks discusses the major issues in measuring economic returns (e.g., CFROI) that are displayed as a time series. For a history of the CFROI development see Bartley J. Madden, 1999. *CFROI Valuation: A Total System Approach to Valuing the Firm*. Oxford: Butterworth-Heinemann. See Timo Salmi and Ilkka Virtanen, 1997, "Measuring the Long-Run Profitability of the Firm: A Simulation Evaluation of the Financial Statement Based IRR Estimation Methods," *Acta Wasaensia* No. 54.

[49] H. Thomas Johnson, "Lean Dilemma: Choose System Principles or Management Accounting Controls—Not Both." In Joe Stenzel, ed., 2017, *Lean Accounting Best Practices for Sustainable Integration*. Hoboken, NJ: John Wiley & Sons.

But, the pragmatic theory of the firm suggests that doing both is needed to promote value creation. Consider how accounting data is needed in order to calculate economic returns (ROIs) achieved by a firm and to help management make smart resource allocation decisions. Why continue with incremental improvements to a business unit that realistically can never earn the cost of capital? However, Johnson is on target with his emphasis on controlling those key variables that cause the accounting results. For example, radically reducing inventories to "improve" RONA (return on net assets) *before* first transitioning to a far more efficient lean process can easily worsen results. So, there is a *crossover problem* involving a transition from accounting data used for decision making at higher levels to process control variables measured at lower levels of the firm where the work is done.

The crossover problem, illustrated in Figure 5.10, spotlights the need for a deeper understanding of value creation and the kind of information that is truly useful.[50] As we improve our understanding, expect our language to become more precise for describing how the system functions and how to manage improvements.

Language is perception's silent partner.[51] Julio Olalla notes that: "We live in language in the same way that fish live in water: it is transparent to us … We are unaware that language is *shaping* the world as we see it."[52]

For example, those in business continually deal with management's goal of reducing *costs*. For many, the meaning of the word *cost* is rooted in the language of accounting. That word can easily shape the world into independent activities thereby promoting actions to minimize accounting cost without regard to the consequences on the overall system.

Consider the improvement in language (and thinking) when we work toward a goal of reducing *waste* (any activity that does not add value)

[50] H. Thomas Johnson and Anders Bröms, 2000, *Profit Beyond Measure: Extraordinary Results through Attention to Work and People*. New York: Free Press.

[51] See Chapter 3 of Bartley J. Madden, 2014, *Reconstructing Your Worldview: The Four Core Beliefs You Need to Solve Complex Business Problems*. Naperville, IL: LearningWhatWorks.

[52] From the Foreword to Chalmers Brothers, 2005, *Language and the Pursuit of Happiness*. Naples, FL: New Possibilities Press.

FIGURE 5.10 The crossover problem

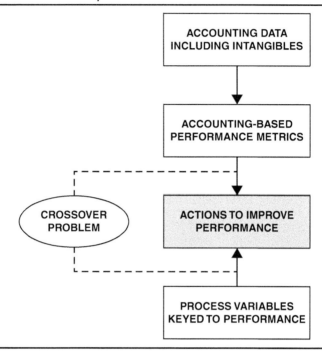

along the entire *value stream*. The value stream is all of the actions that transition raw materials to a product delivered to a customer. The same concept applies to service firms as well as manufacturing firms. The value stream concept helps shape our worldview to embrace *horizontal* flows as opposed to *vertical* silos with their own stand-alone accounting costs.

The usefulness of our current language used to manage firms can be assessed by its effectiveness in answering six critically important questions.

1. **How best to communicate to employees a cause-and-effect logic that is operationally useful for them and connects to strategy, resources, and value streams?** Both products sold and services delivered to customers involve a value stream that has a horizontal flow through many localized activities, typically organized as silos within the firm and its suppliers. The value stream

mindset is helpful for understanding how value is created as well as identifying waste (non-value-adding activities).[53] Disconnected from the perspective of lower-level employees is the process whereby management sets strategic objectives, develops resources, and allocates resources.

2. **How best to organize improvements with an eye on the key constraint?** At any point in time, management should be able to identify the key constraint arising within the system (i.e., the firm). The analysis may suggest that improving the localized efficiency of one component degrades the efficiency of the overall system. For example, suppose the bottleneck (key constraint) is located at B downstream from activity A. Hence, improving A (install faster machine) can easily worsen the bottleneck situation at B.

3. **How best to utilize process variables in order to link to accounting-based data and to ROI measurement?** Process variables provide guideposts for those performing work but are not expressed in accounting language that translates to an ROI. This is a significant measurement problem.

4. **How best to design a learning process inside the firm for generating useful data (quantitative and qualitative) on intangibles?** There are three major needs: (1) improved decision-making for investing in intangibles; (2) improved process for incorporating intangibles into the language of accounting in order to generate more useful track records of economic returns and reinvestment rates for a firm and its business units; and (3) better explanations for investors as to how a firm creates long-term value.

5. **How best to design compensation packages that optimize the balance between short-term performance and building**

---

[53] Dan Jones and Jim Womack, 2011, *Seeing the Whole Value Stream*. Cambridge, MA: Lean Enterprise Institute. The authors note: "We drew the path of a humble cola can. This simple product with only three parts (barrel, top, and 'pop-top') traveled 319 days through nine facilities owned by six companies in four countries to progress from ore in the ground into the hands of the customer. Yet during this long march only three hours of value-creating activities were performed and the great majority of the steps—storing, picking, packing, shipping, unpacking, binning, checking, reworking, and endless movements of information to manage the system's complexity—created no value at all."

long-term value, which may involve significant outlays for intangibles? This work would benefit from experience in using the life-cycle framework to understand long-term value creation as reflected in stock prices. In particular, one should appreciate the process of value creation illustrated by Amazon's quarterly earnings shortfalls due to making exceptionally large investments in new businesses which coincided with rising stock prices. Similarly, Netflix made large investments which tempered their quarterly earnings but resulted in a sharply rising subscriber base and a rising stock price.

6. **How best to organize data about the firm's operations and management's decisions (especially strategic decisions) that shows how well or poorly these activities utilize components of the knowledge-building loop illustrated in Figure 2.1: purposes, worldview, perceptions, actions and consequences, feedback, and the validity of core assumptions in the knowledge base?** A core proposition in this book is that if you could choose just one thing for a firm's management to get right in order to survive and prosper over the long term, that would be a firm's knowledge-building proficiency.

There are many ongoing approaches designed to improve communication in order to facilitate value-creating decisions. This is an obvious commonsense need to fill. Although these various approaches do not attempt to deal with all of the key questions posed above, some of these approaches represent significant steps to improve decision-making.

For instance, the Balanced Scorecard is designed to coordinate activities to achieve long-term strategic goals. Measurements are focused on financial performance, customer knowledge, business processes, and capabilities. The architects of the Balanced Scorecard, Robert Kaplan and David Norton, note that: "Every measure selected for a Balanced Scorecard should be an element in a chain of cause-and-effect relationships that communicate the meaning of the business unit's strategy to the organization."[54] Moreover, they recommend an Office of Strategic Management to coordinate activities across functions and business units (conceptually similar to value stream maps used by lean thinkers).[55] This important thinking about coordination is shared by Toyota, which gives remarkably wide responsibility to their Chief Engineers (CEs). At Toyota, CEs have responsibility for developing new vehicles but no authority over the functional groups doing the work. Their success depends upon their skill in building knowledge and effectively communicating with others—the essence of a value-creating language. The following is a glimpse into the role of CEs and their emphasis on building knowledge:

> It's clear that the chief engineers are target-driven and timing-driven, yet always willing to step back and reflect on the range of options that are available. One thing about the Lexus and the Prius is the "no-compromise" attitude of the chief engineers. At some point, with the intense time pressure to do a seemingly impossible job, one would expect the leader to say, "OK, let's pick a direction and just get on with it." But repeatedly throughout the Prius development, Uchiyamada [CE Takeshi Uchiyamada] would step back and say, "Let's stop and reflect. Let's rethink what this project is about. Let's test every possible design for a hybrid engine in the world. Let's have a design competition and get all the styling studios to generate competitive designs." Suzuki [Ichiro Suzuki, who has the reputation of being the Michael Jordan of Toyota's CEs] decided to do what had never been done in engine technology, aerodynamics, and fuel economy through experimenting and trying new ideas. … Exploring all possible alternatives and considering pros and cons of each while consulting all partners who have something to offer allows Toyota to execute fast, once a decision is finally made, without backtracking to remake decisions.[56]

---

[54] Robert S. Kaplan and David P. Norton, 1996, *The Balanced Scorecard: Translating Strategy into Action.* Boston: Harvard Business Press, p. 31.
[55] Robert S. Kaplan and David P. Norton, 2008, *The Execution Premium: Linking Strategy to Operations for Competitive Advantage.* Boston: Harvard Business Press.
[56] Jeffrey K. Liker, 2004, *The Toyota Way: 14 Management Principles from the World's Greatest Manufacturer.* New York: McGraw-Hill, p. 64.

Perhaps a useful name for those who specialize in this type of coordination is *system conductor,* similar to the role of an orchestra conductor. Much can be learned about a value-creating language by studying the thinking and communicating processes used by Toyota CEs and others who orchestrate highly effective coordination in complex environments. The qualitative nature of these studies sharply differs from those using quantitative accounting-based data; however, such studies can yield valuable insights about how knowledge is created and communicated, leading to value creation involving thousands of people, which is of the utmost importance to understand.

In their book, *The End of Accounting and the Path Forward for Investors and Managers,* Baruch Lev and Feng Gu promote an industry-specific Strategic Resources and Consequences Report designed to communicate how a firm can potentially achieve economic returns above the cost of capital (competitive advantage). The report is organized in a logical sequence with detailed information that addresses: developing resources (e.g., R&D outlays), resource stocks (e.g., patents), resource preservation, resource deployment, and value created. This proposal is in the spirit of Integrated Reports (Chapter 5) but with a far greater emphasis on business economics. Importantly, the spotlight is put on intangibles which can be unique and difficult for competitors to duplicate as opposed to tangible assets that are easily copied.

Keep in mind that today's accounting system was mainly shaped in the early 1900s to support manufacturing products in batches—a push system which is diametrically opposite to a preferred pull system that ties manufacturing to customer orders using lean processes designed to reduce waste throughout the entire system. Standard cost accounting is about minimizing cost per unit produced, which encourages local efficiencies, not overall system efficiency. For manufacturing firms, standard cost accounting is designed to reward maximum production and work-in-process inventories and penalize unused capacity. Both lean proponents and Theory of Constraints (TOC) proponents strongly object to standard cost accounting and instead tie measurements to value streams using a systems mindset. TOC founder, Eli Goldratt, often made presentations titled "Cost Accounting—Public Enemy Number One of Productivity."[57]

The above discussion about accounting language, specifically the language of standard cost accounting, returns us to the knowledge-building loop of Figure 2.1, which has purposes as one component. Note the divergent purposes between standard cost accounting and overall system efficiency:

> Lean companies make money by maximizing flow on the pull from the customer, not by maximizing resource utilization. Lean companies realize that maximizing resource utilization leads to overproduction, inventory, and large batches. ... Lean companies relentlessly eliminate waste to create available capacity to meet increasing customer demand—and generate more profits. Again, standard cost information will send the wrong message—that resources are being underutilized even though customer-focused operational performance such as improved on-time shipments, are improving. Operational performance in a lean [manufacturing] company is measured by improvements in cycle time, productivity, quality, flow, and cost. Standard cost information does not provide any relevant performance measures in any of these areas. Indeed, standard costing systems provide information that motivates people to take actions that sabotage lean operational improvement.[58]

The use of accounting data should be in the context of value creation and not the standard cost accounting that is attuned to the manufacturing world of the early 1900s. At one level of analysis, value creation is about a comparison of ROI versus the opportunity cost of capital. A more comprehensive level addresses market value created and involves present value calculations of future net cash receipts. As explained in Chapter 4, an especially useful way to forecast net cash receipts is via the life-cycle variables

---

[57] Eric Noreen, Debra Smith, and James T. Mackey, 1995, *The Theory of Constraints and Its Implications for Management Accounting*. Great Barrington, MA: North River Press.

[58] Brian Maskell and Nicholas Katko, "Value Stream Costing: The Lean Solution to Standard Costing Complexity and Waste." In Joe Stenzel, ed., 2007, *Lean Accounting: Best Practices for Sustainable Integration*. Hoboken, NJ: John Wiley & Sons.

of economic returns and reinvestment rates that incorporate long-term mean-reversion.

Another way to express the critical ROI versus cost of capital comparison is to deduct a capital charge from a firm's income. The resulting *residual income* (first used by General Electric) involves a deduction computed as the product of a firm's assets multiplied by its cost of capital.[59] The residual income concept has been popularized as EVA (economic value added).[60]

What is the difference between EVA track records and the life-cycle track records using CFROIs, which are displayed throughout this book?

We can differentiate these concepts by focusing on purpose. The purpose of residual income/EVA is to draw attention to the direction and magnitude of value created (positive) or dissipated (negative) for ongoing business units and firms (not startups). This is a step in the right direction away from earnings and earnings per share growth rates as a guide to a firm's performance. However, users of EVA in business environments need to be mindful of the previously discussed crossover problem. Managing with an accounting-based metric like EVA at lower levels of the business can be at cross-purposes with managing improvements guided by process variables.

The purpose of life-cycle track records is to gain insights as to levels and trends in economic returns and reinvestment rates; to understand the key issue determining a firm's current market value—its economic returns or reinvestment rates, or both; to facilitate comparisons with competitors on a global basis; to raise questions as to the adjustments (especially for intangibles) made to calculate economic returns and reinvestment rates; and to provide plausible checks regarding forecasts of future fade of economic returns and reinvestment rates. Consequently, we see that EVA's gain in simplicity, by compressing all the life-cycle variables into a single number, is

---

[59] David Solomons, 1965, *Divisional Performance: Measurement and Control.* Homewood, IL: Richard D. Irwin.

[60] G. Bennett Stewart, 1991, *The Quest for Value.* New York: HarperBusiness. EVA is a registered service mark of Stern Value Management, Ltd. (originally by Stern Stewart & Co. in 1994) for financial management and consulting services in the area of business valuation, and is registered as a trademark by Institutional Shareholder Services Inc. (originally by EVA Dimensions LLC in 2008) for a number of uses.

a shortcoming for deeper analysis.[61] For example, EVA users often use some version of a CAPM/Beta equity cost of capital which involves an estimate of Beta and an estimate of the equity risk premium. These estimates are subject to wide variation and can have a significant impact on the final calculation of EVA, such as switching from a positive EVA to a negative EVA. But this dilemma is obfuscated by the single compressed EVA number.

What we see is the unavoidable tradeoff between simplicity and complexity. For example, CFROIs and reinvestment rates are inflation adjusted, which is essential for analyses that cover long time periods and especially important for cross-comparisons with firms on a global basis. However, inflation adjustments entail significant effort whose incremental cost may not exceed the benefit for managers whose firms operate in a low-inflation environment.

Here is an important issue when interpreting a time series (track record) of EVAs for a business unit or firm. Is a year-to-year increase in EVA due to a higher reinvestment rate in above-cost-of-capital projects or a reduction in reinvestment in below-cost-of-capital projects? The former is more difficult to do and is encouraging for favorable fade in the future, whereas the later tends to be a short-term benefit and less sustainable as to value creation over the long term. In contrast, life-cycle track records provide a clear visual explanation of the interrelated impact of economic returns, cost of capital, and reinvestment rates on value creation.

In summary, the above discussion of six critically important questions involves knowledge building, especially the role of language in shaping our perceptions. Research that improves our answers to these questions will likely involve seeing behind the assumptions in the words we use and thereby sharpening our language for value creation.

---

[61] For a discussion of some of the measurement problems with EVA, see Greg Milano, 2019, "Beyond EVA," *Journal of Applied Corporate Finance* 31(3): 116–125. The author explains the advantage of a return measure based on gross assets, as used in the CFROI calculation. The problem with using a return measure based on net assets, as used in the EVA calculation, is that as assets age their accumulated depreciation charges rise. This produces a declining net asset amount thereby artificially boosting the calculated return on net assets and EVA.

Part III

Value Creation

6

LIFE-CYCLE POSITION, ADAPTABILITY, AND ORGANIZATIONAL STRUCTURE

*Founders and entrepreneurs set the tone as they form their new orga-
nizations, so leaders clearly create culture from the outset. But as these
organizations mature, their cultures determine what kind of leaders they
choose. They develop a very clear idea of what leadership is supposed to
be in that environment, and they select people for senior jobs who match
that profile. The same thing happens throughout the ranks. A young
organization draws on a variety of talents to achieve success, but as it ages,
it develops strong beliefs, expressed in job descriptions, about what kinds of
talent are needed and then recruits only those people. Talent management
in the very mature organization then becomes a subtle process of the
culture just re-creating itself, of hiring only people who "fit" in both
the technical culture (how tasks get done) and the social culture (how
relationships work in the organization). When the outside environment,*

*or microculture, changes, organizations arrive at a moment of truth: We
need innovation, yet we can't get our people to do it!*

—Edgar Schein[1]

*If we can agree that the economic problem of society is mainly one of rapid
adaptation to changes in the particular circumstances of time and place, it
would seem to follow that the ultimate decisions must be left to the people
who are familiar with these circumstances, who know directly of the relevant changes and of the resources immediately available to meet them. We
cannot expect that this problem will be solved by first communicating all
this knowledge to a central board which, after integrating all knowledge,
issues its order. We must solve it by some form of decentralization.*

—Friedrich Hayek[2]

LIFE-CYCLE GUIDEPOSTS

The firm's competitive life-cycle was introduced in Chapter 4 and illustrates significant stages throughout a firm's life. Even though competition
inevitably forces economic returns toward the cost of capital, for a period
of time a firm can overcome the typical fade pattern due to competition
and produce increasing economic returns (e.g., as previously noted, Apple's
subsequent surge in profitability after Steve Jobs returned to the company).

At any point in time, a firm or one of its business units can be positioned
on the competitive life cycle. The critical management task for each specific
life-cycle stage is shown in the bottom of Figure 6.1.

In the high innovation stage, top priority should be given to test the
validity of those assumptions that are critical to future business success.
Management should be especially careful about automatically assuming
that what worked in the past will work in a much different future. In
2004, Michelin management agreed with the forecast made by the consumer research firm J. D. Powers and Associates that within six years, 80%
of new cars would be sold equipped with Michelin's run-flat tires. Many

[1] Edgar Schein in a conversation between Edgar H. Schein and Peter A. Schein, 2019, "A New Era for
Culture, Change, and Leadership," *MIT Sloan Management Review* Summer 60(4): 52–58.
[2] F. A. Hayek, 1945, "The Use of Knowledge in Society," *American Economic Review* 35(4): 519–530.

FIGURE 6.1 Competitive life-cycle stages and key management tasks

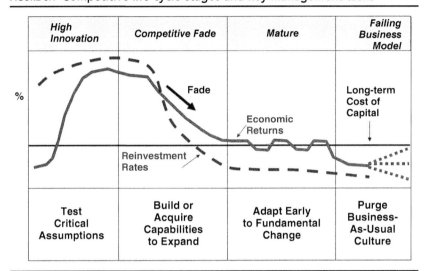

years before, Michelin invented the radial tire which quickly gained wide adoption. Management assumed that their new invention of run-flat tires would follow a similar path to commercial success. But the introduction of run-flat tires resulted in a major financial loss to Michelin primarily due to ignoring the role of service centers. The owners of the service centers were not motivated to purchase the expensive equipment to repair run-flat tires *and* incur training expenses to gain Michelin certification—significant upfront costs with only the prospect of meaningful revenue in the distant future if run-flat tires were widely adopted.[3]

FOCUSED EXECUTION OF AN INNOVATIVE BUSINESS MODEL—NETFLIX

A different business outcome followed a key assumption about consumers that led to Netflix pioneering the delivery of personalized entertainment over the Internet after starting in 1997 as a DVD-rental-by-mail operation.

---

[3] Ron Adner, 2012, *The Wide Lens: What Successful Innovators See That Others Miss.* New York: Penguin Group, pp. 17–23.

The original DVD rental business offered higher quality compared to low resolution videotapes. Netflix cofounder and CEO, Reed Hastings, recalls when he formulated the key assumption:

> I had a big late fee for *Apollo 13*. It was six weeks late, and I owed the video store $40. I had misplaced the cassette. It was all my fault. I didn't want to tell my wife about it. And I said to myself, "I'm going to compromise the integrity of my marriage over a late fee." … I started thinking, "How come movie rentals don't work like a health club, where, whether you use it a lot or a little, you get the same charge?"[4]

Not only was this core assumption confirmed, but Netflix has continued to successfully experiment (test assumptions) with different ways to create value for customers. Netflix's DVD business attracted competition from Amazon and Walmart. With a focus on the long term, Hastings and his partner Marc Randolph early on recognized both the potential for video-on-demand to obsolete the firm's DVD business and the importance of Netflix being flexible as to technology. They positioned Netflix to decentralize entertainment via the Internet.

Blockbuster used physical stores for distribution, which eventually became an anchor making it difficult to change course to a video-on-demand business model and compete with Netflix. Blockbuster management had an opportunity in 2000 to acquire Netflix for $50 million and declined, which will probably rank as the biggest missed deal of the century. What Blockbuster management did not see was the potential for fast-learning, highly motivated entrepreneurs to create value at a huge scale through early and smart strategic moves with a sharper eye on the future than their competitors.

On their website, Netflix management sums up their current business model:

> Netflix is a global Internet entertainment services network offering movies and TV series commercial-free, with unlimited viewing on

---

[4] Matthew Honan, "Photo Essay: Unlikely Places Where *Wired* Pioneers Had Their *Eureka!* Moments," *Wired Magazine*, March 24, 2008.

any Internet-connected screen for an affordable, no-commitment monthly fee. Netflix is a focused passion brand, not a do-everything brand: Starbucks, not 7-Eleven; Southwest, not United; HBO, not Dish.

We are about the freedom of on-demand and the fun of binge viewing. We are about the flexibility of any screen at any time. We are about a personal experience that finds for each person the most pleasing titles from around the world.[5]

Figure 6.2 displays Netflix's life-cycle performance.

The life-cycle chart in Figure 6.2 shows CFROIs sharply declining after 2010 while asset growth rates were maintained at extraordinarily high rates (approximately 35% per year). Management purposively sacrificed short-term profitability in order to make huge investments, particularly in original programming, to secure the leadership position in online entertainment. The success of this strategy was reflected in Netflix's rapid growth in subscribers. From 2002 to 2018, Netflix's shareholders outperformed the S&P 500 approximately 100-fold (see bottom panel). In 2016, the magnitude of Netflix's growth was emphasized by Vladimir Medinsky, Russian Minister of Culture, when he asserted that Netflix was on the government payroll and the White House had figured out "how to enter every home, creep into every television, and through that television, into the head of every person on earth, with the help of Netflix."[6]

As Netflix transitioned from a successful startup to an established firm in the competitive fade stage, top priority was given to expansion with new capabilities as needed. Netflix launched a new streaming video product in 2007 when existing technology was slow with poor resolution. However, the firm invested heavily to improve their streaming technology well in advance of competitors. Note that Netflix's software to evaluate subscribers' preferences can also inform management as to the type of original content movies and TV series that will likely be well received. Netflix's high reinvestment rates facilitated expansion into original content of high quality and increased its global subscriber base. The firm has excelled in

---

[5] https://www.netflixinvestor.com/ir-overview/long-term-view/default.aspx accessed on 19 July 2019.
[6] Tom Parfitt, June 24, 2016, "Netflix Is Just a CIA Plot, says Kremlin," *The Times*.

FIGURE 6.2 Netflix 2000 to 2018

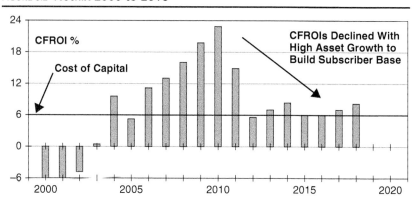

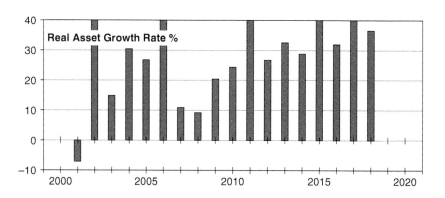

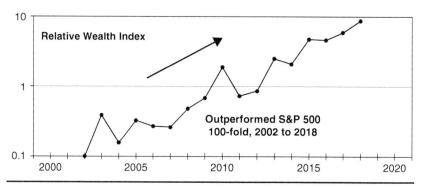

Source: Based on data from Credit Suisse HOLT global database.

knowledge building, especially in building local knowledge in countries outside the United States. Local knowledge includes insights about political, institutional, cultural, and technical issues facilitating a remarkable expansion to 190 countries in seven years.[7] This suggests sustained high CFROIs in the future, which has been duly noted by investors as shown in the bottom panel of Figure 6.2. However, competition is relentless, and the preeminent original content provider, Disney, has entered the streaming service business; this may well dampen Netflix's future growth.

Netflix is a huge winner in the New Economy. We would expect such a firm to be grounded in a robust, knowledge-building, value-creating culture. On the firm's website is an extensive description of the Netflix culture which is condensed into five points.

- Encourage independent decision-making by employees.
- Share information openly, broadly, and deliberately.
- Be extraordinarily candid with each other.
- Keep only our highly effective people.
- Avoid rules.

Feedback is an especially important component of the knowledge-building loop of Figure 2.1 and is critical to the Netflix culture in terms of sharing information and being extraordinarily candid.

> We believe we will learn faster and be better if we can make giving and receiving feedback less stressful and a more normal part of work life. Feedback is a continuous part of how we communicate and work with one another versus an occasional formal exercise. We build trust by being selfless in giving feedback to our colleagues even if it is uncomfortable to do so. Feedback helps us avoid sustained misunderstandings and the need for rules.[8]

In the competitive fade stage, a firm is generating high economic returns with significant reinvestment rates. Maintaining such stellar life-cycle

---

[7] Louis Brennan, 2018, "How Netflix Expanded to 190 Countries in 7 Years," October 12, https://hbr.org/2018/how-netflix-expanded-to-190-countries-in-7-years.
[8] https://jobs.netflix.com/culture accessed July 19, 2019.

performance (favorable future fade rate) requires management to seize opportunities to create significant value that may exceed the firm's current capabilities. The so-called management truisms of "stick to the knitting" and "focus on the core" are a recipe for fast fade.

Amazon has avoided the type of culture (described by Edgar Schein at the beginning of this chapter) which perpetuates particular skills/talents resulting in a firm becoming incapable of significant innovation in a world that experiences significant change. Here Jeff Bezos describes Amazon's innovation process.

> Companies get skills-focused, instead of customer-needs focused. When [companies] think about extending their business into some new area, the first question is "Why should we do that—we don't have any skills in that area." That approach puts a finite lifetime on a company, because the world changes, and what used to be cutting-edge skills have turned into something your customers may not need anymore. A much more stable strategy is to start with "What do my customers need?" Then do an inventory of the gaps in your skills. Kindle is a great example. If we set our strategy by what our skills happen to be rather than by what our customers need, we never would have done it. We had to go out and hire people who know how to build hardware devices and create a whole new competency for the company.[9]

INNOVATION IN THE OPERATING ROOM—INTUITIVE SURGICAL

Figure 6.3 illustrates the life-cycle performance of Intuitive Surgical. In the early years, the firm was in the high innovation startup stage proving its technology. In 2001, the FDA approved the da Vinci robotic surgical system for prostate surgeries with the goal of less invasive surgery, reduced surgical errors, and faster patient recovery times. By 2018 nearly 5,000 da Vincis were employed in operating rooms for one million surgeries per year. As shown in Figure 6.3, high economic returns and high asset growth rates have been sustained during the competitive fade stage of Intuitive

---

[9]Interview, April 16, 2008, "Bezos on Innovation," *Bloomberg Businessweek*.

FIGURE 6.3 Intuitive Surgical 2000 to 2018

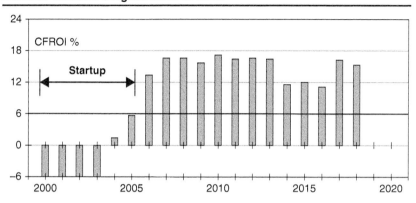

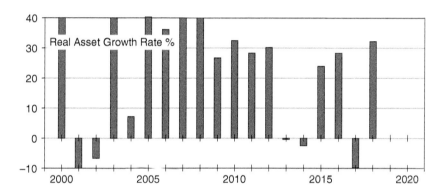

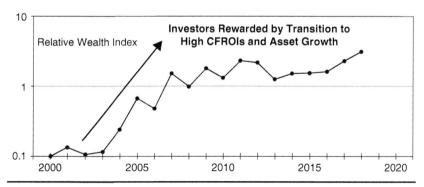

Source: Based on data from Credit Suisse HOLT global database.

Surgical's life cycle. As to expanding its capabilities, the firm has developed expertise in systems, instruments, stapling, energy, and vision while moving beyond its mainstay prostate operation to include hernia and lung procedures. Recent technological R&D has addressed augmented reality, big data analytics, and artificial intelligence.

Figure 6.3 shows the firm in the startup part of the high innovation stage occurring from 2000 to 2005. During this period, large investments were made in order to develop its robotic technology. Investors began realizing the firm's potential from 2003 to 2005 when the stock sharply outperformed the S&P 500, illustrated with the rising relative wealth index in the bottom panel of Figure 6.3. The top and middle panels of this figure document that the firm did deliver exceptional life-cycle performance 2006 to 2018, which resulted in significant shareholder rewards.

Intuitive Surgical aptly exemplifies an important point made in Chapter 1 (see Figure 1.1): the benefits to society from a successful business innovation far exceed the benefits to the firm's shareholders. Although difficult to precisely quantify, a strong case can be made that the past and future benefits to patients from robotic surgery far exceed the rewards to Intuitive Surgical's shareholders.

By way of background as to the impact of CEOs who manage high-technology firms, an important study focused on "Inventor CEOs" who have a personal track record of being awarded patents.

> We show that firms led by Inventor CEOs are associated with a greater volume of registered patents, more highly cited patents, higher innovation efficiency, and a greater propensity to produce ground-breaking, or disruptive innovations. ... CEOs with high impact inventor experience, as well as CEOs who maintain first-hand involvement in their firm's innovation, have an incrementally positive effect on their firm's patent output and impact. ... Firms exogenously switching from Inventor to non-Inventor CEOs experience a significant decline in corporate innovation ... our results paint a consistent picture of the unique innovation-enhancing capabilities that CEOs with hands-on experience "doing" innovation bring to their firms.[10]

---

[10] Emdad Islam and Jason Zein, forthcoming, "Inventor CEOs," *Journal of Financial Economics*.

Here is a concrete example of one CEO's innovation-enhancing capabilities. Gary Guthart, CEO of Intuitive Surgical since 2010, has a PhD in Engineering Science from the California Institute of Technology, and there is a long list of patents owned by Intuitive Surgical with Guthart listed as one of the inventors. Since he became CEO, his managerial skill coupled to his technical expertise has contributed to the firm's enviable track record. That track record has recently attracted competitors, including Medtronic and a startup, Verb Surgical, funded by Johnson & Johnson and Alphabet (Google).

Intuitive Surgical creates value primarily through the intangible (human) capital of its employees, which differs from the Old Economy with winners achieving scale advantages through tangible capital (factories). The next section reviews how management of an Old Economy firm did not wait for Silicon Valley startups to disrupt its business.

NOTHING RUNS LIKE A DEERE

John Deere represents an especially strong brand for farmers. The company began in the mid-1800s when John Deere, a blacksmith, constructed a rugged, high-performing plow from a steel sawblade. Noted for its tractors and other farm equipment, the company also manufactures construction, forestry, industrial, and lawn care equipment. All of these products face stiff competition.

As noted earlier, strong brands have an emotional connection to customers. Deere has earned that loyalty through long-term innovation and reliability. During the Great Depression in the early 1930s, for example, Deere lent money to struggling farmers.

From 1960 to the early 1990s Deere was in the mature life-cycle stage earning approximately the cost of capital economic returns (dark horizontal line at 6% real in the top panel of Figure 6.4). The next 25 years displays cyclical and mostly value-creating CFROIs in excess of the cost of capital. What caused this improvement?

FIGURE 6.4 **Deere 1960 to 2018**

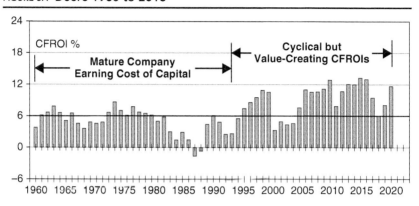

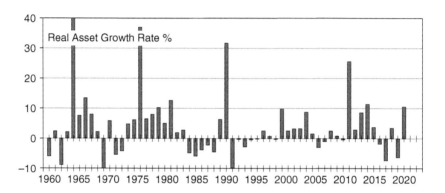

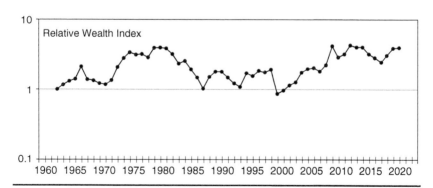

Source: Based on data from Credit Suisse HOLT global database.

Management adapted early to fundamental change: In order to better compete in a changing global environment of heightened competition, management implemented a financial discipline known as SVA (Shareholder Value Added). SVA's objective is to coordinate decision-making, especially resource allocation decisions, to deliver economic returns greater than the cost of capital. Consistent with this renewed focus on value creation and efficient innovation, Deere evolved from a product-centric business to incorporate a platform-centric capability to better compete in the digital world of the New Economy.

Deere intends to be the global leader in precision agriculture that enables farming with Deere products to be automated and more precise across the production process. The Deere platform exploits the Internet of Things (IoT) environment with sensors on their machines and probes in the soil. Software tools, data sharing, and artificial intelligence (AI) help their customers increase yield and decrease costs in all phases of farming.

In 2017, Deere acquired Blue River Technologies, which uses computer vision and machine learning in order to radically reduce the use of herbicides by spraying only where weeds are growing. Management has staked out a high-tech future.

> When you say IoT, you normally think of things that fit in your pocket. The "T" for us is ten-ton tractors. Our large equipment now has … modems, with WiFi and Bluetooth, and that does two-way communication so it collects data off your farm and sends it to the cloud. It also takes instructions from Deere or from dealers or other software companies and sends it to the machine … tells the machine what to do.
>
> Our roadmap is calling for machine learning and AI to find their way into every piece of John Deere equipment over time. What we do with our eyes can be done more accurately with a camera and a computer, with a system that retains that data and never forgets, and gets smarter with every pass of the field. This also applies to our construction and heavy equipment divisions.[11]

---

[11] Interview with John Stone, SVP of John Deere's Intelligent Solutions Group, Scott Ferguson, March 12, 2018, "John Deere Bets the Farm on AI, IoT," *Light Reading*.

SMITH CORONA AND NCR

The key managerial task for firms in the failing business model stage is to purge a business-as-usual culture and reject an obsolete business model ill-suited to today's changing world. But this can be difficult for top management whose past successes and promotions were likely achieved because they skillfully executed the existing business model. Moreover, reliance on what has worked in the past (assumptions) is not at all easy to purge from one's knowledge base absent concrete feedback about change taking place that is likely to impair the existing business model. Successful adaptation entails major resource allocation decisions, the redirection of existing capabilities and the building of new capabilities, and at times, the acceptance of a much smaller and refocused company that can efficiently deliver value to customers at its smaller size. Let's briefly review the histories of two firms that were in the failing business model stage of their life cycle, Smith Corona and NCR. The former eventually went bankrupt while the latter was revitalized.

In the late 1800s, the Smith Premium Typewriter Company redirected its expertise in mechanical processes and manufacturing techniques for firearms to making and selling typewriters. In 1926, the firm merged with Corona Typewriter Company. The combined entity, Smith Corona, quickly gained the leading share of the typewriter market in the United States. After World War II, the firm produced a major innovation, the world's first portable electric typewriter and, by 1980, had a 50% share of the typewriter market. After being acquired by Hanson Trust in 1986 and doing an IPO in 1989, Smith Corona filed for bankruptcy just six years after its IPO.

Feedback ideally facilitates new knowledge building that is critical in directing innovation both for existing products and new products that may significantly differ from existing products. Smith Corona developed a capability in electronics but only applied this skill to enhance typewriters and word processors. With falling profits, management did initiate workforce reductions and asset sales but these funds merely continued business as usual.

The core problem was a serious lack of knowledge-building proficiency that resulted in top management and the board of directors *committing to new products based on a faulty assumption about the power of the Smith Corona brand*. They assumed that the well-known Smith Corona brand could be advantageously used in products for home and office use that were not typewriters. Their failure to early on rigorously test this assumption led to a multitude of undifferentiated and unsuccessful products, manufactured for the most part by other firms, and carrying the Smith Corona name. Consumers were not impressed because they viewed the quality implied by the Smith Corona brand as belonging specifically to typewriters.[12]

In addition, management was exceedingly slow to recognize how personal computers would sharply decline in price while simultaneously making huge improvements in user functionality. More adverse change was afoot since the small stores that had deep relationships with Smith Corona were being put out of business by new super-stores such as Walmart. All the while, the firm's culture was rooted in the slow changes to typewriters that occurred over 100 years, not the seismic changes in the blink of an eye that accompanied the personal computer revolution.

With hindsight one can analyze a company's long-term history and pinpoint "causes" of a decline in profitability and even bankruptcy. Oftentimes, such an analysis suggests that the root causes were either strategic errors or slowness in developing new capabilities. However (as readers might anticipate), I believe the root cause of either exceptionally good or bad long-term performance lies in the firm's knowledge-building proficiency. The captain of the firm's knowledge-building ship is the CEO. When CEOs adapt to a changing environment at a snail's pace, maintain organizational structures ill-suited to a new world, and make strategic mistakes, this is emblematic of a flawed knowledge-building process. The fix, if it is not too late, is a new CEO highly skilled in building knowledge and bringing business experience and leadership skill that enables him or her to hit the ground running.

---

[12] Erwin Danneels, 2010, "Trying to Become a Different Type of Company: Dynamic Capability at Smith Corona," *Strategic Management Journal* 32(1): 1–31.

This may be one of those "obvious once you think about it" observations. Yet, top management positions are often assigned to those with stellar track records in decision-making within a system attuned to what worked well in the past with minimal attention to an executive's skill in orchestrating knowledge, especially feedback about the external environment. That knowledge-building skill enables a manager to excel in different contexts, much like Lou Gerstner's managerial skill (quoted in Chapter 2) that enabled him to successfully restructure IBM.

When a firm has been managed for a long time by one or more CEOs accustomed to success in a slow-changing competitive environment, expect a firm-wide culture with processes (our way of doing things) with deep roots. This is because these processes have had a long undisturbed time to grow deep roots, even though more efficient ways of doing things may be achievable.

Let us now review how NCR faced no less a difficult situation due to a failing business model.

The NCR story begins as the National Cash Register company founded by John H. Patterson in 1884. In 1911, NCR sold 95% of the world's cash registers, and later its product line expanded to include adding and accounting machines. These were complex electromechanical products designed and manufactured in one integrated facility in Dayton, Ohio. In 1938, an in-house research effort began to explore electronics. In the early 1950s, NCR added a fourth product line—digital computers—and acquired Computer Research Corporation (CRC). NCR management viewed computers as distinct from its other products and believed that computers represented an evolution not a revolution.[13]

Management extrapolated the past slow evolution of cash register innovations, which NCR basically controlled, to apply to computers in the future. They concluded the firm's existing organizational structure focused around electromechanical technologies was satisfactory. Product development attuned to slow-moving change remained intact, quite contrary to

---

[13] Richard S. Rosenbloom, 2000, "Leadership, Capabilities, and Technological Change: The Transformation of NCR in the Electronic Era," *Strategic Management Journal* 21: 1083–1103.

CRC's forward-looking founders focused on fast-paced change. Eventually, CRC's manufacturing personnel were laid off. An ill-conceived joint venture was formed with General Electric given responsibility for manufacturing computers. NCR's R&D staff remained in Dayton surrounded by a legacy of mechanical engineering. Business-as-usual reinvestment was maintained in yesterday's technologies. At the massive manufacturing facility in Dayton, thousands of mechanical parts were made, even including screws—nothing was outsourced. Manufacturing costs were excessive, and inefficient work processes proliferated, insulated by union work rules.

Retail firms, the mainstay of NCR's long-term business relationships, wanted computerized point-of-sale systems; but NCR salespeople responded by demonstrating the newest features to existing products that they asserted would maintain a wide cost advantage over any future computerized products. IBM soon gained dominance in the computer industry with the introduction of its 360 series. Meanwhile, William Anderson was running NCR's business in Japan and delivering impressive results. He was unusually skilled in learning about what customers really needed, and he even developed an electronic cash register suited to local needs.

Think for a moment about the degree of difficulty in restructuring NCR as profits plummeted in the early 1970s and 100,000 employees were entrenched in a culture of fossilized processes that guaranteed failure in the new electronics world. That task went to William Anderson, who became CEO in 1972.

In contrast to Smith Corona's failure to make a radical break from the past, Anderson literally declared martial law for NCR. Upon assuming his leadership role, he quickly taped a video to employees plainly communicating that business as usual no longer works: "Complacency and apathy—these are NCR's greatest sins. Until we see a return to profitability, something akin to martial law will be in effect in Dayton."[14]

Keep in mind that Anderson survived being a POW in a Japanese prisoner camp during World War II. His biography reflects an individual with

---

[14]Linda Grant Martin, 1975, "What Happened at NCR after the Boss Declared Martial Law?" *Fortune*, September: 100–104.

unique determination and skill in learning about change, in leading people, and in organizing resources to deliver products and services that genuinely created value for customers.[15] He made his mark in Japan outside of the stifling bureaucratic culture of Dayton.

Fortunate for Anderson, NCR's board of directors fully supported the needed organizational restructuring initiated by Anderson. New product development was moved from Dayton to self-contained business units that primarily out-sourced the supply of electronic components. The sales force was organized to focus on particular types of customers complemented by field engineers to service customers. Large-scale layoffs were unavoidable. Anderson's deep knowledge of customers led him to reverse NCR's strategy of treating computers as a distinct product independent of NCR's other products. He believed that NCR had to connect its terminals to host computers manufactured by NCR thereby delivering to customers a complete system. As Anderson successfully orchestrated the transition to electronic systems, NCR's 3% CFROIs at the beginning of his tenure rose to 10% prior to NCR merging with AT&T in 1991. Sadly, the AT&T bureaucratic culture resulted in the wholesale loss of NCR's senior management, and the merger proved to be a financial disaster. NCR again became a public company in 1997.

Smith Corona's bankruptcy and NCR's successful restructuring illustrate how top management's worldview based on assumptions rooted in past experiences shape perceptions and actions taken or not taken. Particularly important is a CEO's cognitive process for perceiving the world and learning about change.

THE ABCs OF ORGANIZATIONAL STRUCTURE

As firms grow large, they tend to add layers of management and silos of expertise in order to increase control of operations. This results in a proliferation of rules and regimented ways to achieve targets set by the next higher-up management level. The end result is a bureaucratic,

---

[15]William S. Anderson, 1991, *Corporate Crisis: NCR and the Computer Revolution*. Dayton, OH: Landfall Press.

command-and-control hierarchical structure with decisions made at the top that translate into marching orders for those at the bottom of the hierarchical pyramid. Information is limited to those who need it according to their position in the hierarchy. This structure is labeled type-A in Figure 6.5.

Many have argued that 21st-century organizations can create far more value for customers and other stakeholders by transitioning to an organizational structure that flattens the hierarchical pyramid.[16] Such a structure focuses on teams comprised of individuals doing the work of efficiently serving customers. In Figure 6.5, organization type-B reflects sharply reduced layers of management (shrunken pyramid).

During his tenure as CEO of Nucor from 1965 to 1996, Ken Iverson nurtured a flattened, type-B organizational structure focused on supporting teams in the steel mills so that managers enabled an environment that frees employees to determine what they do and should do, to the benefit

FIGURE 6.5 Three types of organizational structure for business firms

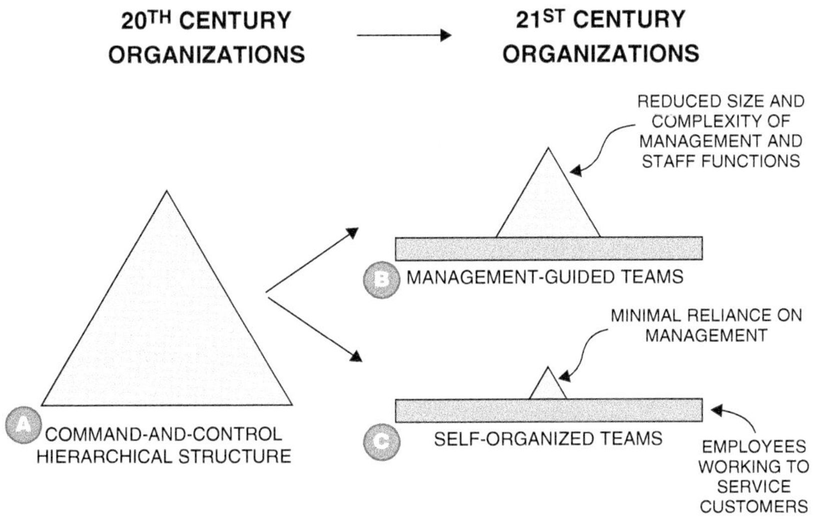

20TH CENTURY ORGANIZATIONS → 21ST CENTURY ORGANIZATIONS

REDUCED SIZE AND COMPLEXITY OF MANAGEMENT AND STAFF FUNCTIONS

B MANAGEMENT-GUIDED TEAMS

MINIMAL RELIANCE ON MANAGEMENT

A COMMAND-AND-CONTROL HIERARCHICAL STRUCTURE

C SELF-ORGANIZED TEAMS

EMPLOYEES WORKING TO SERVICE CUSTOMERS

---

[16] Frederic Laloux, 2014, *Reinventing Organizations: A Guide to Creating Organizations Inspired by the Next Stage of Human Consciousness*. Brussels, Belgium: Nelson Parker. Also see a report published in 2017 by Gallup, *State of the Global Workplace*, which highlights findings from Gallup's ongoing study of workplaces in more than 140 countries.

of themselves and the business. Recall the discussion in Chapter 3 about Toyota's preeminent lean manufacturing system focused not on managers telling employees what to do, but employees guided by mentors who are skilled in asking questions that help employees solve problems, all the while employees are improving their knowledge-building skills.

When a firm's CEO (perhaps a founder) has been at the helm for a long period, the firm's organizational structure can evolve into a shape preferred by the CEO. Key ingredients to Netflix's culture, noted earlier, include sharing information broadly, being extraordinarily candid with each other, and avoiding rules. These desirable type-B characteristics are far easier to achieve for a firm like Netflix, which has had the same CEO for its entire existence. Changing from a type-A (especially so for a large firm) to a type-B is an exceptionally difficult challenge. Why? At all levels of the firm, people have evolved a worldview of how to do things rooted in assumptions based on experiences within a command-and-control hierarchy. Not so easy to change, which is why type-B firms face difficulty with integrating managers who have spent a long time working in type-A environments.

What can we learn from type-C firms that have nearly eliminated management and transferred most or all of the control and responsibility for running the firm to those employees doing the work? Let us review some type-C firms beginning with Morning Star Company, the world's largest tomato processor.[17] The company operates in an extraordinarily decentralized manner.

Chris Rufer has been the leader of Morning Star since he started the company in 1970. The company began as a trucking operation and

---

[17] Sharda S. Nandram, 2015, *Organizational Innovation by Integrating Simplification: Learning from Buurtzorg Nederland*. Basel, Switzerland: Springer. This book is a comprehensive analysis of Buurtzorg Nederland, a type-C firm that has significantly improved health care for patients served. In the Foreword to the book, the firm's founder Jos de Bok wrote the following:

> In 2006 Buurtzorg Nederland was established. Some friends with a big ambition wanted to change the Dutch homecare into community care. Many patients were troubled by the fragmented way care was delivered and many nurses were frustrated because they couldn't perform the way they wanted to. We chose an organizational model which focuses on meaningful relationships and no hierarchy. We wanted to use IT in a way that it served the nurses. We wanted to work with people who could be proud of what they achieve: day in day out! We wanted to show that it's much more effective and sustainable to work this way and yes: we wanted to change the world (a little bit).

still distributes processed tomato products with its trucks, in addition to harvesting the tomatoes. Their website describes a unique vision of self-management focused on efficiently serving customers and generating superior economic performance. Annual industrial sales are approximately $350 million and, although financial statements are not public, the firm's performance is generally acknowledged to be superior.

> The Morning Star Company was built on a foundational phi-losophy of Self-Management. We envision an organization of self-management professionals who initiate communication and coordination of their activities with fellow colleagues, customers, suppliers and fellow industry participants, absent directives from others. For colleagues to find joy and excitement utilizing their unique talents and to weave those talents into activities which complement and strengthen fellow colleagues' activities. And for colleagues to take personal responsibility and hold themselves accountable for achieving our Mission.
>
> To be an Olympic Gold Medal performer in the tomato products industry. To develop and implement superior systems of organizing individuals' talents and efforts to achieve demonstrably superior productivity and personal happiness. To develop and implement superior technology and production systems that signifi-cantly and demonstrably increase the effective use of resources that match customers' requirements. To provide opportunity for more harmonious and prosperous lives, bringing happiness to ourselves and to the people we serve.[18]

It is refreshing to read about Morning Star's blending of demonstrably superior productivity (Olympic Gold Medal performer) and personal hap-piness. This is the path to a sustainable firm that resonates with the four-part purpose of the firm (Chapter 1), which includes win-win relationships with employees and the need to at least earn the cost of capital over the long term; otherwise, the firm's stakeholders are guaranteed to suffer.

Many studies about Morning Star conclude that its colleagues (employees) are exceptionally motivated, productive, and enjoy their work environment.[19] Notable is an absence of managers so that colleagues

---

[18] Website www.morningstarco.com, accessed July 26, 2019.
[19] Gary Hamel. 2011, "First, Let's Fire All the Managers," *Harvard Business Review*, December, pp. 48–60.

interact in order to negotiate and agree on goals and responsibilities. No job titles and no promotions. Compensation is peer-based. An especially important component in the firm's self-management system is its Colleague Letter of Understanding (CLOU). The author of a CLOU negotiates with other colleagues most impacted by that person's work on personal goals and performance metrics. Colleagues work as part of business units with their own profit and loss statements, which can require negotiated customer-supplier agreements. Colleagues make decisions on ordering equipment or whatever they feel is needed to fulfill their CLOUs. Large expenditures require agreement with a wide number of colleagues.

This system of self-management works for Morning Star. Most remarkable is how bureaucracy has been essentially eliminated and colleagues work in a way that is productive, builds teamwork, is beneficial to customers, and is fulfilling (sense of genuine accomplishment). Since promotions and related job titles are eliminated, colleagues advance by way of adding responsibilities and peer recognition. Information is widely shared—no information silos like those in conventional type-A pyramid organizations. Performance of units and individuals is regularly reviewed by colleagues. Conflict resolution is achieved through mediating colleagues and is critical in maintaining a balance between freedom and responsibility. Striving to build up one's reputational capital (and also one's peer-determined compensation) is a hand-in-glove fit with teamwork, which is a hallmark of Morning Star's self-management system.

One criticism of Morning Star is that the firm's type-C structure may not handle radical innovation well. This situation has not impacted Morning Star due to the stability of the tomato processing industry with its reduced concern for product obsolescence and reliance on incremental improvements for processing tomatoes. The previously mentioned Ken Iverson, while CEO of Nucor, not only orchestrated a lean type-B organization but was the key person responsible for a bet-the-firm technology decision to invest in an untested (at scale) innovation—mini-mills that use electric arc furnaces to melt scrap steel. Would a type-C steel company, in circumstances similar to Nucor, make such a bet-the-firm decision? In a similar vein, would Intel have been better served by a type-C organization instead of having Andy Grove calling the shots to abandon manufacturing dynamic memory (its primary source of revenue) and switch to manufacturing microprocessors?

In contrast to Morning Star, Valve is a type-C firm in a fast-paced, volatile industry. In 1996, Gabe Newell and Mike Harrington started Valve as a traditional game company with a core competency in writing software code. Today, the firm has characteristics of an entertainment/software/platform company. Valve is populated by innovative employees who work in a decidedly flat organization with almost nonexistent management control. Employees are self-directed in that they select projects to work on that potentially will make good use of their skills and create genuine value for customers. The firm stresses knowledge building and especially experiments involving predictions and comparisons to forecasted results, thereby evaluating assumptions. Over the years, Valve created many popular games. In 2008, the firm released Steam, which is a platform of tools and services for game developers and publishers which quickly grew to 20 million users and over 500 games. Peer-driven performance reviews are used to better connect compensation to value created. Extreme importance is accorded to hiring the right people. As its *Handbook for New Employees* states:

> Across the board, we value highly collaborative people. That means people who are skilled in all the things that are integral to high-bandwidth collaboration—people who can deconstruct problems on the fly, and talk to others as they do so, simultaneously being inventive, iterative, creative, talkative, and reactive. These things actually matter far more than deep domain-specific knowledge or highly developed skills in narrow areas. This is why we'll often pass on candidates who, narrowly defined, are the "best" in their chosen discipline.
>
> We value "T-shaped" people. That is, people who are both generalists (highly skilled at a broad set of valuable things—the top of the T) and also experts (among the best in their field within a narrow discipline—the vertical leg of the T).

Valve's self-reported financial data show sales per employee and profit per employee greater than either Google or Facebook. Why? Valve hires exceptionally talented people able to effectively collaborate within an organizational structure designed to aggregate individual knowledge so that diversity-based, crowd-sourced, and highly effective decisions emerge. Simply put, employees evaluate projects by voting with their feet as to joining or not.[20]

One view of Valve's hyper-flat structure is that it is ideally suited to the creativity of highly skilled, innovative people *and* the collaborative culture that is so carefully nurtured. However, should not one be skeptical of such a type-C structure imposed on, say a global manufacturing firm with tens of thousands of employees making products like refrigerators and stoves, not computer games? It so happens that such a type-C firm exists. The corporate history of the Haier Group is a remarkable story.

ORGANIZATIONAL EXPERIMENTATION AT THE HAIER GROUP

In 1984, Zhang Ruimin became CEO of a small, near-bankrupt Chinese manufacturer of low-quality refrigerators. Ruimin is an example of a knowledge builder who relies on experimentation and feedback to orchestrate innovation not only for product design but also for the firm's organizational structure. Today, Haier Group is a multinational consumer electronics and home appliance firm that earns economic returns well in excess of the cost of capital and holds the leading global share of whitegoods (refrigerators, ovens, etc.). Figure 6.6 displays Haier's life-cycle track record from 2000 to 2018.

The Haier story can be viewed as a study of instilling dynamism in a country one company at a time. From a value-dissipating firm of 800 employees in 1984, the firm, at the beginning of 2019, had over 87,000

---

[20]Teppo Felin and Thomas C. Powell, 2016, "Designing Organizations for Dynamic Capabilities," *California Management Review* 58(4): 78–96.

FIGURE 6.6 Haier Group 2000 to 2018

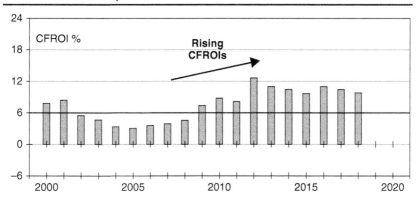

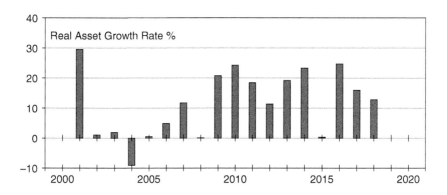

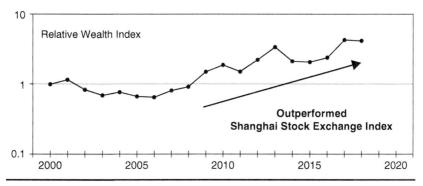

Source: Based on data from Credit Suisse HOLT global database.

employees who efficiently deliver value to customers with a relentless focus on innovation.

From 2000 to 2006, as seen in Figure 6.6, CFROIs declined below the long-term, inflation-adjusted (real), benchmark cost of capital of 6%, and Haier's stock underperformed the Shanghai Stock Exchange Composite Index as illustrated in the bottom panel. The improved financial performance since 2006 exceeded investor expectations, and the stock outperformed due to a sharp rise in CFROIs coupled to significant asset growth, including the 2016 acquisition of General Electric's appliance division for $5.4 billion.

Zhang Ruimin is an unusual CEO in that he views Haier's organizational structure as evolving in tandem with a continual knowledge-building process keyed to delivering high value to customers. In an interview he noted: "One of the biggest differences is our ability to remake and overhaul ourselves. Many companies' ways of thinking and operating have ossified and become hard to change, especially their organizational structures."[21]

The Haier revitalization journey from the failing business model life-cycle stage began with Ruimin, shortly after becoming CEO, getting employees' attention as to the abysmal level of manufacturing quality. A total of 76 refrigerators with significant defects were destroyed with a sledge hammer by Ruimin and other employees even though each refrigerator was worth an employee's salary for two years. The dismal morale of employees and the decrepit condition of the Qingdao General Refrigerator Factory was evident in Ruimin's first rule: do not pee on the factory floor. Early on, he understood the key ideas of Lean Thinking and spoke of production flowing like a river with minimal inventories.[22] So, the revitalization began with upgrading the firm's manufacturing processes. From 1984 to 1991, Ruimin managed a command-and-control hierarchical structure to dramatically improve quality, build a brand name

---

[21] Art Kleiner, 2014, "The Thought Leader Interview: Zhang Ruimin," *Strategy + Business* Winter 77: 96–102.

[22] Jeannie J. Yi and Shawn X. Ye, 2003, *The Haier Way: The Making of a Chinese Business Leader and a Global Brand.* Dumont, NJ: Homa & Sekey Books.

that represented quality to consumers, and gain the dominant share of the Chinese market for refrigerators.

He saw opportunity in acquiring firms that were inefficiently managed but delivered quality products. From 1991 to 1998, Haier acquired many such firms. During this time period, Ruimin shifted from a command-and-control hierarchy to a decentralized organizational structure that transferred power to individual business units. From 1998 to 2005, Haier entered the most competitive international markets believing that his employees had the necessary skills to successfully compete. He also further evolved the organizational structure to operate with "zero distance" from customers., that is, eliminate any bureaucracy that impedes value creation. In terms of Figure 6.5, Haier was becoming a type-C organization with self-managed teams responsible for generating profits and allocating resources. This is a remarkable large-scale experiment in radically reducing layers of managerial control.

Zhang Ruimin further transitioned Haier in 2012 to a platform-based enterprise so that local employees can provide extensive customization and make customers lifetime users of Haier products and services. Ruimin's "rendanheyi" organizational structure replaces middle management with thousands of self-governing microenterprises. He explains:

> In 2005, with the Internet economy in mind, we began making innovations in our business model that would help us adapt. We called our new model *rendanheyi*. *Ren* refers to the employees, *dan* means user value, and *heyi* indicates unity and an awareness of the whole system. The term *rendanheyi* suggests that employees can realize their own value during the process of creating value for users. This new model was intended to foster co-creation and win-win solutions for employees and customers.[23]
>
> For the first few years, our performance didn't really pick up. .... Some of our shareholders expressed concerns. .... In our shareholders' meetings we explained that this is the model that we believe will lead to success, especially in this changing world

---

[23] Zhang Ruimin, 2018,.\ "Why Haier Is Reorganizing Itself Around the Internet of Things," *Strategy + Business*, Summer 91.

where we were entering the Internet era. . . . Our performance started picking up in 2016. Our stock price doubled that year. In 2017, our stock price doubled again. This pick-up in performance was no coincidence. It was the accumulated effect of many years of working in the micro-enterprise model.[24]

Haier's strategy of mass customization and zero distance to customers is evident in its water purifiers which eliminate pollutants specific to each of 220,000 Chinese communities. Project teams closest to customers decide on resource allocations, and they have the freedom to obtain resources either inside or outside the firm. In addition, Haier's innovative, fast-paced culture has a reputation for nurturing, rewarding, and retaining high-performing employees. This management of talent may well be the key to the firm's success with its radical decentralization. Here is a perceptive assessment of Haier's culture that supports the foundational value of knowledge building: *"Rather than pursuing scalable efficiency, Haier is experimenting with a corporate culture that can drive scalable learning."*[25]

Keep in mind that Ruimin's unique skill in decision-making and leadership was essential for Haier's transition to a type-C organization. Moreover, it is doubtful that the adoption in 2012 of the platform business model would have emerged solely from self-organized teams, absent his leadership. A strong case can be made that, for large, complex type-C firms, continued success requires a strong leader who promotes autonomy for teams/micro-enterprises while still orchestrating major strategic decisions as circumstances warrant.

Haier's organizational structure promotes efficiency at the micro (firm) level similar to the efficiencies realized by a free-market economy at the macro level. It is an understatement to say that this organizational evolution for a large multinational firm is uniquely important to building knowledge that could be applied to thousands of other firms.

---

[24] Knowledge@Wharton, "For Haier's Zhang Ruimin, Success Means Creating the Future," April 20, 2018, http://knowledge.wharton.upenn.edu/article/haiers-zhang-ruimin-success-means-creating-the-future/

[25] Bill Fischer, Umberto Lago, and Fang Liu, 2013, *Reinventing Giants: How Chinese Global Competitor Haier has Changed the Way Big Companies Transform.* San Francisco: Jossey-Bass, p. 220.

Recall from Chapter 1 that the starting point of the firm's four-part purpose is a vision that is both inspiring and motivating. In that regard, Zhang Ruimin commented about his vision for Haier's Internet-based platform:

> Today, we offer our resources to society, providing a Haier branded business platform to makers. This means that those innovators who are full of entrepreneurial passion, can develop new products within the Haier platform.
>
> More than 100 small companies have been bred and hatched on Haier's cloud platform. They have left Haier to form stand-alone entrepreneurial enterprises. There are also social entrepreneurs making use of the Haier Internet platform to create businesses. … The makers on the Haier platform are both the entrepreneurs and the builders of our platform. … Haier strives to be a home and a community for great makers.[26]

To sum up: Haier is a compelling experiment in progress to learn about transitioning from a type-A organizational structure to a type-C. What else might we learn about innovation in China? That is addressed in the next section.

VALUE CREATORS DRIVE DYNAMISM IN CHINA

Entrepreneur is an entrenched word in our everyday language referring to one who innovates, usually by starting a new company. At a deeper level, entrepreneurs focus on a problem and develop or adapt a solution that potentially can create value for customers. The beginning point is knowledge building that results in value creation. Entrepreneurs over the age of 40 are five times more likely to succeed compared to entrepreneurs under 30. Those who studied engineering do better than those who studied business. Most entrepreneurs develop their ideas while working at large firms.[27]

Suppose the large firm green-lighted the innovative idea, and the person promoting the idea was given responsibility to build a team, develop

---

[26] Hu Yong and Hao Yazhou, 2017, *Haier Purpose: The Real Story of China's First Global Super-Company*. Oxford: Thinkers 50.
[27] Carl J. Schramm, 2018, *Burn the Business Plan: What Great Entrepreneurs Really Do*. New York: Simon & Schuster.

the product, and execute a marketing plan. Would that person wearing a corporate hat be less of an entrepreneur? The key point is that *value creator* may be a more useful term for those, in general, who deliver significant benefits to customers by solving problems that may or may not require the startup of a new firm. The common thread is value creation. In my experience with students, they all want to be value creators while far fewer aspire to be an entrepreneur. Isn't value creator an accurate description of Zhang Ruimin at every stage of building Haier into a large multinational firm and a showcase of Chinese innovation?

China's economic resurgence has been fueled by manufacturing and investment enabling hundreds of millions of people to escape poverty. Dynamism is flourishing in China and reflected in jobs that bring discovery, opportunities to solve problems and to build new skills, and rewards that exceed monetary compensation. There is a tremendous growth of startup businesses and a steady rise in pioneering companies that have become global leaders, for example, Alibaba in e-commerce and retail, the Internet and AI technology company Baidu, the gaming and social media company Tencent, Lenovo, the dominant manufacturer of personal computers plus other electronic products, and Huawei, the world's largest patent filer, with global leadership in telecommunications and consumer electronics.

The rapid pace of innovation by Chinese companies is a radical departure from the days when China was viewed as a copycat economy. Today, there is a unique confluence of conditions that are highly supportive of business innovation.[28]

- Tremendous geographical diversity and range of consumer needs
- Regulatory environment that favors Chinese companies
- Expanding middle class with rising consumer demands
- Markets where good enough products give companies a toe-hold followed by rapid experimentation and improvement

---

[28]Xiaolan Fu, 2015, *China's Path to Innovation*. Oxford: Cambridge University Press. See also Yu Zhou, William Lazonick, and Yifei Sun, 2016, *China as an Innovation Nation*. Oxford: Oxford University Press; and George S. Yip and Bruce McKern, 2016, *China's Next Strategic Advantage: From Imitation to Innovation*. Cambridge, MA: MIT Press.

- Heightened competitive environment equips survivors for continual fast-paced innovation and global expansion
- Return of highly educated and skilled Chinese who want to work for Chinese companies
- Culture that promotes networking and joint ventures, coupled to substantial R&D investment
- Availability of venture capital
- Centralized leadership structure for fast decision-making

The last bullet point regarding centralized leadership is particularly important and connects back to the earlier discussion of organizational structure. Mark Greeven, George Yip, and Wei Wei have extensively studied how Chinese companies innovate and they note:

> Decision making in most Chinese companies is centralized with a strong leader. ... Because many Chinese companies are young and lack bureaucratic management structures, they tend to be less formal and listen more to decisive bosses.
> The organizational structures of Chinese innovators tend to be either flat or flexible. ... Xiaomi [type-B firm that is a leader in smart hardware and electronics] ... with eight thousand employees has only three organizational layers. ... According to traditional management theory, it is not possible to manage in such a flat but large organization, but Xiaomi succeeded. The seven cofounders direct one layer of directors, who in turn manage the engineers and salesforce directly.[29]

The takeaway from this brief discussion of Chinese innovation is that other countries, loaded with type-A firms, had best consider shedding bureaucratic layers in order to compete with China's rising innovation powerhouse firms. A related takeaway is that changing a firm's organizational structure involves performance measurement and effective language, which was reviewed in Chapter 5.

---

[29] Mark J. Greeven, George S. Yip, and Wei Wei, 2019, *Pioneers, Hidden Champions, Changemakers, and Underdogs.* Cambridge, MA: MIT Press, pp. 125-126.

7

ACHIEVING PROGRESS THROUGH KNOWLEDGE BUILDING AND VALUE CREATION

We do think that capitalism—or more precisely, the free enterprise system—in its ideal form is the best system to allocate resources and rewards. But the forms of capitalism that are experienced in most countries are very far from the ideal. They are a corrupted version in which vested interests prevent competition from playing its natural, healthy role. Many of the accusations against capitalism—that it oppresses workers, creates private monopolies, and allows only the rich to get richer—apply not to a true free enterprise system but rather to the corrupt, uncompetitive versions that we observe around the world.

Capitalism's biggest political enemies are not the firebrand trade unionists spewing vitriol against the system but the executives in pin-striped suits who extol the virtues of competitive markets with every breath while attempting to extinguish them with every action.

—Raghuram G. Rajan and Luigi Zingales[1]

---

[1] Raghuram G. Rajan and Luigi Zingales, 2004, "Making Capitalism Work for Everyone," *Journal of Applied Corporate Finance* 16(4): 101–108.

There is no broad-based intellectual movement focused on understanding the dynamics of progress, or targeting the deeper goal of speeding it up. We believe that it deserves a dedicated field of study. We suggest inaugurating the discipline of "Progress Studies."... Why did Silicon Valley happen in California rather than Japan or Boston? Why was early-20th-century science in Germany and Central Europe so strong? Can we deliberately engineer the conditions most hospitable to this kind of advancement or tweak the systems that surround us today?

This is exactly what Progress Studies would investigate. It would consider the problem as broadly as possible. It would study the successful people, organizations, institutions, policies, and cultures that have arisen to date, and it would attempt to concoct policies and prescriptions that would help improve our ability to generate useful progress in the future.

—Patrick Collison and Tyler Cowen[2]

This chapter highlights the main takeaways from this book; emphasizes the usefulness of life-cycle track records for boards of directors, managers, investors, academic researchers, and business students; describes low-hanging fruit for spurring economic progress through changes in the regulatory state; and contemplates how the proposed new discipline of Progress Studies might evolve.[3]

THE NEW ECONOMY AND THE PRAGMATIC THEORY OF THE FIRM

The World Economic Forum in its *Future of Jobs Report* identified complex problem solving, critical thinking, and creativity as the most desirable skills in order for people to excel in the 21st century workplace.[4] This resonates

[2] Patrick Collison and Tyler Cowen, July 30, 2019, "We Need a New Science of Progress," *The Atlantic,* https://www.theatlantic.com/science/archive/2019/07/we-need-new-science-progress/594946/.
[3] It should prove useful to make a top priority for Progress Studies the definition of "progress." On the one hand, many researchers prefer specificity that facilitates econometric studies with readily available quantitative data. On the other hand, we should consider the advice of Adelbert Ames in Chapter 2 to work with important variables that are not easily quantified and also that "the value of an experiment is directly proportional to the degree to which it aids the investigator in formulating better problems." Hence, the definition of progress should relate to hard-to-measure cultural variables involved with dynamism, which has been a major focus for Edmund Phelps (see Chapter 1).
[4] World Economic Forum, 2016, *Future of Jobs: Employment, Skills and Workforce Strategy for the Fourth Industrial Revolution.* Switzerland: Cology/Geneva.

with the main theme of this book that knowledge-building proficiency is the key to long-term value creation by individuals, business units, and firms. A corollary theme is that resources are best allocated by management (including entrepreneurs) less concerned with hierarchical control mechanisms, and instead, intent on developing a knowledge-building culture keyed to innovation and constructive change. Such a culture rewards and motivates those who reveal obsolete assumptions; analyze problems to unravel root causes—ranging from process improvements that involve all employees to strategic choices made by top management; perceive significant change at an early stage; and figure out how to better serve customers in a changing world—that is, fast and effective traversing of the knowledge-building loop (Figure 2.1). But such a fast-paced, innovative world leaves behind those workers with obsolete jobs. They need training to become better value creators in the new economic environment.

In the New Economy, investors grapple with practical problems in analyzing firms in order to make investment decisions. This process is more complex compared to the Old Economy. For instance, how many "Value" investors have missed the New Economy's intangible-intensive winners (e.g., Amazon, Facebook, Alphabet/Google, and many more) due to their high PEs (price to earnings multiples)? Those earnings are based on standard accounting rules which are not attuned to intangible assets, especially platform business models that benefit from network effects. Worse yet, Value investors tend to buy low PE firms (e.g., Barnes & Noble, J. C. Penney, Sears, and many more) that subsequently suffered as consumers felt better served by their Internet-enabled competitors. The old rules for value investing keyed to selling high PE firms and buying low PE firms are ill-suited to the New Economy. Those who viewed the stock market as somewhat of a mystery in the Old Economy, must be genuinely puzzled by the challenge of analyzing value creation in the New Economy.[5] The New Economy, focused on human capital and a firm's

---

[5] Jeffrey B. Madden, 2019, "The World Has Changed: Investing in the New Economy," *Journal of Wealth Management* 22(2): 87–98.

intangible assets, spotlights the slowness inherent in rigid hierarchical organizations designed for pre-Internet mass production where workers were told how to do a job and not trained to be problem solvers capable of developing improved processes.

While this book raises questions about a firm's organizational structure, broader questions are being debated about capitalism as the means for a society to achieve economic progress. Those concerned with income inequality argue that capitalism exacerbates a situation where increasing financial rewards accrue to the top income earners while making matters worse for those near the bottom. *Should not economic progress mean enhanced prosperity for all?*

In writing about capitalism, I frequently use the term *free-market capitalism* to emphasize the point made in the opening quote by Rajan and Zingales that critiques of capitalism most always center on corrupt, uncompetitive versions nurtured by "executives in pin-striped suits." Another useful term is *crony capitalism* with its lobbying and exerting of power to orchestrate laws and regulations that benefit powerful firms and organizations by minimizing competition that would ultimately benefit consumers. The capitalism debate becomes more productive by making the distinction between free-market capitalism and crony capitalism.

To help us understand free-market capitalism, let's first acknowledge that business firms are the economy's engine for value creation—the powerful tide for economic progress that can lift all boats. Consequently, it is imperative to continuously build up our knowledge about better ways to organize and manage firms, leading to improved decisions. The decision makers range from those inside the firm, which includes the board of directors, management at all levels, and employees, to those on the outside, including investors and other stakeholders, plus lawmakers and regulators impacting business.

How can we evaluate the pragmatic theory of the firm, or any other theory of the firm, as to its contribution to our understanding of progress? In the beginning of Chapter 1, I offered six such metrics. With these metrics, I'll evaluate the pragmatic theory of the firm discussed in the previous chapters.

1. **Clarity about the firm's purpose:** Invariably, debates about the role of capitalism in society scrutinize the purpose of the firm. Clarity about the firm's purpose can defuse the seemingly never-ending argument between proponents of maximizing shareholder value versus proponents of stakeholder primacy. An important conclusion of this book is that maximizing shareholder value is the result of a firm successfully achieving its four-part purpose:

- Provide a *vision* to behave ethically while making the world a better place so that work provides more than a paycheck.
- *Survive and prosper* with a knowledge-building, adaptable culture that enables the firm to at least earn the opportunity cost of capital over the long term.
- *Sustain win-win relationships* with all of the firm's stakeholders. Consider the many firms that have miserable scores on employee engagement, perhaps more accurately labeled as management failure. Getting to a win-win relationship between management and employees surely benefits not only employees but everyone who is impacted by the quality of their work.
- *Take care of future generations* through the design of products and manufacturing processes that simultaneously minimizes waste and improves efficiency, and also eliminates pollution before it occurs.

The purpose of the firm is the foundation for the pragmatic theory of the firm.

2. **Source of competitive advantage:** A recurrent theme in the company examples presented in this book is that attributes of successful firms, such as winning strategies and early adaptation to change, are rooted in a firm's knowledge-building proficiency—the central element in the pragmatic theory of the firm. If management asserts that employees are their

firm's greatest asset, should not that translate into a continual top priority to nurture and sustain a knowledge-building culture and, in so doing, nurture and sustain competitive advantage?

An often neglected source of competitive advantage is a firm's organizational structure. Neglected perhaps because pay and power in an existing hierarchical structure is accorded to managers of the bureaucracy. There is little incentive for them to change. However, the Haier Group (Chapter 6) reveals how a CEO of a large firm experimented and successfully eliminated organizational impediments to value creation.

3. Understanding the firm's market valuation: The pragmatic theory of the firm applics systems thinking to the firm in general and in particular to understanding the firm's market valuation. The bullet points listed below highlight how the life-cycle framework, described in Chapter 4, facilitates systems thinking. It provides a useful perspective on financial and valuation issues that is economically sound, although different from mainstream finance's reliance on CAPM (Capital Asset Pricing Model) thinking. The life-cycle framework focuses on the individual firm as the unit of analysis stripped of any assumptions about risk and return in an assumed equilibrium environment.

- A firm's degree of success in efficiently providing value to customers results in a net cash receipt stream that ultimately drives its market valuation. A useful way to articulate these cash receipts is via a time series of economic returns and reinvestment rates (i.e., a firm's life-cycle track record).
- Life-cycle track records highlight the impact of managerial skill and competition playing out over time, and benchmark a firm's financial performance versus the cost of capital while delivering insights about a firm's long-term shareholder returns versus the general market.
- Viewed as a valuation system, the life-cycle valuation model employs a forward-looking, market-implied discount rate that depends on the forecasting procedures used for net cash receipts. This sharply contrasts with the conventional practice of inserting a discount

rate which is estimated independently of how the valuation model orchestrates cash flow forecasts.

- On average, stock prices represent astute expectations of a firm's future life-cycle performance. Decoding investor expectations embedded in stock prices helps to establish a crucial benchmark as to what a firm needs to exceed in order to outperform the general market.

- The CAPM mindset, with its notion of volatility (Beta) corresponding to investor risk, has reached far beyond finance, influencing thinking in economics, management, and accounting. A useful complement to investor risk is the concept of firm risk as driven by obstacles to achieving the firm's purpose. Firm risk helps management analyze and potentially control significant sources of future shortfalls in financial performance.

- Investors can incorporate the perceived benefits of intangible assets, such as brands, via a more favorable fade of economic returns and reinvestment rates. The same fade adjustment process can be used to "adjust for risk," and instead of changing a discount rate, an alternative fade forecast is employed that provides an intuitive, visual feel for what one is doing.

- An awareness of the importance of a firm's knowledge-building proficiency coupled to the life-cycle framework provides guideposts for analyzing excess shareholder returns. This can yield important insights that have too often been missing from the numerous correlation-based studies using financial variables as described in Chapter 5.

4. **Source of improved operating performance:** In the Old Economy dominated by firms utilizing a command-and-control, hierarchical organizational structure, managers were promoted and given bonuses for developing workarounds for problems, for firefighting, and for telling employees how to achieve the targeted accounting goals. Recognizing that the New Economy is dominated by human capital and intangible assets, the pragmatic theory of the firm emphasizes

human capital as the central means to sustain continual improvement in operations. Chapter 3 described three major performance approaches: Lean Thinking, TOC (Theory of Constraints), and OPM (ontological/phenomenological model). The knowledge-building loop assists in understanding each approach as well as the differences between them. The same knowledge-building mindset can help evaluate any proposed way to "work smarter" in order to improve operating performance.

A major improvement in operating performance may require a different strategy. The source of such a strategy fundamentally resides in knowledge building. Rather than attempting an accurate forecast of the long-term future, such a strategy requires crafting options to exploit the future as it unfolds. Richard Rumelt writes:

> When a leader characterizes the challenge as underperformance, it sets the stage for bad strategy. Underperformance is a result. The true challenges are the reasons for the underperformance. Unless leadership offers a theory of why things haven't worked in the past, or why the challenge is difficult, it is hard to generate good strategy.
>
> Many writers on strategy seem to suggest that the more dynamic the situation, the farther ahead a leader must look. This is illogical. The more dynamic the situation, the poorer your foresight will be. Therefore, the more uncertain and dynamic the situation, the more *proximate* a strategic objective must be. The proximate objective is guided by forecasts of the future, but the more uncertain the future, the more its essential logic is that of "taking a strong position and creating options," not of looking far ahead.[6]

In other words, knowledge building is the start of the development of good strategy.

5. Source of improved managerial decisions: Application of the pragmatic theory leads to better decisions because it emphasizes systems thinking and relationships among variables. This helps managers understand how efficiency of one local component of the system is necessary to promote continuous improvements, yet insufficient because overall system efficiency results from how all components work together. Of

---

[6]Richard P. Rumelt, 2011, *Good Strategy Bad Strategy: The Difference and Why It Matters.* New York: Crown Business, pp. 55 and 111.

the many examples discussed in this book, a particularly important one is the crossover problem (see Chapter 5) where accounting-based performance metrics tied to accounting costs—when applied at lower levels of the firm—can interfere with improving the overall process. The reason involves language, which has a silent but strong impact on our thinking. Specifically, accounting costs, as previously pointed out, imply that components of a system are independent of one another, so optimizing local efficiencies must therefore optimize system efficiency. This is not necessarily true.

By using life-cycle track records for a firm and its business units, management and the board can significantly improve resource allocations. The track records constitute a reality check when juxtaposing the past next to a forecasted future life cycle. The next step is to answer the question: Do the planned investments in the business make economic sense? More specifically, as described in Chapter 6, a business's life-cycle stage helps identify management's critical task. In the high innovation stage, for example, focus on quickly proving or disproving the critical assumptions about how value for customers is efficiently delivered. In the competitive fade stage, expand the opportunities for the firm to gain competitive advantage and add new capabilities as needed. In the mature stage with economic returns approximating the cost of capital, management and boards should replace the "grow the business" mindset with an imperative to simultaneously improve existing operations and redirect resources to potential high-return opportunities that may even compete with existing businesses—not an easy task. In the failing business model stage, decisive leadership (perhaps new leadership) is needed to purge the business-as-usual culture, similar to John Anderson's revitalization of NCR Corporation.

6. **Analysis of firms:** Analysis of a firm (especially a long-term, historical study) would improve if life-cycle track records were included. This is especially so for strategic analyses and security analyst reports that involve comparisons with competing firms since life-cycle track records facilitate insights not easily obtained otherwise. Absent life-cycle track records, company analyses typically range from one extreme of highly detailed Excel

spreadsheets with mountains of numbers but little insights as to value creation or dissipation to the other extreme of little quantification. Hence, qualitative language abounds about "growth," "profitability," "competitive advantage," and the like made by writers who are uninformed about the firm's economic returns versus the cost of capital and whether asset growth is actually creating or dissipating value.

A typical Wall Street security analyst report focuses on dissecting a firm's latest quarterly earnings report and forecasting near-term quarterly earnings. This format serves as a template to facilitate writing the next report. However, what is rarely encountered is an in-depth analysis of a firm's knowledge-building culture and related issues such as the logic behind strategic options, the extent of lean manufacturing expertise, the degree of employee engagement, etc., each more difficult to quantify compared to quarterly report data on sales, margins, taxes, and earnings.

LIFE-CYCLE TRACK RECORDS ARE A SCORECARD AND A LEARNING TOOL

The pragmatic theory of the firm applies systems thinking to improve our understanding of firms and our measurement tools, and to upgrade decision-making. Consequently, I use the label "pragmatic" as contrasted with theories focused on issues such as why firms exist or what they hypothetically maximize.

Life-cycle track records are an exceptionally useful tool for advancing value creation. Although widely used by money management firms, they are not yet widespread as part of the conversations among top management and the board of directors. However, when money managers present to top management life-cycle track records of the firms they are managing, the conversations invariably shift to fundamental issues about long-term value creation. If similar conversations could occur between management and investors, this would help management secure an investor base with a long-term owner's mindset.

On the one hand, investors well-versed in the life-cycle framework have a viable long-term owner's mindset, and they are expected to support high-value-creation-potential investments that will depress near-term quarterly earnings *if management has demonstrated superior value-creation skill in the past.* On the other hand, we might expect these same investors to oppose sizable investments and favorable executive compensation for managements that have *demonstrated decidedly below average skill,* especially when they have presided over a firm that is in the failing business model life cycle stage. So, a viable long-term owner's mindset is rooted in sound economics with an eye on long-term value creation and on fixing value-dissipating businesses and the sooner the better. Shouldn't shareholders expect this of a firm's board of directors?

Hopefully, this book will accelerate the use of life-cycle track records as part of a common valuation language among managements, boards, and investors. To this end, the section "Integrated Reports, Life-Cycle Reviews, and Intangibles," in Chapter 5 discussed Life-Cycle Reviews as a key element for improving both the measurement of past financial performance and the allocation of resources to the benefit of future performance. The core concept behind Life-Cycle Reviews is that management's strategy for a business unit and its planned reinvestment should be placed in the context of the unit's track record of economic returns in relation to the cost of capital and its reinvestment rates. Isn't this common sense? Moreover, Integrated Reports may communicate important ESG (environmental, social, and governance) information, yet none of this matters if a firm steadfastly fails to earn the cost of capital—the hallmark of value dissipation.

A firm's life-cycle track record is a critical readout of a firm's success in achieving its four-part purpose. These track records demonstrate how well a firm serves its customers and, in so doing, benefits society.

Life-cycle track records provide a superior "bottom line" compared to accounting earnings. They provide a direct link to market valuation and offer an economically sound means to link management compensation to value created—far better than linking compensation to growth in earnings per share. The preponderant challenge is handling the accounting treatment of human capital/intangibles, which requires ongoing experimentation that should be the responsibility of chief financial officers. Waiting for accounting rule-makers to solve these issues will be unacceptably long. *Innovation* is needed by CFOs and their staffs to overcome limitations of today's accounting conventions. This is fertile ground for finance/accounting researchers to jointly work with corporate staffs to develop industry-specific accounting treatments that advance value creation in the New Economy. The kind of innovation needed was briefly addressed in the Chapter 5 section, "System Principles and Effective Language," that identified situations in which our existing language is deficient. For example, new measurements (better language) are needed to link process variables to accounting-based ROIs. Language improvements and experimentation walk hand-in-hand.

Throughout this book, I have illustrated that the firm is best understood using systems thinking. Moreover, the firm as a system acts and is acted upon within a broader socioeconomic system with important consequences. The next section discusses public perception concerning two interconnected issues—capitalism as a system to facilitate the greater good and the behavior of large corporations. Public perception is particularly important to managements and boards of directors of large corporations.

POLITICS AND THE GREATER GOOD

In an earlier chapter, I emphasized that maximizing shareholder value is best viewed as the result of firms successfully achieving a purpose broadly consistent with the four-part purpose noted above. That view continues to gain acceptance. On August 19, 2019, the Business Roundtable issued an open letter, "Statement on the Purpose of a Corporation," asserting support for the free market system and a commitment to deliver value to all of their stakeholders: customers, employees, suppliers, communities, and shareholders. The letter was endorsed by 181 of the 188 CEO members. It is a major step away from the singular goal of maximizing shareholder value, with related concerns of management excessively focusing on short-term earnings. Keep in mind that to survive and prosper while acting responsibly toward all stakeholders requires a firm to at least earn its cost of capital over the long term.

Is this letter simply a politically astute move that means little in terms of behavior or is it a sign of major changes on the horizon? Will this letter impact corporate funding for lobbying to influence legislation and regulation? Does this letter mark an acceleration of a transition away from rigid hierarchical control with a pyramid of management levels to a flatter organization with less compensation to top management and more compensation to lower-level employees who are creating value? Perhaps these questions reflect impatience on the part of those wanting a level competitive playing field where compensation is directly tied to value creation at all levels of the firm and CEO pay is treated as a message to employees about a win-win partnership focused on value creation. The ideal competitive playing field for firms has regulations that may well be politically motivated but still agree with common sense while not putting an excessive burden on business in a quest for a marginal social benefit.

For example, I like being able to read about the ingredients in my cereal box. I appreciate the FDA's oversight to keep bad stuff out of our food supply. However, those in business, especially in small businesses, operate under an enormous regulatory load that has accumulated over decades with thousands of regulations whose costs greatly exceed their benefits. Politicians can pass laws and incentivize regulators to ostensibly make the world a better place, as they proclaim in their speeches, but politicians who don't own businesses or who never operated one do not always understand the pain of excessive regulatory costs that unnecessarily increase consumer prices, reduce investment, and curtail the creation of new jobs.

After many years as a Democratic senator and passing numerous onerous regulations on business, George McGovern left Congress and eventually acquired the leasehold on Connecticut's Stratford Inn. His worldview changed. In an October 21, 2012, op-ed in the *Wall Street Journal,* "A Politician's Dream Is a Businessman's Nightmare," he noted:

> I wish that during the years I was in public office, I had this firsthand experience about the difficulties businesspeople face every day. That knowledge would have made me a better U.S. senator and a more understanding presidential contender.
>
> I lived with federal, state and local rules that were all passed with the objective of helping employees, protecting the environment, raising tax dollars for schools, protecting our customers from fire hazards, etc. While I never doubted the worthiness of any of these goals, the concept that most often eludes legislators is: [should] we make consumers pay the higher prices for the increased operating costs that accompany public regulation and government reporting requirements with reams of red tape. It is a simple concern that is nonetheless often ignored by legislators.

Lawmakers and regulators experience limited feedback about the actions and unintended consequences from the rules they impose.[7] There is growing awareness of the benefits from periodically repealing all regulations and replacing them with regulations that can produce benefits well in excess of their costs. Repeal and replace is about a shared concern for undoing the damage caused by well-intentioned but economically dysfunctional regulations that apply static rules to a dynamic system often generating unintended consequences. This is low-hanging fruit.

A Rhode Island Democratic governor and a Democratic legislature in 2016 initiated repeal and replace while transitioning to a greatly improved online regulatory system. Idaho's 8,200 pages of regulations were repealed on July 1, 2019, and replacements evolved in a bipartisan manner based on experience with how regulations performed in the past. Ohio is one of the most heavily regulated states, and its 2019 budget includes a provision to sharply reduce the regulatory load, as did Virginia in 2018.[8]

---

[7] Patrick A. *McLaughlin*, Jerry Ellig, and Michael Wilt, 2017, "Comprehensive Regulatory Reform," Mercatus Policy Primer. See also Daniel Carpenter and David A. Moss, 2014, *Preventing Regulatory Capture: Special Interest Influence and How to Limit It.* New York: Cambridge University Press.

[8] James Broughel, May 9, 2019, "Idaho Repeals Its Regulatory Code," *The Bridge,* Mercatus Center at George Mason University. James Broughel, August 2, 2019, "A Dark Day for Red Tape in the Buckeye State," *Wall Street Journal.*

The fundamental reason that repeal and replace is gaining momentum is that replacing bad regulations with good regulations helps all members of society and paves the way for economic expansion.

In contrast, the goal of many Washington lobbyists is to explicitly tilt the playing field by securing special treatments for the large corporations that hire them. Not much has changed since 1922 when Franz Oppenheimer wrote *The State: Its History and Development Viewed Sociologically.* He argued that there are two ways to acquire wealth—the economic means through creating value for others and the political means by coercing and lobbying to gain advantage through laws and regulation. The latter involves transfers of wealth, typically by favoring one group by creating costs that are excessively burdensome for their competitors (or potential competitors), under the guise of promoting the general welfare. Also, lobbyists can persuade politicians to not pass legislation that would bring heightened competition to the firms that hire the lobbyists. For such firms this can be a very high return on the resources spent for lobbying.[9]

This political problem falls into the category of "wickedly difficult" to fix. Today, most voters don't understand the long-term consequences of what is happening, and politicians want to keep it that way. The flipside of benefits to firms that hire lobbyists is the campaign contributions sent by those firms to politicians. Legislation passed by politicians is implemented by regulators who have wide latitude as to what and how they regulate. Regulators and the regulated have a close working relationship. The regulated provide most all of the data that regulators need to do their jobs. Importantly, when regulators leave their government jobs, they often take higher-paying jobs with large firms in the industries they have been regulating.

How could this situation possibly change? Will managements have an epiphany and decide that for the greater good they will cease all lobbying? Similarly, will regulators forgo thinking about their future careers at higher-paying jobs in industry? The situation will change if and when

---

[9] Fred S. McChesney, 1997, *Money for Nothing: Politicians, Rent Extraction, and Political Extortion.* Cambridge, MA: Harvard University Press.

the costs to continue the status quo exceed the benefits. Step one is to work toward transparency that effectively communicates to voters what is taking place.

> The emergence of the Internet and electronic rulemaking dockets are changing the dynamics of the regulatory process. Regulation is no longer solely the purview of Washington-based lobbyists. Members of the public now have more opportunities to engage in the regulatory debate. As agency processes are made more transparent via the Internet, the once-arcane world of regulation will become more accessible to a much wider public, with the potential for making regulators and regulations more accountable to the people. Additionally, social media and other Internet technologics lower the cost of group formation and collective action so that citizens will be better able to educate themselves about the regulations that affect them and to take action to make their voices heard.[10]

Have you not felt hopeless about the lack of accountability as to how government spends the money raised from tax revenues and borrowings? Help is on the way from an important citizen initiative, www.openthebooks.com, which has a banner on its website, "Every Dime. Online. In Real Time." The goal is to put every government expense—local, state, and federal—online in easy-to-access format. Another not-for-profit initiative with a similar goal is www.usafacts .org. These initiatives may foreshadow bipartisan efforts to restructure the regulatory state to minimize lobbying and cronyism in order to secure a more level competitive playing field and spur economic growth. Transparency can jumpstart engagement by the heretofore silent public who gets energized to make change happen. If management and the board believe that they have a strong case for regulatory change in order to level the competitive playing field, they should participate in the emerging transparency movement. So too for taking an active role in communicating their firm's purpose and what that means for society.

---

[10] Susan E. Dudley and Jerry Brito, 2012, 2nd edition, *Regulation: A Primer*. Mercatus Center at George Mason University and the George Washington University Regulatory Studies Center.

Why are there so few CEOs who vigorously defend free-market capitalism?[11] Do they believe that society has given them a perpetual license to operate with no accountability? Perhaps the answer to both questions is that the larger and more powerful the corporation, the more attractive is the return on lobbying to tilt the competitive playing field in their favor. They do not want to engage in public debates in which they might need to defend their lobbying behavior and, besides, "We would be at a competitive disadvantage if we did not lobby." As previously noted, this is a wickedly difficult problem to solve.

An important ongoing debate about capitalism focuses on inequality; and, at a deeper level, should we trust the economic system in general, and large corporations in particular, to operate fair and ethically? The U.S. capitalistic system with its deep-rooted cronyism/lobbying enabled many financiers who played a role in the financial crisis of 2007–2009 to walk away keeping not-fairly-earned (as perceived by many) immense incomes. Deeply disappointed were the many supporters of a free-market capitalism that embodies a level playing field wherein the highest earnings go to those who genuinely provide the highest value to consumers.[12] IBM CEO Ginni Rometty neatly summarizes: "Society gives each of us a license to operate. It's a question of whether society trusts you or not. We need society to accept what it is that we do."[13]

Consider the financial crisis of 2007–2009 and the precarious financial health of many large banks during that time. This was a period of "innovative" financial products such as negative amortization loans, which were very profitable in the short term for the issuing financial institutions. These loans facilitated trading up in order to buy more expensive homes because the early monthly payments were less than the interest expense,

---

[11] Three CEOs—John Allison, T. J. Rodgers, and John Mackey—who carried the torch for free-market capitalism are discussed in Chapter 1 of Bartley J. Madden, 2016, *Value Creation Thinking*. Naperville, IL: LearningWhatWorks.
[12] Keep in mind that sports figures and entertainers who occupy the highest rung on the income ladder avoid criticism because they compete on a level playing field where consumers (or owners of sports teams) vote as to the entertainment value created.
[13] Alan Murray, 2019, "A New Purpose for the Corporation," *Fortune* September, pp. 88–94.

which might have succeeded if the purchased home continued to strongly appreciate. We know how that worked out. Many buyers of these loans suffered severe losses. Let's examine why BB&T Bank was the best performing major bank during this financial crisis.

BB&T Bank refused to sell negative amortization loans to its clients. John Allison, who was the bank's chairman for 20 years, describes the bank's culture:

> If you want to have passion and energy in your life, you must have a sense of purpose in your work. ... I ask the employees of BB&T: Are you truly making the world a better place to live through your work? Are you really helping your clients achieve economic success and financial security? Are you providing the quality of advice that ensures that they make better decisions?
>
> You should never do anything that you believe will not be in your client's best interest, even if you can make a profit in the short term. ... Life is about creating win-win relationships.[14]

The financial crisis of 2007–2009 was about too many managements in the financial sector adrift due to not being committed to a purpose grounded in building long-term value and earning client trust. Ever more extensive laws and regulations are not a substitute for earned trust.

PROGRESS STUDIES

The quote from Patrick Collison and Tyler Cowen, at the beginning of this chapter, promotes a new field of study—Progress Studies. This is strikingly important and seems so obvious once we think about it. However, we should not underestimate the challenge of building knowledge when researchers and students alike have preconceived beliefs coupled with the need for Progress Studies to include empirically grounded insights that may overturn strongly held assumptions by those on the political Left and Right. Since Progress Studies is about knowledge building within the

---

[14] John A. *Allison*, 2013, *The Financial Crisis and the Free Market Cure: Why Pure Capitalism Is the World Economy's Only Hope.* New York: McGraw-Hill, p. 241.

educational environment, let's begin with the environment on college campuses and the study of business and economics in particular.

The purpose of education should be to increase our knowledge base with verifiable and useful assumptions ("truth") and, most importantly, teach us ways to recognize and overcome the biases and limitations in our knowledge-building process (see the knowledge-building loop of Figure 2.1, which has been utilized throughout this book). In so doing, we have a better chance to make good decisions, to do well at work, and to live more satisfying lives that can contribute in some measure to making the world a better place. The knowledge-building process enables us to purge faulty assumptions thereby providing a useful guidepost to shape worldviews attuned to value creation.[15] Awareness of how we build knowledge facilitates a healthy skepticism and a motivation to criticize and potentially improve our assumptive world. A desirable result of this constructive skepticism is asking penetrating questions that may result in profoundly useful discoveries. And another is being able to have civil and productive debates with those holding far different political ideologies as long as both share a commitment to building knowledge and a willingness to consider data that upsets one's strongly held beliefs.[16] This is an issue on many college campuses. A good dose of straight thinking is reflected in the University of Chicago's January 2015 "Report of the Committee on Freedom of Expression," which includes this quote from Hanna Holborn Gray, former President of the University of Chicago:

> Education should not be intended to make people comfortable, it is meant to make them think. Universities should be expected to provide the conditions within which hard thought, and therefore strong disagreement, independent judgment, and the questioning of stubborn assumptions, can flourish in an environment of the greatest freedom.

[15]The perceptions-actions and consequences-feedback part of the Knowledge-Building Loop is a condensed version of the scientific method.
[16]In the spirit of civil and productive debates, a well-crafted book that can upset strongly held beliefs of those on the Left and the Right is Oren Cass, 2018, *The Once and Future Worker: A Vision for the Renewal of Work in America*. New York: Encounter Books.

The questioning of stubborn assumptions integral to Progress Studies requires a pluralistic inquiry that is not beholden to mainstream views in either business schools or economics departments. For example, this book makes a strong case that the firm is the engine of economic progress and it can be advantageous to focus on the firm as the unit of economic analysis. Neoclassical economics, as described in Chapter 1, minimizes the role of the firm, and more specifically, economists are inclined to utilize micro and macro theories which do not require in-depth knowledge of how firms operate.

An especially fertile line of inquiry for Progress Studies is the process of nurturing and sustaining a value-creation (knowledge-building) culture in the firm. Similarly, identifying the best method at any point in time to nurture and sustain a society's culture of dynamism is also uniquely important.[17] Perhaps the culture inside the firm and the culture in the outside environment are much more connected than we currently understand.[18] Perhaps the economists Vernon Smith and Bart Wilson are correct when they state: "For the science of economic betterment in the twenty-first century to be a study of humankind, it must likewise be an inquiry into human social betterment."[19]

Consider the development of business schools and the role of beliefs about knowledge building. After World War II, management accounting and quantitative thinking flourished. This promoted quantitative analyses of component parts of the system (i.e., the firm) and wide use of accounting data to manage business systems in order to hit calculated optimum accounting targets.[20] Management accounting and quantitative methods

---

[17] For insights on the emergence of Germany in the mid-1800s and related dynamism, see M. Norton Wise, 2018, *Aesthetics, Industry, and Science: Hermann Von Helmoltz and the Berlin Physical Society.* Chicago: University of Chicago Press.

[18] Valentina A. Assenova, 2019, "Why Are Some Countries More Entrepreneurial than Others? Evidence from 192 Countries over 2001–2018." SSRN working paper https://ssrn.com/abstract=3449762. Assenova notes: "Drawing on the largest available longitudinal sample comprising 192 countries over 2001–2018 … the evidence shows … social norms being the most strongly associated with entrepreneurialism and rates of organizational founding."

[19] Vernon L. Smith and Bart J. Wilson, 2019, *Humanomics: Moral Sentiments and the Wealth of Nations for the Twenty-First Century.* Cambridge, UK: Cambridge University Press.

[20] For insights on the limits of data-driven decision-making, see Roger L. Martin and Tony Golsby-Smith, 2017, "Management Is Much More Than a Science," *Harvard Business Review,* 95(5): 129–135.

have deep roots and have significantly influenced thinking about how to improve a firm's financial performance.[21] In recent decades, the accelerating adoption of quantitative methods in business schools and highly mathematical models in economics raises the possibility that high-level mathematics and insightful thinking may be viewed as one and the same. Consequently, systems thinking may be downgraded in importance if it interferes with the application of quantitative tools. This concerned Peter Drucker:

> There is one fundamental insight underlying all management science. It is that the business enterprise is a system of the highest order: a *system* whose parts are human beings contributing voluntarily of their knowledge, skill, and dedication to a joint venture. And one thing characterizes all genuine systems, whether they be mechanical like the control of a missile, biological like a tree, or social like the business enterprise; it is interdependence. ... For what matters in any system is the performance of the whole; this is the result of growth and of dynamic balance, adjustment, and integration, rather than of mere technical efficiency. ... Primary emphasis on the efficiency of parts in management science is therefore bound to do damage. It is bound to optimize precision of the tool at the expense of the health and performance of the whole.[22]

One would hope that systems thinking plays a major role in future studies of progress.[23] In Chapter 3, I described three innovative approaches to improve performance (i.e., progress), which were not developed in the

---

[21] Warren Bennis and James O'Toole argue that business schools have mistakenly evaluated faculty based on publications in top journals that favor theory and advanced econometric studies. This drives teaching away from the messy, tough choices important in running a successful business and from the practical know-how to get plans implemented and desired results produced. See Warren G. Bennis and James O'Toole, 2005, "How Business Schools Lost Their Way," *Harvard Business Review*, May 83(5): 96–104. See also, Srikant M. Datar, David A. Garvin, and Patrick Cullen, 2010, *Rethinking the MBA: Business Education at a Crossroads*. Boston: Harvard Business Press.

[22] Peter F. Drucker, 1973, *Management: Tasks, Responsibilities, Practices*. New York: Harper Business, p. 508.

[23] Systems thinking is critical to improving the FDA's regulatory process. Enabling patients, advised by their doctors, to make informed decisions about the use of not-yet-approved drugs would bring needed competition to the FDA's regulatory process to the ultimate benefit of patients. See Bartley J. Madden, 2018, 3rd ed., *Free to Choose Medicine: Better Drugs Sooner at Lower Cost*. Arlington Heights, IL: Heartland Institute. An early publication of the Free to Choose Medicine proposal was instrumental in Japan implementing this initiative for regenerative medicine drugs. The Japanese version is called conditional approval, see www.freetochoosemedicine.com.

customary way that business and economics professors operate. The customary process is that articles published in the top journals constitute the best source of important, new knowledge and in turn this is eventually codified in the textbooks that guide student learning. However, with a pluralistic mindset we should be open to new ideas, especially those that demonstrate effectiveness, even if not developed in leading journals. Such is the case for: (1) Lean Thinking, as practiced by preeminent lean firms such as Toyota and Danaher; (2) the Theory of Constraints originated by Eli Goldratt; and (3) the work of Werner Erhard, which in recent years has been expanded into the ontological/phenomenological model (OPM). These three approaches involve a *cognitive revolution*, not minor organizational changes or adopting "best practices" without concern for nurturing a knowledge-building culture, and deserve further research as part of Progress Studies, including classroom discussions. Although these three approaches are currently taught to a limited degree in business schools, they deserve much greater emphasis to the ultimate benefit of students.

For many, Lean Thinking is synonymous with a worldview of waste elimination throughout the entire system (value stream) for a product or service. Less visible is the culture that engages employees in applying scientific thinking (hypotheses about root causes of problems and experiments) in order to continually improve processes. Lean companies that have sustained superior performance invariably reflect a deep and ongoing commitment by top management to orchestrate a learning culture. Helping employees effectively deal with uncertainty improves their human capital (personal skills) and results in earned success because they creatively contribute to their firm's progress. In other words, their jobs provide more than a paycheck. The common mistake is to focus excessively on learning about lean tools to the exclusion of learning about lean's knowledge-building culture.

Goldratt's mega-bestseller novel *The Goal* is an entertaining way for business students and others to learn about identifying and fixing bottlenecks. However popular this book is in business schools, it does not address Goldratt's thinking process that is applicable to problem solving in general.[24] His logical trees for mapping cause and effect and revealing hidden assumptions are time-consuming to construct but overall time-saving in discovering the root causes of seemingly complex problem situations. He always stressed that one should overcome the common perception of reality as complex; avoid accepting conflicts as unsolvable and tradeoffs being unavoidable—instead, after revealing hidden assumptions, find a simple solution that avoids compromises; always strive for win-win relationships; and be skeptical of believing one knows something with absolute certainty. Business schools should emphasize learning about Goldratt's thinking process.

The idea of a cognitive revolution certainly applies to OPM. The Erhard-Jensen Ontological/Phenomenological Initiative supports a worldwide program to assist academic institutions in equipping students for on-the-court experiences of being a leader that utilize a much improved understanding of how our worldviews automatically shape our perceptions.[25] The foundation for this approach resides in an awareness of how our brains function in constraining the future to be tightly linked to our past experiences so that one's being and acting is synchronized to the predicted future. To achieve breakthrough performance, leaders need to creatively transform the current context, enabling others to aspire to a far different future. Along these lines, successful lean transformations of below-average performing firms often begin with a radical change by implementing lean processes in a selected manufacturing plant in order to unambiguously demonstrate to employees that breakthrough performance is achievable in the future.

It would be beneficial for the study of capitalism to include how capitalism is perceived. Consider the contrast between capitalism and socialism. Perhaps current polls that show surprising support for

---

[24] *See* Chapters 23–27 of James F. Cox III and John Schleier, Jr., eds., 2010, *Theory of Constraints Handbook*. New York: McGraw-Hill. In particular, Chapter 25 by Lisa Scheinkopf discusses an especially important innovation by Goldratt—logical trees which expedite the discovery of root causes of problems. Two short and insightful books about Goldratt's innovative way of thinking about problems include Eliyahu M. Goldratt and Efrat Goldratt-Ashlag, 2008, *The Choice*. Great Barrington, MA: North River Press; and Yishai Ashlag, 2014, *TOC Thinking: Removing Constraints for Business Growth*. Great Barrington, MA: North River Press.

[25] https://beingaleader.net/the-initiative

socialism do not reflect an admiration for life in Venezuela or Cuba, nor a misreading of history as to the different prosperity outcomes for East Germany versus West Germany and North Korea versus South Korea. Is it not plausible that proponents of free-market capitalism have erred by focusing almost entirely on the societal benefits of competition? The efficient allocation of resources via competition appeals to economists since this spurs innovation and advances our standard of living. In so doing, resources move away from firms that are becoming obsolete. However, everyday people typically don't think about competition being the driving force of a rising standard of living. But they do recognize how competition leaves in its wake people hurt by what economists label "creative destruction." I believe that this phrase, made famous by Joseph Schumpeter, should be creatively removed from our vocabulary because it is incomplete, misleading, and sends the wrong message.

Technology advancements including robotics, digitization, and artificial intelligence raise fear of job losses while simultaneously improving firms' financial performance. The economic argument that new jobs are being created may be true but offers little comfort to those left behind. We need to provide a helping hand for those left behind and for young people trying to get in the game. Surely, there are innovative ways that business firms can orchestrate mutual benefits through expanded training programs with minimal government involvement.[26] Our educational system for young people certainly seems ripe for disruptive innovation.[27] We owe people, young and old, equal opportunity to rise as high as their skills, determination, and insight can take them.

Young people joining a firm's workforce seek engagement with an enterprise that realistically can make the world a better place. So, too, for

---

[26] On the topic of a helping hand to those left behind, some important ideas of Glenn Hubbard are covered in Tunku Varadarajan, May 19–20, 2018, "A Conservative Economics of Dignity," *Wall Street Journal*, p. A11. In addition, see Edmund S. Phelps, 2007, *Rewarding Work: How to Restore Participation and Self-Support to Free Enterprise*. Cambridge, MA: Harvard University Press.

[27] Clayton M. Christensen, Michael B. Horn, and Curtis W. Johnson, 2008, *Disrupting Class: How Disruptive Innovation Will Change the Way the World Learns*. New York: McGraw-Hill. For some tough-minded insights see Bryan Caplan, 2018, *The Case against Education: Why the Education System Is a Waste of Time and Money*. Princeton, NJ: Princeton University Press.

customers who want to buy from firms that operate with a purpose consistent with the four-part purpose promoted in this book.

Critics of capitalism assert that people are motivated to behave in selfish ways. However, those selfish actions are actually incentives to make mutually beneficial transactions even though each party is focused on meeting their own needs, not the other party's needs. As Adam Smith suggested with his metaphor of the invisible hand, such actions are the means to advance the common good.

Both successful business relationships and transactions between buyers and sellers occur due to mutually beneficial outcomes—not a zero-sum game in which if you win, I must lose. For example, how do you react to potential business partners who assert that their foundational principle is "greed is good"?[28] In contrast, how do you react to potential business partners whose track records demonstrate that they believe in win-win outcomes and are committed to serving customer needs?

A free-market economy is built on trust. When transactions involve strangers, institutions or firms establish rules that ensure neither side gets hoodwinked. At a macro level, laws protect property rights and do other useful tasks to facilitate human betterment through trade (i.e., the multitude of transactions that make up our day). Paul Rubin sums up with three points:

> First, the term "competition" implies a winner and a loser, but in a market both participants (buyers and sellers) gain. Second, the fundamental unit of an economic relationship is a transaction, and because both parties gain from a transaction, it is cooperative. Third, competition has an important role in a market, but its role is to ensure that transactions (cooperation) occur on the best possible terms with the best possible agents.[29]

---

[28] Before Ivan Boesky was convicted for insider trading, he spoke favorably of greed during a commencement speech to business students at the University of California at Berkeley. Those comments led to Gordon Gekko's (actor Michael Douglas's) famous lines in the movie *Wall Street*: "The point is, ladies and gentlemen, that greed, for lack of a better word, is good. Greed is right, greed works. Greed clarifies, cuts through, and captures the essence of the evolutionary spirit."

[29] Paul H. Rubin, 2019, *The Capitalism Paradox: How Cooperation Enables Free Market Competition*. New York: Post Hill Press, p. 15.

Integrating cooperation into the explanation of the free market system makes sense.

In summary, my view is that an important role for Progress Studies is to better understand the evolutionary process in which firms build knowledge, create value, and generate progress—a bottom-up, concrete body of knowledge using the individual firm as the unit of analysis. This book is a step in that direction.

ABOUT THE AUTHOR

Bartley J. Madden is an independent researcher. His current research focuses on value creation and knowledge building as opposite sides of the same coin. Madden retired as a managing director of Credit Suisse HOLT after a career in investment research and money management that included the founding of Callard Madden & Associates. His early research was instrumental in the development of the cash-flow return on investment (CFROI) valuation framework that is used today by money management firms worldwide.

His website, www.LearningWhatWorks.com, details a wide range of intellectual interests, including inventions related to information processing innovations for the New Economy and public policy initiatives. An early version of his book, *Free to Choose Medicine: Better Drugs Sooner at Lower Cost,* was translated into Japanese and played a significant role in Japan's implementation of their version of *Free to Choose Medicine* to facilitate early, informed access to regenerative medicine drugs; see www.freetochoosemedicine.com.

INDEX